# DIVISIONAL PERFORMANCE: MEASUREMENT AND CONTROL

# DIVISIONAL PERFORMANCE

## measurement and control


DAVID SOLOMONS

Professor of Accounting
Wharton School of Finance and Commerce
University of Pennsylvania

RICHARD D. IRWIN, INC. Homewood, Illinois 60430
IRWIN-DORSEY INTERNATIONAL London, England WC2H 9NJ
IRWIN-DORSEY LIMITED Georgetown, Ontario L7G 4B3

This edition published by arrangement with the Financial Executives Research Foundation.

First Printing, March, 1968
Second Printing, September, 1969
Third Printing, May, 1970
Fourth Printing, November, 1970
Fifth Printing, August, 1971
Sixth Printing, May, 1972
Seventh Printing, March, 1973
Eighth Printing, April, 1974

Library of Congress Catalog Card No. 65-28460

Printed in the United States of America

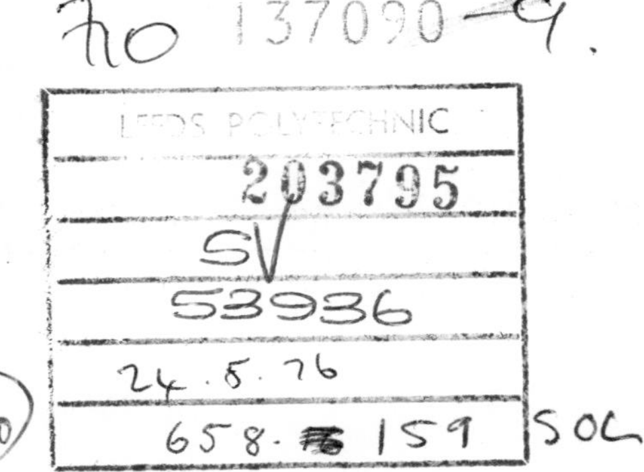

# Preface

The organizational structure of a corporation is the result of many factors. As sales volume grows, and as product lines diversify, the divisionalized form of organization becomes a logical one for many corporations. But progress inevitably brings problems (just as the resolution of problems brings progress) and the change from a one-unit operation to a multiunit operation means that management must operate under difficult ground rules.

The reporting of performance of divisions, and the rating of a division manager and their assistants based on division earnings, created a situation in which a conflict of interest arose. A general manager might make a decision which benefited his division's earnings and his personal compensation but which might not be the best decision from the company viewpoint. Moreover, division managers objected to the reduction of their earnings through accounting practices which were designed to reduce the payment of taxes in the current year, by reason of increased depreciation or other charges which reduced book earnings. As a result of this tax accounting, cash flow would be increased but the net income on which performance was based would be decreased. Then other decisions affecting relations between divisions might increase earnings of one division at the expense of another division and perhaps also the company. These questions needed investigation and research to suggest acceptable solutions.

In view of the importance of the divisionalized corporate structure, the Trustees of the Research Foundation decided, in 1961, that there was need for a definitive study concerned with the accounting control of decentralized business operations. Such operations would include not only those which are geographically separate from the controlling center (distant plants, branch offices, etc.) but also those separated from the controlling center organizationally rather than geographically (e.g., autonomous divisions, subsidiary companies, and service establishments).

Such a study was not intended to be a mere empirical recital of current practices but, rather, an eclectic view in which the researcher's views would have equal weight with the best practices observed. It was likely that in some areas there probably would be no practices which adequately and satisfactorily dealt with the questions involved. In this way the Trustees felt the report of the researcher would truly enable the reader to gain insights into ways of measuring and controlling divisional performance.

To Professor Solomons, for his research and for his original thinking, and to the members of the Steering Committee and the Review Panel listed on page x of this book, the Trustees of the Research Foundation gratefully acknowledge their appreciation for the combined constructive effort which has developed in this area.

*Dudley E. Browne, President*
*Financial Executives Research Foundation 1965-1966*

# Contents

## Project Group

Composed of the members of the Steering Committee, the Review Panel, the Board of Trustees, and the Staff of the Foundation.

Frank M. Brettholle, Vice President and Controller
H. J. Heinz Company

David W. Chappuis, Controller
Celanese Corporation of America

L. Russell Feakes, General Controller and Assistant Treasurer
Johnson & Johnson

L. Keith Goodrich, Executive Vice President
McGraw-Hill, Inc.

Donald P. Jones, Comptroller
Sun Oil Company

Frank L. Linton, Vice President and Comptroller
Allied Chemical Corporation

Frederick J. Muth, Vice President and Controller
Armstrong Cork Company

Robert E. Pfenning, Comptroller
General Electric Company

John E. Rhodes, Controller
Schlumberger, Limited

Thornton R. Smith, Controller
Johns-Manville Corporation

C. Roger Stegmaier, Comptroller
Campbell Soup Company

STAFF:

W. Joseph Littlefield, Research Director
Financial Executives Research Foundation

# Introduction

The purpose of this study is to investigate the financial relations existing between the central management of a divisionalized company and the management of its several divisions; and, as a result of such investigation, to arrive at recommendations which would make for the more effective coordination and control of divisional operations in accordance with the objectives of the corporation. The study was sponsored by Financial Executives Research Foundation. Twenty-five companies, whose names are listed on page xiii, participated in it. All of them were visited, a number of them both at head office and at divisional level, and I was able to talk freely with their financial executives.

It was not my objective simply to make a survey of existing practices, for which purpose a much broader coverage by questionnaire would have been more suitable. Rather, I wanted to uncover the pros and cons of different practices, and then to form my own judgment about their relative merits. The result is no mere neutral description of current methods. Though I cannot hope to have my judgments endorsed by all who read this book, I can and do hope that those who do not agree with me will find something to think about in my reasoning and, as a result, see their own judgments in a clearer light.

At many points, it has been difficult to prevent the study from turning into a general examination of management accounting. The fact is, of course, that many of the problems which beset divisionalized companies plague other companies also. I have tried to concentrate on those aspects of financial control which are peculiar to the divisional form of organization but, as is obvious from the space given to such matters as depreciation, direct costing, and LIFO, I cannot claim to have kept clear of more general issues. I can only plead that the discussion of divisionalization would have been woefully incomplete had I done so.

Though the needs of tax accounting and management accounting are widely recognized to be different, it is perhaps not so widely recognized that many companies are paying a substantial, though concealed, price for tax savings when, in the pursuit of these savings, they adopt accounting methods which do not serve the needs of management and may even positively mislead it. This point, which is not peculiar to divisionalized companies, kept on obtruding itself as the study proceeded. It is not what is generally meant when people talk about the impact of taxation on business. Perhaps the point deserves more attention from financial executives than it has heretofore received.

It is a pleasure as well as a duty to acknowledge the help which I have received from so many quarters. W. Joseph Littlefield, the research director of Financial Executives Research Foundation, has given me his support and advice at every turn. The members of the project steering committee—Donald P. Jones, chairman, L. Russell Feakes, John E. Rhodes, Thornton R. Smith and C. Roger Stegmaier—made numerous valuable suggestions both as the study proceeded and in their review of my manuscript. Dr. Samuel R. Sapienza gave me the benefit of his comments on a large portion of the manuscript which he read, and I enjoyed several discussions with Dr. Tibor Fabian on Chapter VI. James K. Schiller provided much assistance in the early stages of the project, and contributed especially to Chapter VI. John Negrey and Jonathan Harris assisted me ably at later stages of the work. Mrs. Ruth Rich and Mrs. Ceil Smith Thayer, formerly of Financial Executives Research Foundation, Mrs. Muriel Schock, Miss Roberta Webster, and especially Mrs. Jane Semple, all of the Wharton School, and my wife, Miriam, helped, between them, to turn a frequently baffling manuscript into a book. Last, though perhaps most importantly even though they must remain nameless, I must thank the executives of the participating companies who gave so generously of their time to discuss their problems with me. If, as a result of what I learned from them, there is in this book any illumination of those problems, I shall indeed be gratified.

*David Solomons*
*Wharton School of Finance and Commerce*
*University of Pennsylvania*

*November 1965*

## COMPANIES PARTICIPATING IN THE STUDY

American Can Company

American Radiator and Standard Sanitary Corporation

Armstrong Cork Company

Atlantic Refining Company, The

Chilton Company

Crane Co.

E. I. du Pont de Nemours & Co., Inc.

Du Pont of Canada Limited

Electric Storage Battery Company, The

Frick Company

General Electric Company

Johns-Manville Corporation

Johnson and Johnson

Merck and Co., Inc.

Olin Mathieson Chemical Corporation

Raytheon Company

Scott Paper Company

Shell Oil Company

Smith Kline & French Laboratories

Sperry Rand Corporation

Stanley Works, The

Sun Oil Company

Sylvania Electric Products Inc.

United Aircraft Corporation

United Gas Improvement Company, The

DIVISIONAL PERFORMANCE: MEASUREMENT AND CONTROL

# THE ORGANIZATION OF DIVISIONALIZED BUSINESS

## CHAPTER I

The terms "divisionalization" and "decentralization" are sometimes used as if they were interchangeable. They are, however, not synonyms, for the devolution of authority to make decisions, which is the essence of decentralization, is often carried to considerable lengths in businesses which are not divisionalized. Such businesses may have widely dispersed plants, sales offices and research facilities, each the responsibility of its own manager who may be given wide latitude as to how his operation is to be conducted. Divisionalization, however, adds to decentralization the concept of "delegated profit responsibility." A division has been defined as "a company unit headed by a man fully responsible for the profitability of its operations, including planning, production, financial and accounting activities, and who usually, although not always, has his own sales force. The division may be a unit of the parent company or it may be a wholly or partially owned subsidiary."[1]

In a truly divisionalized business the authority which devolves on the head of the division covers not only *how* the operations of the division shall be carried out but also, within limits, *what* those operations shall be. The reservation "within limits" is important, and we shall have to examine it further. But, within the general authority given to him, the head of a division—the divisional general manager

[1] *Division Financial Executives,* Studies in Business Policy, No. 101, New York: National Industrial Conference Board, 1961.

(or DGM as we shall call him from now on)—will usually have a degree of discretion as to what products he sells and at what price; what manufacturing operations are to be performed; what sales areas are to be served; and what research projects are to be pursued. He will also have the power to decide how these activities are to be carried on.

There is, unfortunately, no uniformity as to the way the word "division" is used. In some companies it is used interchangeably with "department," so that the organization chart will show a marketing division, a controller's division and so on. In other companies, the word connotes a marketing area, production being organized differently. This is not the way the word will be used here. For our purposes, and in line with more generally accepted practice, a segment of a business will be recognized as a division when it exercises responsibility for both producing (or purchasing) and marketing a product or a group of products. Anything less than this degree of responsibility makes it impossible to hold divisional management answerable for the profitability of the segment of the business it controls; and as the delegation of profit responsibility is the essence of divisionalization, in the following text no business segment will be recognized as a division unless it is a profit center. However, to add to the terminological confusion, we must note that a few large companies use the term "product department" to mean what we are calling a division.

The above definition makes it clear that responsibility for production and marketing (in a manufacturing company) or buying and selling (in a distributive enterprise) is the minimum extent of responsibility necessary for the existence of a division. This is not meant to imply that a division must market all the products it makes or make all the products it markets. It is quite common to find one division "buying" a product from another division and marketing it with others it makes itself. As an example, in one chemical company, two types of antifreeze having different chemical bases are made in different divisions, but one of these divisions alone handles the marketing of both types. Transfers of products between divisions play an important part in making divisionalization work, and they will be discussed more fully in Chapter VI. This is not the only way in which a division may have to cooperate with other parts of the business, and indeed it will be argued later that some degree of cooperation between divisions, going hand in hand with a substantial degree of independence, is an essential characteristic of sound divisionalization.

There are many different patterns of divisionalization within the broad definition already given, and the distinction between divisional and nondivisional, or functional, organizations may itself become quite blurred in some cases. However the nature of the distinction will be better understood if we look more closely at typical organizations in the two categories.

### *Divisional and functional organizations compared*

There is no better way of comparing the two types of organization than to look at an organization chart for a representative company of each type. Shorn of considerable detail, Figure 1 shows the organization chart of a mining and manufacturing company. There are three operating departments—mining which takes the raw material from the ground, manufacturing which transforms raw material into a number of different products, and marketing which sells the manufactured product in different markets and services the consumer. These three operating departments are served by seven staff departments—finance and accounting, personnel, public relations, purchasing, exploration, legal, and research and development. None of the three operating departments is responsible for more than a part of the process which turns the ore in the ground into a building product in a New York apartment, or into a part for an automobile speeding on a midwest highway. There is a multiplicity of products and a great variety of markets to be served; but no department is exclusively responsible for any product or for any market.

Turn, by contrast, to Figure 2. This shows, in summary form, the manner of organizing divisionalized operations in the electric battery industry. The three main domestic divisions of the company in question are those making lead-acid batteries for automotive use, producing dry batteries and flashlights and making lead-acid, nickel-alkaline and other kinds of batteries for industrial applications such as motive power, railway, telephone, aircraft, engineering, submarine and missiles electric power.

This company has a number of features which are worthy of comment. In the first place, the range of products handled is less diversified than is the case in many divisionalized companies—the term "packaged power" covers all the more important activities of the company. What really differentiates the divisions from each other is that they are operating in quite different markets. The automotive division is selling to automobile, truck and tractor manufacturers (for

## FIGURE 1
## Organization of a Mining and Manufacturing Company

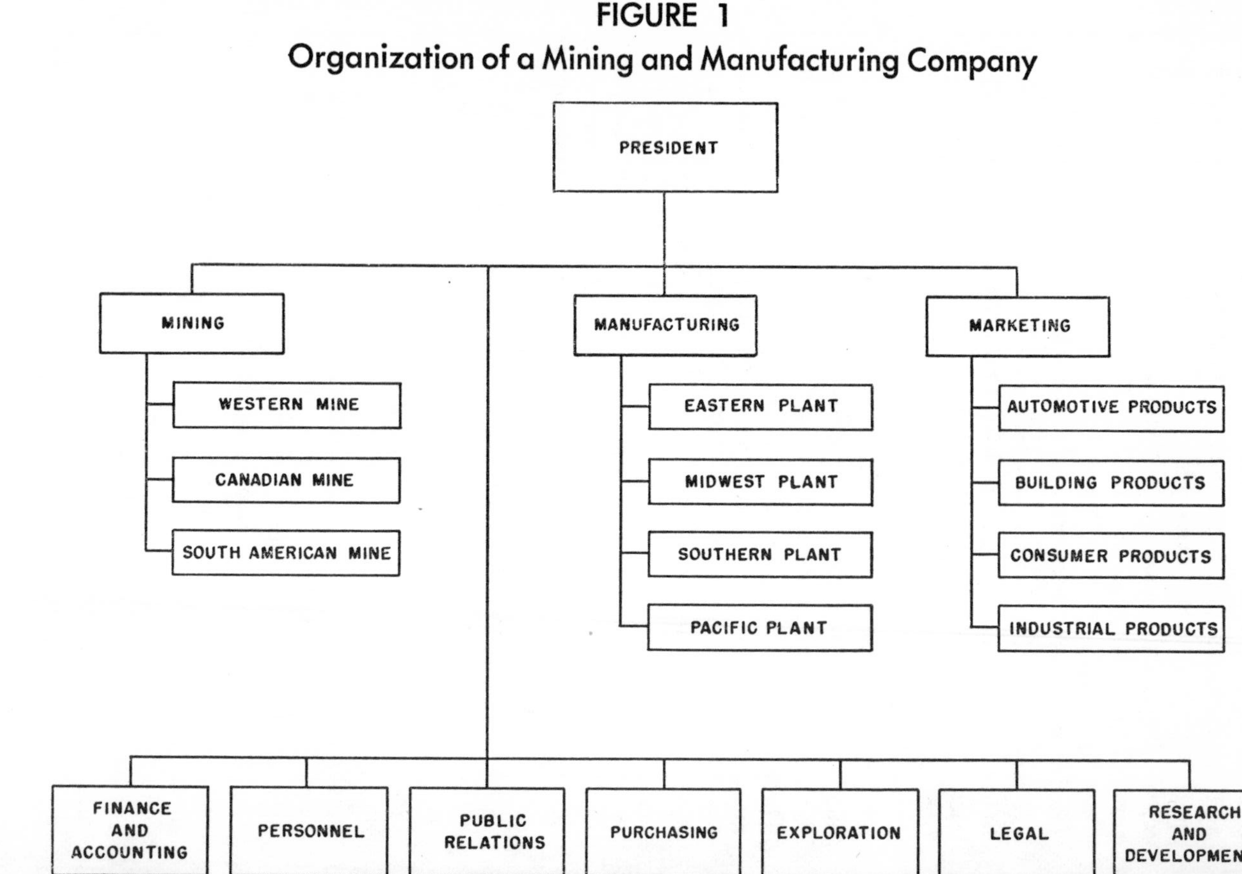

## FIGURE 2
## Organization of a Divisionalized Company in the Electric Battery Industry

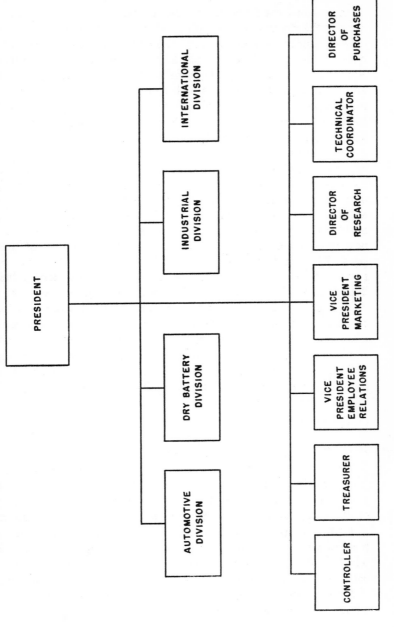

PRESIDENT

AUTOMOTIVE DIVISION

DRY BATTERY DIVISION

INDUSTRIAL DIVISION

INTERNATIONAL DIVISION

CONTROLLER

TREASURER

VICE PRESIDENT EMPLOYEE RELATIONS

VICE PRESIDENT MARKETING

DIRECTOR OF RESEARCH

TECHNICAL COORDINATOR

DIRECTOR OF PURCHASES

original equipment) and to automotive parts and specialty distributors, various mass marketers and the like (for replacement equipment); the dry battery division is selling to distributors for redistribution to numerous retail outlets; the industrial division is selling to manufacturers and users of battery-powered materials-handling equipment, to railroads, telephone companies, governmental agencies and to other industrial users of batteries. It is not so much the technical problems of production which distinguish these divisions from each other (though these exist also), but more importantly the marketing problems which confront them.

The company provides a good example of the importance of market orientation in the organization of divisions in other respects also. Batteries are used extensively in many kinds of boats and ships. Those used on the larger commercial type vessels are the heavier type batteries and are sold as original equipment to shipbuilders, and the replacement batteries for these are sold to ship chandlers. This business is appropriately handled by the industrial division of the company. Pleasure boats, on the other hand, are served mainly by marinas, which in many respects resemble automobile service stations. This business is therefore handled by the automotive division.

Though this company draws the boundaries between divisions according to the markets served (and this is probably the most common basis for divisionalization), other bases can be found. Technical considerations relating to manufacturing processes are one. Quality differences in the product may be another, as in the case of the automobile manufacturers—but this is really a marketing distinction also, as is a regional basis of divisionalization, according to the geographical market area served by the division.

### *Why do companies divisionalize?*

The growth of divisionalization in recent years suggests that, when given certain prerequisites for success, it has certain advantages which are more than just those of decentralization and specialization. Four of these special advantages are of perhaps predominant importance.

First, a divisional organization secures decentralization in a form particularly appropriate to a company seeking diversification, or which is already some way down that path. Its various activities may each have to be organized differently, and they will demand somewhat different skills. A divisional structure makes it relatively easy for such a company to combine diversity with unity.

Second, as one writer puts it, "a great improvement is believed to result in any firm when the creative talents of responsible individuals are encouraged to develop in a climate of individual responsibility, authority and dignity—a climate that is made possible by the decentralization of decision-making."[2] Let us add, it is the "decentralization of decision-making" which distinguishes divisionalization from mere "decentralized administration of decisions already made."[3]

Third, since the principal objective of divisional management is the long-run maximization of the division's contribution to the profitability of the corporation as a whole, there is (ideally, at least—the practical difficulties will be taken up later) a readily available measure of divisional success in the form of profit contribution. Because top management can measure the success of divisions, it can afford to give them a substantial degree of freedom in their administration of the resources entrusted to them. The more difficult it is, in a particular situation, effectively to measure divisional performance by the profit test, the more circumscribed is divisional freedom of decision-making likely to be. The difficulty is likely to arise whenever a division's affairs cannot be sufficiently disentangled from other parts of the business. Ultimately, a point is reached when the "division" loses the right to be regarded as a genuine division at all. But because of the many gradations encountered in the amount of autonomy enjoyed by divisions of different companies—a subject to which we return later—no attempt will be made to define just where this point lies.

Fourth, divisional operations provide a first-rate training ground for the development of the company's future senior management. Running a division presents most of the problems of running a separate business, if on a smaller scale, in a way which no subordinate function of a centrally administered firm can do. The scale need not be small in any except a relative sense. A division of an industrial giant such as du Pont or the General Electric Company may be as large as all but one or two of the other businesses within that industry.

### *Prerequisites for success*

For divisionalization to succeed, certain conditions must be present. The most important of these, clearly, is that each division should be

[2] John F. Burlingame, "Information Technology and Decentralization," *Harvard Business Review*, Vol. 39, No. 6, November-December 1961, p. 122.

[3] R. B. Heflebower, "Observations on Decentralization in Large Enterprises," *Journal of Industrial Economics*, Vol. 9, No. 1, November 1960, p. 8.

sufficiently independent of other divisions, both in respect of its production facilities and its marketing organization, to make its separate profit responsibility a reality. In some industries such independence is impossible, and we need only look at an oil company to see why this should be so. In the oil industry, a multitude of products flow from a single refinery. Some of these can be marketed separately —asphalt is an obvious example—but, since they have a common source of supply, anything resembling self-contained product divisions for the main products is impossible.

This does not mean that divisions must be completely self-contained to operate successfully. In fact, they hardly ever are so. Without going outside the oil industry, we can find companies which have split off the production and marketing of chemicals as a separate division or group of divisions. These, to be sure, are not independent of the rest of the business, for the feed stocks from which petrochemicals are obtained are refinery products. However, the existence of an independent market for these semiprocessed materials, allowing a realistic transfer price, and the necessity for considerable further processing within the chemical division itself, together with the obvious differentiation between the marketing problems of chemicals and gasoline, all ensure sufficient independence of chemicals from the rest of the business to make divisionalization of at least this part of the company's operations an effective method of securing decentralization.

Though substantial independence of divisions from each other is a necessary condition of successful divisionalization, if carried to the limit it would destroy the very idea that such divisions are integral parts of any single business. The divisions would then become so many unrelated businesses. What could the central management contribute to their success (except, perhaps, the provision of some common services of a more or less routine nature such as data processing)? Top management could hardly be expert in more than one or two of the diverse businesses in which the divisions were engaged. The corporate directors would, in fact, be operating a closed-end investment fund with a controlling interest in each of the investments. This is not a truly divisionalized business but rather a collection of separate businesses. Divisions should be more than investments, for they should contribute not only to the success of the corporation but to the success of each other. They may do this by using a common raw material, and therefore making it possible to buy it more cheaply in bulk. They may, by product transfers, help each other to complete a product line. They may provide complementary products (like RCA's phonographs and records) so that one division's products help to create the demand for the other's. They may be able to share technical know-how, or market information (as where a company operates both manufacturing divisions and a wholesaling division).

Two tests may be suggested to determine whether the divisions of a business logically "belong" together. One is for the corporate management to ask itself the question in relation to each division, "Why are we in this business?" The other is to ask, "What industry is the company in?" With the present-day movement towards diversification, more and more companies will find it difficult to give clear answers to the second question though not, it is hoped, to the first. Difficulty in answering both these questions implies that a sound basis for divisionalization does not exist. Having called for a substantial degree of independence as the first prerequisite for successful divisionalization, we may now postulate some degree of interdependence as the second.

It is a further condition for full success that relations between divisions should be so regulated that no division, by seeking its own profit, can reduce that of the corporation. This is not the same as saying that no division may seek a profit at the expense of another; but whenever one division does increase its profit at the expense of another, the amount it adds to its own profit must exceed the loss it inflicts on the other. This is no more than common sense. Divisions are very often in competition with each other, sometimes directly. More often, it will be found that products offered by different divisions, and primarily intended to meet different needs, do overlap in some markets and can be substituted for each other. Electronic tubes and semiconductors, hand tools and power tools, Buicks and Oldsmobiles—these will serve to illustrate the point.

The very fact that divisions are principally judged on the profits they can make carries with it the danger that a division may, if it can, make an easy profit at the expense of another division rather than go after a harder-to-get profit at the expense of a competitor. In spite of some striking examples of companies—highly successful ones, at that—which have sharply competing divisions, the best way to deal with this situation is probably not to let it arise. This may be achieved by so drawing the lines between divisions that competition between them is minimized. This may mean that certain products or markets may have to be transferred from one division to another. Such reorganization, in the short run, may be painful, but if it is in the best interest of the corporation, the pain had best be endured.

But even when interdivisional competition has been diminished in this way, the possibility of a conflict of interest between the company and one of its divisions may still arise. One of the challenges of divisionalization is to devise financial arrangements which make it as difficult as possible for a division to make a profit at the expense of the corporation. Interdivisional competition in marketing is not the only way this may come about. A division may hold another up to ransom, in an extreme case, by supplying materials or components that it needs only at exorbitant prices. One division's profit is another's loss, and it is probable (though not certain) that the corporation as a whole will suffer from such behavior. What is called for, therefore, is a system of transfer prices which will make such extortion impossible, or at least difficult. This and other aspects of interdivisional relations will be taken up in Chapter VI.

A fourth condition for the success of divisionalization is a degree of self-restraint on the part of the corporate administration in issuing directives to the divisions. The point is well put by the former chairman of the board of the General Electric Company in his book *New Frontiers for Professional Managers:*

> A major challenge posed by the decentralization philosophy is the challenge to lead by persuasion rather than command. This is inherent in the very idea of decentralization. . . . A centralized organization implies control from a central point, with close supervision and issuance of orders and mandatory courses of action, so that the centralized control can be effective. Decentralization, on the other hand, implies freedom for individuals everywhere in the organization to act on the basis of their own knowledge of the particular conditions that apply to the particular problem at hand. . . . In this situation the manager's work is to lead others by drawing out their ideas, their special knowledge and their efforts. Since self-discipline rather than boss-discipline is the hallmark of a decentralized organization, the manager resorts to command only in emergencies where he must admit temporary failure to make the situation and the necessary course of action self-evident.[4]

---

[4] Ralph J. Cordiner, *New Frontiers for Professional Managers,* New York: McGraw-Hill Book Company, Inc., 1956, pp. 74-5.

### *Divisionalization is not always the right answer*

From the way in which the case for divisionalization has just been put, it will be clear that it is not by any means to be regarded as a universal panacea, and for many companies it is not the right answer, even if the above conditions for success can be satisfied. In the first place, it is expensive in terms of administrative talent. However careful the organization is to avoid the duplication of authority, having head office staff personnel overlooking divisional personnel will generally lead to a more expensive administrative organization than a centralized company would need. This point may be particularly significant for a medium-sized firm which can achieve delegation of much decision-making without divisionalization. It was noted earlier that a division of one of the largest divisionalized companies such as General Electric may be as large as or larger than most other companies in its industry; and this point has been cited as evidence that, since such giants do not think it worth while breaking these large divisions up into smaller units or subdivisions, breaking a smaller company up into divisions may not be advisable either.[5]

There are, to be sure, other dangers in divisionalization. It may take top management some time after the new organization has been adopted to adjust itself to its new role. The skills of direct operating responsibility which it formerly needed are not quite the same as the skills in planning divorced from operations, in coordination and in remote control, these being the functions left to it under divisionalization. There may also be a scarcity of the financial understanding which successful divisionalization demands. Fortunately, there are alternatives to either full delegation of profit responsibility on the one hand, or full centralization of control on the other. Divisionalization may be restricted to subsidiary activities with control of the main business continuing at the center, or a reorganization of the management structure to reduce the number of people reporting to the top may enable the company to continue under a centralized regime without loss of efficiency. Nothing that has been said in our earlier discussion should be taken to imply that divisionalization is suitable for companies of all sizes in all situations.

---

[5] See John Dearden's article, "Mirage of Profit Decentralization," *Harvard Business Review,* November-December 1962, pp. 140-154, for a discussion of this argument and of other snags in divisionalization.

## Division of Responsibilities Between Head Office Staff and Operating Departments

There is a great variation from company to company in the amount of authority given to divisions, and also in the degree to which services such as data processing, credit sanction, engineering and the like are provided centrally. To some extent, these variations reflect differences in the nature of the companies' operations. The amount of diversification and geographical dispersion of divisional activities, as well as the confidence which top management has in divisional management—a function in part of the latter's length of service with the company—will all have some bearing on this matter. However, to some extent, too, such variations will simply reflect differences in philosophy between top managements, or will indicate the amount of experience top management has acquired of the working of decentralization.

If there is such a thing as a typical pattern of evolution of a decentralized organization, it probably goes something like this. A company of modest size, and in a well-defined line of business, is operating quite effectively with a functional organization. All important decisions are being undertaken by a management committee consisting, probably, of the president, executive vice president, and vice presidents in charge of manufacturing, marketing, finance, and research and development. Then, as the business grows, new products are added. Specialized plants have to be built for them. Specialized sales forces have to be developed, and the tremendous volume of decision-making which accompanies growth turns the management committee into a bottleneck.

With this growth there is a violent swing towards decentralization. Divisions are set up and every possible function is transferred to them—production, marketing, purchasing, training, labor relations, traffic, accounting. Management of the company's cash resources and pension fund and basic research will probably remain headquarters functions, with applied research and development handed over to divisions. The divisions prepare forecasts and plans of their operations which are approved by top management, but very little effort is made to call them to account when their actual performance deviates from their plans. Capital expenditures alone will probably remain under close control, since the company's solvency might be jeopardized by loose supervision in this area.

So long as business remains good, the company will probably continue along these lines for some time. But, as soon as a recession strikes, there is liable to be a reaction. Complete, or almost complete, decentralization is seen to be expensive. Services are being duplicated. The company's collective buying power is not being harnessed to get the best prices on its purchases. The failure to hold divisions closely accountable for their performance, together with the costly decentralized set-up, results in a sagging rate of return for the company as a whole. Moreover, all divisions are probably answerable to the president, and his attempt to oversee so many diverse activities makes his advice, when a division asks for it, less effective than it should be.

This situation leads to the third stage in the company's organization, the one which the more successful divisionalized companies have now reached. Divisions continue to have the maximum amount of freedom in their day-to-day operations, but are called to account strictly for the result of these operations. Where divisions are at all numerous, some logical grouping can usually be found—perhaps as between those divisions primarily serving the private sector and those mainly working under government contracts, or those supplying a mass market and those dealing in custom-built products—and between the president and the divisions are interposed group vice presidents, each having a span of control narrow enough to make effective control possible. Control here does not, of course, mean continual interference with decision-making, for this would be a negation of the divisional philosophy. It means, rather, oversight and calling to account, the very purpose of which is to make freedom of operations possible; for so long as any serious departure from previously approved plans has to be promptly answered for—which does not necessarily mean punished, of course—the detailed dictation of how these plans are to be implemented becomes quite unnecessary.[6]

With this tightening of control will probably go some recentralization of services. Data processing is one which the development of large-scaled computers has made it economical to centralize; and this often carries with it the centralization of credit and collection work.

---

[6] This idea is explored by Raymond Villers in "Control and Freedom in a Decentralized Company," *Harvard Business Review,* Vol. 32, No. 2, March-April 1954, pp. 89-96.

Economic forecasting and market research; executive development and training (especially if divisional personnel are not too scattered); purchasing of basic materials used by several divisions, packing materials and service supplies such as light bulbs; clerical services at regional warehouses shared by two or more divisions; engineering design of new facilities and equipment; the provision of insurance cover; and the specialized job of traffic planning (but not the day-to-day routine of making shipments)—these are all examples of service functions which can, in most circumstances, be most effectively and economically performed centrally. They will probably, therefore, be brought back to headquarters when the judgment is reached that decentralization has gone too far.

Many companies have "gone divisional" through acquisitions or mergers, usually as part of a diversification process. In such cases, the first stage of the evolution just described will have been skipped. The company may, if it is not careful, then find itself in the second stage, that of overdecentralization, with a number of sprawling divisions each tending to go its own way. Here again, the survival of the corporation as a profitable business will require a tightening of central control and some centralization of services.

How, then, is the company likely to be organized when it has settled down in this third stage of its divisionalized existence? How is responsibility for its operations likely to be divided between the corporate headquarters and the divisions? Since the company's organization will be reflected in the methods of financial control appropriate for it—and it is financial control in which we are primarily interested—it is desirable to look a little more closely at the way a divisionalized company might be organized, at the responsibilities handed over to divisions, and at those retained in the hands of the corporate headquarters staff. As has already been made clear, no two companies will be found to be organized exactly alike. We must resist the temptation to judge one form of organization as being better than another without a full knowledge of all the facts, which probably are not fully available to those outside the company.

In a recent survey,[7] some evidence is to be found of the diversity of organization in divisionalized companies, especially as it affects the level of management bearing the responsibility for making decisions

[7] John Maughan, "Who Makes the Profit Decision?" *Dun's Review and Modern Industry,* Vol. 80, No. 3, September 1962, p. 28.

of various kinds. Of the approximately 300 companies covered by the survey, not all of them are necessarily divisionalized in the sense in which the term is used here. The percentages of the total in which various kinds of decision are taken at particular management levels are shown in Figure 3.

This is not an area in which great reliance can be placed on statistical tabulations. The answer to the question "who makes this or that kind of decision?" is seldom clear-cut. Most decisions are the result of compromise or of consultation: and even when one man (say, the president) does clearly make a formal decision on some topic (for example, a new capital investment), an important part of the decision-making process has previously been carried out by the person responsible for gathering and presenting the data on which the decision is to be based, for in the selection of the data and in the way they are presented, great influence on the ultimate decision can be wielded. Furthermore, decisions of a particular kind, even in a single company, may be taken not at one but at several levels. Using the same example (decisions on capital expenditure), the level at which plans are approved will almost always vary with the amount of money involved. Small expenditures can usually be authorized by a plant or department manager, sums up to a higher limit by the DGM, still larger sums by a vice president or the president, and so on up to board level. How are we to tabulate, in any simple statistical way, who makes investment decisions? But there is still a further difficulty in the way of giving simple answers to these questions. There is an old proverb about paying the piper and calling the tune. Thus, in Figure 3, nine per cent of the companies represented permit decisions to introduce a new production process to be taken at a level below that of department manager—presumably, that is to say, at foreman or supervisor level. Yet, apparently, not a single company gives these lower echelons the right to authorize new investment. This must limit their power to introduce new processes to making relatively trivial changes in existing processes, for process changes of any importance usually call for substantial expenditures. The same thing is true of new product introductions.

The interesting thing which emerges from Figure 3 is not so much the actual percentages shown but rather that, in all but one of the decisions listed, no less than six different levels of management are said to have decision-making authority, and in the remaining one, packaging redesign, five different levels are involved. The picture is

## FIGURE 3
### Profits and the Pyramid of Power

| | BOARD | CHAIRMAN | PRESIDENT | EXECUTIVE COMMITTEE | VICE PRESIDENT | DIVISION MANAGER | DEPARTMENT MANAGER | LOWER |
|---|---|---|---|---|---|---|---|---|
| INVESTMENT/CAPACITY | 9.8% | 1.2% | 25.8% | 11.1% | 28.4% | 23.4% | | |
| NEW PRODUCTION PROCESS | 2.5 | 1.2 | 7.5 | 5.1 | 38.9 | 35.0 | | 9.0% |
| NEW PRODUCT INTRODUCTION | | | 16.0 | 8.6 | 39.5 | 32.0 | 2.4% | 1.2 |
| INVENTORY CHANGE | | | 13.1 | 6.5 | 38.1 | 35.5 | 1.3 | 5.2 |
| DISTRIBUTION CHANGE | 1.2 | | 21.8 | 6.4 | 30.7 | 23.0 | 16.6 | |
| ADVERTISING BUDGET | 3.8 | | 15.3 | 10.2 | 23.0 | 24.3 | 23.0 | |
| PACKAGING REDESIGN | | | 7.3 | 4.4 | 23.5 | 32.3 | 32.3 | |

How far down the corporate ladder are the basic profit decisions made? This table gives the answers. The rank of the man who decides and the proportion of Presidents' Panel companies in which he is permitted to make each of these seven basic decisions are shown.

Source: Reprinted by special permission from *Dun's Review* and *Modern Industry* September 1962. Copyright 1962, Dun & Bradstreet Publication Corporation.

one of great diversity. But out of the diversity another pattern emerges; there is a large group consisting of about three-quarters of the companies divided between those who give most of the decision-making power to the division manager and those who give it to a corporate vice president. This "split down the middle" does bring into clear focus the difference of opinion which exists about the merits of divisional autonomy.

The dangers and difficulties of making generalizations about the "do's and don'ts" of divisional organization have already been noted. It is, however, worth mentioning that arguments that appear to be about organization and decentralization in fact often turn out to be arguments about the quality of the men assigned to various levels of responsibility. As Walther H. Feldmann, of Worthington Corporation, puts it in referring to decision-making authority, "The real danger lies not in the level at which decisions are made but in not having sufficiently competent people in lower levels of management."[8] If only there were enough capable men and women to go round, arguments about where decisions should be made would be much less important than they are.

### *The chief executive officer and his lieutenants*

Variations in practice become apparent as soon as one tries to identify a company's chief executive. In some companies this is the chairman of the board of directors, in others it is the president. Some companies do not have a chairman, in which case the position of the president is unambiguous as the chief executive who is responsible only to the board of directors collectively for all the company's operations. Where there is both a chairman and a president, at least four different relationships may exist between them. The chairman may simply preside over board meetings, leaving all active administration to the president, so that the latter is in much the same position as if there were no chairman. Or the chairman may have the right, subject only to board control, to determine policy, leaving the president to supervise its implementation. The chairman may take on the responsibility for supervising all operating divisions, leaving the president to control the staff departments at corporate headquarters. Or these roles of chairman and president may be reversed. This reversal took place recently in one very large company, when the former

[8] *Dun's Review* and *Modern Industry,* Vol. 80, No. 3, September 1962, p. 29.

president who had had operating responsibility succeeded to the chairmanship of the company. In his new role he retained his old responsibilities, giving to the new president, who had formerly occupied a senior staff position, the staff responsibilities previously exercised by the former chairman.

It is clear that, whatever arrangement is arrived at, the coexistence of a chairman and a president can only be successful if their roles are precisely defined by the board of directors. Even then conflicts may arise. We need not come down on one side of the argument or the other as to what those roles should be. However, in order that our own terminology should be clear, it should be noted that, in what follows, the chief executive of the company will be referred to as the president, and it will be assumed that the chairman, if there is one, has no authority outside the board room.

If the divisions involved number no more than four or five, then the DGMs (who may or may not be vice presidents) will probably be answerable directly to the president. If, as was suggested earlier, there are too many divisions for one man to control directly, the interposition of group executives (who will almost always be vice presidents) will facilitate effective control. Each will be responsible for a number of divisions, and will function between the DGMs and the president or management committee.

Where group executives exist, it is usually found that they need little or no staff except a secretary. If this is not the case, there is probably something wrong, for their purpose is not to head up another layer of staff departments standing between divisions and corporate headquarters. It is, simply, to act for the president in matters relating to the control of divisions to the fullest extent that his duties can be delegated, using the corporate headquarters staff for consultation and advice as necessary.

Most divisionalized companies make some use of a committee structure as part of their top management organizations. This, however, takes so many different forms that it is difficult to generalize about it. In one notable case of a very large company, the management committee, consisting of the president, group vice presidents, and the vice presidents in charge of staff departments, is in almost continuous session. All directives to divisions, other than those which need board authority, are issued solely by this committee. In many other companies, directives are issued only by the president, on the optional advice of staff officers. In such cases, regular meetings of the president, staff vice presidents, and DGMs will usually still be held for the exchange of information. At these meetings the DGMs report on the principal developments within their groups. Without such meetings, it is easy for these men to forget that the corporation is bigger than their own units. Moreover, by providing a forum in which new ideas in one division may be passed on to others, the general level of performance within the company cannot help but be raised.

There are any number of further variants of the committee system which may be encountered. Sometimes the operating committee which exercises control over divisions consists only of the president, group vice presidents, and the chief financial officer (who may be a vice president, the controller, or the treasurer). In such cases the DGMs may meet independently to exchange ideas, with staff officers sitting in at any meeting they choose to attend if the agenda of the meeting, circulated to them in advance, includes items of interest to them. In addition to committees of officers and managers, there will often be an executive committee of the board of directors to act for it in all but formal matters such as the declaration of a dividend. Sometimes separate committees of the board are formed to watch over each division or group of divisions. With this latter system it is easy for confusion and therefore conflict to arise between the authority of one of these committees and the authority of the president. To avoid this danger, the committees may be given purely advisory powers or the president may have to be a member of all of them. It is perhaps not surprising that few companies have adopted this pattern.[9]

## The Division of Authority Between Staff Departments and Divisions

Figure 2 has already shown the staff departments of one divisionalized company, which happens to be a company with a notably small head office staff. However, this small central staff has been strengthened recently to provide for technical coordination at the corporate level. Formerly, decisions relating to manufacturing methods and engineering were left wholly in the hands of divisions. This

[9] For a contrary view of the efficacy of the committee system, see Robert W. Murphy, "Corporate Divisions vs. Subsidiaries," *Harvard Business Review,* Vol. 34, No. 6, November-December 1956, p. 85.

situation was rather unusual. Most divisionalized companies have staff departments covering the following functions:

1. Manufacturing services, including purchasing;
2. Marketing services, including market research, economic forecasting, and advertising;
3. Engineering services;
4. Research and development;
5. Employee relations;
6. Public relations, including stockholder relations;
7. Legal services, often under the general counsel and secretary of the corporation;
8. Treasury services, including credit management, banking, insurance, corporate investments and pension funds;
9. Controllership services, including accounting, budget coordination, data processing and economic analysis of operations;
10. Tax management; and
11. Internal audit.

Some, but not all, of these departments will have their counterparts in the divisions. Marketing, for example, always will, while public relations usually will not. Legal services may or may not be divisionalized. Each company has to decide for itself which responsibilities shall reside in the divisions, and which shall be borne centrally. As this matter has a bearing on the financial control of divisions, it deserves some attention from us.

In the philosophy of one company, "staff departments have only the authority of knowledge." This applies both to the corporate staff departments and to their divisional counterparts. When applied to the corporate departments, however, the statement aptly expresses the concept that, while direct line authority runs from the board of directors through the president and group executives to the DGMs, the staff departments at headquarters must sell their ideas about how divisions should operate by dint of the value of the guidance they can give. Most companies, as a matter of fact, give their central staff departments duties which go beyond the tendering of advice. The handling of cash and the management of taxes are obvious examples in the financial field. As has already been suggested, this tendency seems to be on the increase.

Even when a service is performed within a division, certain methods may be prescribed by the corresponding corporate staff officer. For instance, the budget manager may prescribe the procedures and timing for budgets. General purchasing department may prescribe the formula for an economic purchase quantity which will be followed by division purchasing agents. The chief accountant will prescribe the code of accounts in broad terms. The chief industrial engineer may prescribe the education and experience qualifications for a man to be hired as a "junior industrial engineer."

Although divisional staff officers are usually directly answerable to the general manager of their divisions, it is inevitable that they should also look to the head of the corresponding head office staff department. He is an expert in their field, and they will often turn to him for guidance—indeed, it will normally be their duty to do so. They will also generally have to look to him for advancement, at least outside their own divisions. To be eligible for promotion to divisional controller, a man must usually be acceptable both to the DGM and the corporate controller. Other divisional staff appointments are perhaps less sensitive than this one, but a similar dual line of authority will generally be found.

*Purchasing.* We turn now to the head office services. Under the heading of manufacturing services, the one function which has most room for variation in the distribution of responsibility between head office and divisions is purchasing. It is obvious that a company will usually be able to buy materials used by several of its divisions on more advantageous terms than any one of them could do singly. This, naturally, produces pressure in favor of centralized purchasing. However, this is offset by the difficulties created by the enormous number of variations in quality and size between the needs of one division and those of another. The compromise solution, which seems to work best, is to have the central purchasing department place master contracts for the supply of the basic raw materials in common use. This leaves it up to individual divisions to make their own arrangements with suppliers about precise requirements and deliveries. Thereafter, the central purchasing department acts in an advisory capacity only, seeking out sources of supply and acting as a central clearing house for purchasing information.

Some of the advantages of centralized buying can be obtained without the necessity of setting up a central buying department. This becomes possible when a material in common use is purchased by one division for all the divisions which use it. Such an arrangement makes it possible for all divisions to share the benefits of the specialized knowledge of certain materials which particular divisions may develop.

To the extent that divisions do their own purchasing, or do it for themselves and for other divisions, some limit will usually be placed on the size of the commitment which a particular unit can enter into without special authority. One company places a dollar limit on the commitment under any one contract. It also limits the amount of inventory resulting from a purchase contract to three months' supply in excess of the standard inventory level for the material in question. If the contract will breach either of these limits, it has to have the approval of a special subcommittee of the operating committee. While the power to make capital expenditures on fixed assets by divisions is always subject to some limitation, it is sometimes forgotten that expenditures on materials and supplies may deplete the company's finances even more. Therefore, even when divisions are given great freedom to decide where and what to buy, some degree of financial control may yet be essential.

*Marketing.* A good test of the degree of real autonomy divisions have is to ask whether they are free to set selling prices for their products. This is a sensitive area where mistakes on the part of divisional personnel can cost the corporation a considerable amount of money. It is not easy to find a path between the extremes of complete divisional freedom to set prices and the complete abrogation of this right, as can be done in the field of capital expenditure projects by placing a limit on the amount that the division can spend without higher authority. A general duty to consult with the marketing staff at headquarters before any important price changes are made may be imposed on divisions; or certain important products may be taken out of the area of divisional competence while the power to set prices for others is left. As between these choices, probably the duty to consult is most consistent with the maintenance of divisional responsibility.

Most companies assign product advertising to divisional advertising departments, while leaving corporate or "institutional" publicity to a central advertising group. An alternative to this arrangement is to have a central advertising department in which there is a section assigned to each division. The difference between these two arrangements may not appear significant, especially in those cases where all the divisional headquarters are located in or close to the head office building. However, the latter scheme gives to the staff vice president in charge of marketing much greater authority to decide how divisional advertising appropriations shall be spent. This applies even when a DGM has to approve the advertising plans for his division before any money is spent, since the initiative is with the central advertising staff, even if the division has the last word.

*Economic forecasting.* This is one service which is best provided centrally. It requires a skill which is not in plentiful supply, and a company will usually be better served in this field by a small high-powered staff serving all divisions than if each division tries to do the job for itself, probably with men of lower calibre. Moreover, the company's general policy must be based on some one forecast. The same is not necessarily true of market research, for the differences between the areas served by divisions may be so great—as great as that between electric toasters and steam turbines, or between synthetic fibers and explosives—that divisions may be best left to survey their own markets. It certainly seems that a divisional marketing department may be somewhat seriously weakened by not being given this responsibility.

*Research.* A common division of function in the research field is to have pure or fundamental research carried out in a central research laboratory, with applied research and development carried out at the division level. Some companies draw a somewhat different distinction by saying that the central laboratory does product research, while the divisions do process research and development. However the work may be divided up, some aspect of innovation is almost always left to the divisions.

But even the work done in the central research laboratory will not, for the most part, be altogether outside the control of the divisions. Many of the projects worked on will fall clearly into the domain of one division or another. For such projects, the cost of which will usually be charged to the appropriate division, the prior agreement of the divisional management to accept the charge should be obtained. Failure to give divisions any financial control of the research to be done in their area would rather seriously impair their autonomy, with a consequent loss of the benefits of divisionalization. The direction which research takes will help to determine the future activities of the divisions, and a question of such a fundamental character cannot be taken completely out of their hands without making a farce of decentralization. Moreover, to charge them substantial sums for the cost of research in which they have had no say is to rob their financial results of much of their significance. Refusal of a division to underwrite a research project in its area of interest must not be the last word, however. There will sometimes be projects of such long-term significance that the company cannot afford to neglect them even though the support of the relevant division cannot be obtained. There will also be projects which do not fall clearly into the domain of any existing division. The president must have the right to authorize work on such projects, with the cost falling into general corporate expenditure.

The more diversified the divisions are, the smaller the role of a central laboratory is likely to be. But even in such a situation, the benefits of centralized buildings, equipment, and routine administration can be secured by having the central laboratory organized into sections. Each section is then linked with a division and works on its problems. This arrangement makes possible a more flexible deployment of men and resources (since research effort changes direction from time to time) than is likely to be obtainable if each division runs its own separate research organization. Of course, this argument has more force if the company is of moderate size than it does if the divisions are themselves as big as large companies.

*Employee relations.* As a minimum, a headquarters employee relations department will function in a purely advisory or consultant capacity. It will consist of a small group of specialists of high calibre. Many companies, however, give them duties beyond this, requiring company-wide uniformity in such matters as union recognition, vacations, sick leave regulations, retirement age, and pension arrangements. Certainly an absence of uniformity in some of these matters complicates transfers of personnel between divisions, though it need not prevent it any more than it inhibits movement of employees from one company to another. Training of a routine kind can well be left to divisional training officers, but the education of specialists is almost always handled most effectively and economically by a single organization acting for all divisions. Executive development can also certainly be best handled centrally, since the exchange of experience between men from different divisions will play an important part in the process of managerial education.

Wage negotiations are handled in many different ways. Almost always, as a minimum, an expert negotiator from headquarters sits in on the discussions to keep headquarters informed and to advise when called on. The actual negotiations may be handled at plant level by representatives of the plant personnel departments, or by negotiators from the divisional employee relations department. It may, in some cases, be taken out of divisional hands and be made the responsibility of the headquarters departments. This invasion of divisional autonomy is most likely where several divisions are dealing with the same union. The situation here is perhaps analogous, in the labor field, to the central purchasing of materials in common use by several divisions.

*Public relations.* This is perhaps the function which can most appropriately be handled centrally, for protecting the "corporate image" is a natural corporate, rather than divisional, responsibility. The same is true, even more obviously, of the corporation's relations with its stockholders. However, some aspects of the job can appropriately be left to divisions. Notable in this category are relations with local communities in which plants or other divisional establishments are located.

*Legal services.* It is usual to find legal matters kept firmly in the hands of the general counsel's department at head office. This is presumably because litigation has to be carried on in the name of the company rather than that of a division. Even so, divisions may have the right to employ local law firms (with the approval of the central department) to handle items of local significance. These may include leases of district sales offices and similar matters. Often, too, where divisional headquarters are located at a distance from corporate headquarters, one or more members of the general counsel's staff will be permanently attached to the divisional headquarters. This procedure is particularly appropriate where there is a considerable volume of patent work in which divisional technical personnel have to work closely with the lawyers.

*Financial services.* There is great diversity in the way that responsibility for a company's financial services is divided between the treasurer's and the controller's departments. In the case of a divisionalized company there is added to this diversity many gradations in the division of responsibility between headquarters and divisions. Many of the organizational questions arising in this area have been fairly exhaustively discussed elsewhere.[10] It is, therefore, unnecessary to go into this matter in great detail. Recent developments in the field of data processing, and their impact on the role of divisional finance staffs, however, are worth at least passing attention. The "information revolution" which is currently quietly going on cannot leave the balance of responsibilities in this area unchanged.

Typically, the treasurer's functions include the control of the company's cash, relations with banks, insurance and real estate management, investment management, the provision of finance, and credit and collections. The controller's functions cover accounting, budgeting, costing, financial analysis and reporting, tax accounting (though this may be a separate function) and internal audit. If a separate data-processing center has been set up, this may also come under the controller's direction, though it may sometimes be a separate operation under a manager directly responsible to a vice president in charge of administration. The precise distinction between the treasurer's responsibilities and those of the controller are not too important for our present purpose, and certainly much less important than the distinction between what is controlled by headquarters and what is left to be done by divisions.

One of the features distinguishing the diversified, divisionalized company from a firm in a single, well-defined line of business is the proportion of cash to sales. The divisionalized business can cut its cash holdings if the seasonal peak cash demands of the divisions do not coincide. So long as these peak demands are consecutive, not additive, a given amount of cash can support a larger volume of business than would otherwise be the case. It is easy to see, therefore, why divisionalized companies go to considerable trouble to minimize the number of separate cash funds held throughout the company. The holding of cash is one of the functions which is, emphatically, not decentralized.

But first the cash has to be collected, and this is just part of a chain of operations covering credit management, billing, collection and ledger keeping. At the present time, few people claim to know for certain how these functions are best organized and how responsibil-

[10] See in particular *Centralization vs. Decentralization in Organizing the Controller's Department* by Herbert A. Simon *et al.*, New York: Financial Executives Research Foundation, Inc., 1954 and *Division Financial Executives,* Studies in Business Policy, No. 101, New York: National Industrial Conference Board, 1961. The NICB Study in Business Policy, No. 98, *Administration of Electronic Data Processing,* 1961 is also relevant.

ities should be divided up. One company makes its plants responsible for billing and makes credit and collection the responsibility of a small number of regional credit units. These, in turn, are answerable to the treasurer. Customers' remittances are directed to the district sales offices throughout the country while accounts receivable are kept at a main accounting center. Another company has its credit, billing and collection handled by divisional headquarters while remittances are sent to a number of regional centers which also serve as regional computer centers at which accounts receivable are kept. A third company makes billing a divisional responsibility, while credit, collection and account keeping are handled at the corporate computer center. Yet a fourth company, which previously centralized its credit and collection work, has recently handed it back to its larger divisions so that all contacts with customers, and accounting for them, are in divisional hands. Of course, the proceeds of cash collections are still centralized.

Economizing on cash is an important advantage of divisionalization, so it is not surprising that divisionalized companies give it a great deal of thought. The use of regional banking centers, with rapid transfer of funds to head office, is common. Customers may even be required to send remittances direct to the bank, or to a post office box controlled by the bank, for transmittal to head office. With the steady transfer of payroll accounting from plant accountants to central or regional computer centers, with the computer writing the pay checks as well as accounting for them, local cash requirements have been greatly diminished, with consequent further economies in cash.[11]

What is the impact of the computer likely to be on the organization of divisionalized companies? Will it, by providing better and quicker information, extend the area of decentralized decision-making? Or is it, because of the tendency to centralize information in the computer, likely to recentralize decision-making as well? No one yet knows the answer to these questions, and it will probably be some years before they can be determined. As things have gone down to the present, even where a centralized computer center has been established, the concentration of data processing at one place has not taken away from divisions much more than such routine matters as keeping accounts receivable and the preparation of payrolls. Even these func-

[11] For further discussion of this subject see *Managing Company Cash,* Studies in Business Policy, No. 99, New York: National Industrial Conference Board, 1961.

tions are already imposing on divisions uniformity in document preparation. But we are only at the beginning. Centralized credit control, which has already accompanied centralized ledger posting in some companies, goes much further. It implies the power to decide to whom divisions shall and shall not sell, unless special powers to overrule the central credit control are reserved to divisions. And, as "integrated data processing" (now much talked about but little practiced) becomes more of a reality, and as computers come to be regarded not merely as data-processing machines but also, and more importantly, as decision-making machines applying decision rules determined by top management, it seems at least possible that decentralization may again come to mean merely the decentralized implementation of centralized decisions. There are many well-informed executives who argue strongly the other way.[12] Whatever the final outcome of this issue, the responsibilities of divisional managements are not likely to wither away so rapidly as to make them no longer worth discussing at the present time.

Treasury functions are much less likely to be found delegated to divisions than are controllership functions. The centralization of cash resources carries with it, as a corollary, the centralization of the power to add to these resources by borrowing, for only the central treasury will have the whole picture of the company's cash position. Divisions, therefore, do not share with the central treasury the right to issue bonds or raise other loans. If they need capital, they get it from the corporate headquarters. The investment of surplus cash, if any, is also naturally a corporate function, and so is the custody of the company pension fund. Divisions are rarely, if ever, given any discretion as to whether they join the pension scheme. The purchase of insurance cover is generally done centrally, as a specialized type of purchase for which it would usually be wasteful to have specialists anywhere but at the corporate headquarters.

If the companies participating in this study are typical, then there can be no doubt that divisional controllers occupy a crucial role in the organization of a division, often taking on responsibilities much wider than their title would suggest. They will often be found in

[12] For a survey of the views of some 300 accountants, controllers, vice presidents and presidents on this question, made in 1958, see Herbert O. Brayer, "Decentralization of Operations and Centralization of Accounting," *Cost and Management*, November 1958, pp. 372-380. In this rapidly changing field, unfortunately, views become obsolete very quickly.

charge of administration generally; and in firms engaged largely in government work, their main preoccupation seemed to be the negotiation of contract prices. Though the dual line of authority to which they are usually subject—operationally to the DGM and functionally to the corporate controller—might be expected frequently to give rise to difficult conflicts of interest, it did not in practice often seem to do so. Indeed, the one occasion when attention was drawn to this problem was in a company which gave the DGMs no authority over the controllers of their divisions but made the controllers directly answerable, through group controllers, to the vice president (finance) at head office. The reason for this arrangement was, of course, to prevent reports on divisional operations from being colored by the views of the DGMs. But, while the end was laudable, the means chosen to effect it created more problems than it solved. Certainly it made it difficult for the divisional controllers to think of themselves, and to be thought of by others in the divisions, as members of a management team.

We have now reviewed a few of the many organizational choices which wait answers to the questions: Should the company divisionalize? If so, what functions shall be delegated to divisions? What kind of corporate headquarters should the company have? Almost any arrangement is possible, from complete divisional autonomy at one end of the scale to complete and detailed domination of divisional management by the president and his staff at the other. Sometimes, indeed, the appearances of delegation to divisions may be no more than a disguise for a high degree of centralization of decision-making about all but trivial matters. In the foregoing review, some indication has been given of where a number of companies, successfully divisionalized, have drawn the line between delegation and centralization. But in the last resort, each case must be judged on its merits. A degree of delegation which suits one company may not suit another, even where most of the relevant facts seem to be identical. For example, two companies similarly organized, and in the same industry, appear on paper to give DGMs about the same degree of freedom. In fact, however, the president of one of these companies is constantly interfering with his divisional management. In the other company, the freedom they appear to possess is real. What actually distinguishes these companies is their history. The second has had its present structure for some years, and the DGMs are well known to, and have the confidence of, the corporate headquarters.

The first company has only recently acquired its divisions by purchasing existing businesses. The managements taken over with the businesses are not yet familiar with, and do not yet have the confidence of, the president. Consequently, he does not feel justified in giving them real freedom to make mistakes. Whether, with the passage of time, genuine and successful delegation will come to that company remains to be seen.

### *Organization within a division*

The organization of a division of a manufacturing company, somewhat simplified for our present purpose, is depicted in Figure 4. The division makes and markets products in one industry and its organization is fairly typical of a division of a company in which decentralization has been carried to considerable lengths. Its products fall into four main groups: two of the division's three plants specialize in one product group each, and the third plant handles two product groups. Each product group has its own marketing manager and sales promotion staff, but the field sales force sells all products of the division, covering the whole country from six district sales offices.

At each of the three plants, the division controller has a cost accountant with a small staff to operate the standard cost systems installed some years ago. The rest of his staff is at divisional headquarters. Similarly, the divisional personnel manager has a representative at each plant to handle recruitment of plant labor and other plant personnel matters, while personnel functions relating to clerical and sales staffs are dealt with at division headquarters. The division has its own laboratory, located at one of the plants, which is engaged in product improvement, finding new uses for existing products, and the improvement of production processes. Basic research is left to the large corporate research establishment.

The six heads of departments shown immediately under the DGM in Figure 4 constitute, with him, the division's own operating committee. They meet together regularly to discuss the division's problems and, once a month, meet with the group vice president responsible for the group of divisions to which this particular division belongs. He is the division's main link with the top management of the corporation, and is always available to the DGM for consultation and advice.

## FIGURE 4
## Organization of a Division of a Manufacturing Company

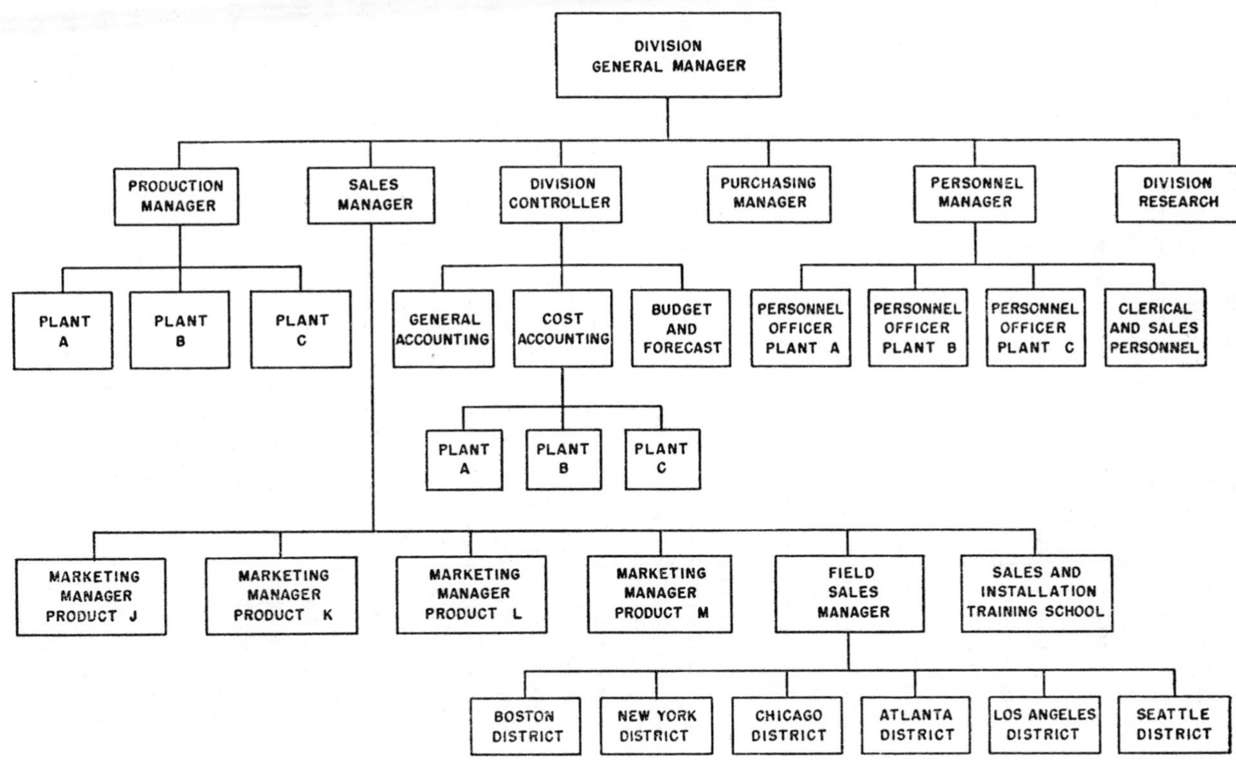

## Divisions or Subsidiaries?

There is one further question which is of some interest, and that is whether a division should be given a separate corporate identity as a subsidiary of the parent company. It may be said at the outset that the tendency in recent years has been markedly against the proliferation of subsidiaries in the domestic market. Many companies which diversified themselves in that way have dissolved their subsidiary companies and continued each separate business as an unincorporated division of the parent firm. While the issue of subsidiary versus division does not seem to be considered by most companies to be one of major importance, it can have some influence on questions of financial control, and for that reason we shall glance at it. The special problems that arise in connection with foreign operations or export will not, however, concern us.

Before the passing of the Revenue Act of 1964, the incidence of federal income tax was one of the most important factors determining whether divisions should be separately incorporated or not. The possibility of claiming a separate surtax exemption for each subsidiary favored their formation, while the fact that a part (15 per cent) of the dividends paid by subsidiaries out of their already-taxed profits was again taxed in the hands of the parent worked in the opposite direction. It is true that this double taxation could be avoided if the parent filed a consolidated tax return, but this means of escape itself cost the company a two per cent penalty tax. The 1964 Act greatly changed the tax position of parent companies and their subsidiaries. By repealing the two per cent additional tax on consolidated returns, it brought the tax treatment of a group of companies more closely into line with that of a single company and removed an impediment from the path of separate incorporation of divisions. The total exemption from tax of the dividends received by a parent company from its subsidiaries, an exemption which the group may elect to enjoy under the Act if it complies with certain conditions, removes another similar obstacle. However, it should be noted that one of the conditions referred to requires the group to limit itself to only one $25,000 surtax exemption instead of taking a full separate exemption for each company in the group. All in all, the effect of the 1964 Act seems likely to diminish the importance of tax as a factor affecting the incorporation of divisions as subsidiary companies.

Other tax considerations favor the perpetuation of subsidiary companies, where they already exist, in certain circumstances. For instance, if a subsidiary has been purchased and it has accumulated tax losses, it is unlikely that it will be liquidated until these losses have been used up by carry-over. Even if the subsidiary does remain in existence after the change of ownership, it must continue its old trade or business substantially unchanged in order to retain the benefit of its tax losses.[13] This provision explains the continued existence of many subsidiaries. The retention of a favorable LIFO base enjoyed by an existing company before it was acquired will also sometimes explain the continued existence as a subsidiary of a company which might otherwise be liquidated. Again, subsidiaries may be formed, or retained where they already exist, to save state taxes. Some states tax "foreign" corporations at higher rates than domestic ones, and it may therefore pay to have a separate locally registered subsidiary handle the company's business in those states. Or, if a company carries on a relatively unprofitable side of its business in certain states, it may pay the firm to have this carried on by one or more subsidiaries. If the unprofitable business were in the hands of an unincorporated division only, the company would perhaps pay state taxes on a proportion of its total profit. This percentage could be determined by taking the proportion of its sales in those states to its total sales, i.e., sales in those states are deemed to be as profitable as all its sales on the average, whereas, in fact, they are less than averagely profitable. Segregating these unprofitable sales in a subsidiary protects the higher profits earned elsewhere from being taxed by states in which they were not earned.

While taxes are a dominant factor influencing the decision whether to incorporate a division as a subsidiary or to retain the corporate form where it already exists, they are not the only factor. A compelling reason to do so arises when, in the process of diversification or expansion, a controlling (but not a 100 per cent) interest is acquired in an existing company so that the minority stockholders continue to participate in it. In a situation such as this, the simple divisional organization is ruled out. A somewhat similar reason for incorporation is encountered when a company starts a new venture jointly with another firm. By far the most convenient form for the venture is a corporation in which both participants hold stock.

Yet, taxes and outside stockholders apart, domestic subsidiaries are

---

[13] See Sec. 382(a) of the 1954 Revenue Code.

still to be found in large numbers. Here are some of the reasons given by companies which have cooperated in this study:

1. One company purchased a large tract of timberland, and found it had acquired a railway. As a regulated public carrier, the railway was retained on a subsidiary basis to save the whole company from being a public carrier. Oil companies owning pipe lines have them held by subsidiaries for the same reason.

2. A subsidiary holding a franchise to do business in a certain state may be continued in order to retain the franchise.

3. Divisions carrying on businesses which are subject to a high risk of public liability claims (e.g., in the construction industry) may be kept as subsidiaries to protect other assets of the corporation from being placed in jeopardy from such claims.

4. The continuance of a separate union contract with a subsidiary may be enough to preserve its corporate existence: and this will be especially true where the rest of the company is not unionized at all.

5. Some states pay subventions to *new* businesses which are set up in their territory. This may be enough to cause the expansion of an existing business to be disguised as a new business. This approach may be achieved by the simple expedient of putting the expansion into the hands of a newly formed subsidiary domiciled in the state in question.

6. Companies sometimes carry on businesses with which they do not wish to be publicly associated, even though those businesses are perfectly legal. As an example, some companies which have made their reputations in the "ethical" drug trade sell patent medicines through subsidiaries.

7. In view of the complex web of contractual relationships which it will have spun around itself, it may be expensive to dissolve an existing subsidiary.

8. The dignity of the corporate officers of a company, control of which has been acquired, may have to be preserved. The simplest way to do this is to continue the acquired company as a subsidiary. Corporate titles such as president and vice president are sometimes used in unincorporated divisions as well, however.

The most obvious case against subsidiaries is that they involve legal formalities and registration requirements which no one would seek for their own sake. On the other side it may be argued that if divisions are to exist as genuinely separate and largely autonomous businesses, this should be reflected in a separate legal identity for them as well, so as to emphasize their relative independence from the parent company to the men responsible for operating them.[14] The fact is, however, that divisions are *not* independent businesses, but only substantially self-contained parts of a larger whole. To give the part a separate legal identity is not particularly appropriate if there is no other reason to do so.

For all operating purposes, the question of division versus subsidiary is of little importance, though for tax purposes and where there are outside shareholders the matter is of greater significance. Each situation must be looked at on its merits; but there is very little doubt that the popularity of subsidiaries has long passed its peak.

## Conclusion

We have examined the organization of divisional companies at some length, and have noted numerous variations in the way responsibilities may be divided, as between the divisions and the corporate headquarters. We might have probed deeper still, and looked at the way in which, within a division, responsibilities are allocated between the operating units of the division—plants, sales offices, service installations and the like—and the staff departments at divisional headquarters. However, since our concern is primarily with the control of divisions, not with control *within* divisions, this discussion of organization will not be pursued further. That it has been taken as far as it has is due to the fact that, before we can consider methods of financial control of divisions, we have to know what their responsibilities are. For example, if a division has no power to determine its selling prices or its advertising appropriations, it is deprived of most of its ability to influence sales revenue. Elaborate methods of analyzing variances between budgeted and actual sales, while they might be of interest to the marketing department at the corporate level, would be of very little concern to anyone in the division. More generally, until a division's responsibilities are known, it is impossible to say whether it can be held truly accountable for its trading results, or how those results may best be measured so as to evaluate as effectively as possible the performance of the division and its management. This question of profit accountability will be taken up and examined in some detail in subsequent chapters.

---

[14] This argument is adduced by Robert W. Murphy in "Corporate Divisions vs. Subsidiaries," *loc. cit.*

# DIVISIONAL ACCOUNTING AND "GENERALLY ACCEPTED ACCOUNTING PRINCIPLES"

CHAPTER II

Recent pronouncements on the postulates and principles of accounting have, for the most part, been directed to the problems of reporting company results to stockholders. When accounting fundamentals are under discussion, little attention tends to be given to the question of whether accounting rules appropriate to the needs of stockholders are also appropriate to the needs of management. It is not just the methods of presenting financial information which are in question here, but the very bases of compiling this information as well. In this chapter we shall take a look at some of these issues, and especially at such of them as have special relevance to the needs of divisionalized firms.

In what follows, the terms "internal" and "external" accounting will be used in preference to the more commonly used "management" and "financial" accounting. There are two reasons for this preference. All accounting in terms of a monetary unit might be called "financial accounting." Therefore, this term does not convey the kind of distinction within the field of monetary accounting which is intended. Moreover, what are usually called "financial accounts" are also used for certain managerial purposes (such as the determination of dividend policy) so that, again, the distinction is blurred. By referring to internal and external accounting, however, the true nature of the distinction can be more accurately conveyed.

Before a judgment can be reached as to the extent to which the principles of external accounting are applicable to internal accounting, there must be some consensus as to what these principles are. We shall take as our starting point for this discussion the Report of the 1961 Management Accounting Committee of the American Accounting Association[1] though we shall depart considerably from the Committee's analysis and conclusions. In Part II of the Report, "the body of postulates, principles, and standards (herein referred to collectively as concepts) which underlie accounting as a general field" are listed as follows:

Entity concept
Enterprise continuity (going concern) concept
Money measurement concept
Cost base and cost flow concept
Realization (recognition) concept
Matching (accrual or periodicity) concept
Objectivity concept
Consistency concept
Materiality concept
Full disclosure concept
Conservatism concept

It is not our aim to evaluate these concepts for the purposes of external accounting. But in assessing their value for internal accounting, which is what we shall try to do, it will probably be impossible to avoid all judgments on these concepts as they are used in other contexts.

### *Entity concept*

The entity concept in accounting is a somewhat pompous way of saying that, before we can account intelligently, we had better identify the person or business unit for which we are accounting; or, at greater length, "The business entity concept provides a basis for identifying economic resources and activities with specific enterprises, and thus for defining the area of coverage appropriate to a given set of records or reports."[2] For external accounting purposes, the ac-

[1] *Accounting Review,* XXXVII, No. 3, July 1962, pp. 523-537. The Committee's term "management accounting" and our term "internal accounting" are interchangeable in the present context.

[2] "Accounting and Reporting Standards for Corporate Financial Statements," 1957 Revision, American Accounting Association, *Accounting Review,* Vol. XXXII, No. 4, October 1957, p. 537.

counting entity is usually a legal person—a corporation, for example—though this is not always so. Consolidated accounts do not relate to a legal entity but, rather, to a group of legal entities (and not even that in any simple sense). In the case of a pooling of interests, it is really quite difficult to say what the accounting entity is. However, the normal case is straightforward enough.

For internal accounting, legal entities have little significance. The accounting entity may be any sector or facet of a business which its management wishes to analyze. We can probably comprehend any such sector or facet of business activity about which it may be desired to collect or present accounting data by categorizing them in one or another of the following classes of entities:[3]

1. Responsibility centers
2. Ventures or market entities
   a. Continuing ventures: focusing on product, market area, type of customer, etc.
   b. Transient ventures: identified as special projects, and either eventually terminating, or being transformed into, or merged with a continuing venture.

The importance of the distinction between these two broad kinds of internal accounting entities is that they serve different purposes. When we are trying to evaluate the performance of a person or persons, it is the results of the appropriate responsibility center which call for attention. This kind of entity is defined by reference to the person bearing the responsibility for it. If, on the other hand, we want to evaluate an activity or a sector of the business (as distinct from the men running it) we must look at the results of the appropriate market entity. This includes the product or product group, the sales region, the market for original equipment as against replacement equipment (if we are in the automotive battery or the tire business) and so on.

The project type of entity will generally have an ephemeral existence. It will be created for a special purpose such as the evaluation of a new line of business, or the contribution made to the business by a new plant, or the extension of an existing one. Usually, once suf-

[3] The classes of entities listed by the AAA Management Accounting Committee (*op. cit.* p. 526) are responsibility entities, product entities and project entities. Numbers 1 and 2b in our list correspond to the first and third in the AAA Committee's list. Our 2a, however, is broader than theirs. "Product" is only one of the things that may identify a venture or a market.

ficient data have been collected to evaluate the project, the project entity will be merged with one of the market entities. The figures relating to it will then become a part of the market entity's figures. Sometimes, however, as in the case of a special seasonal marketing venture, the entity may recur year after year.

In the internal accounting of divisionalized companies, responsibility centers play a vital part. From the DGM, with responsibility for the whole division, down through managers of possible subdivisions to managers of plants and sales district offices, product sales promotion managers, and others, performance is measured by comparing the inputs and outputs for which each is responsible. For accounting purposes, therefore, each is a responsibility center, though with more and more limited responsibilities as we progress down the line.

A division may be incorporated as a subsidiary company, or it may comprise a number of subsidiaries. It may also consist of a part of a subsidiary, and a subsidiary may even straddle two or more divisions. Responsibility centers may or may not correspond, therefore, to legal entities. For the purposes of internal accounting, the only significance of the legal entity is that it will be the entity on which taxes may be levied. The way in which it arranges its affairs may, therefore, affect the tax liabilities it passes on to the responsibility centers which it comprises, or of which it is composed. More will be said about this aspect of the matter later.

It is fairly common to find a divisionalized company bringing the aggregate of its responsibility centers into conformity with the outline of the legal entity through creation of a fictitious responsibility center. This is usually called either the "corporate division" or the "general division." This fiction is created to provide an accounting entity to which nondivisional income can be credited, and nondivisional expenses can be charged. Dividends and interest on corporate investments or a profit on the sale of a head office building are examples of the first. Capital loss on investment is an example of the second. Some companies treat federal income tax as a corporate (i.e., nondivisional) expense also. The idea of the fictitious corporate division is a useful one in that it recognizes explicitly that the whole is greater than the sum of its (nonfictitious) parts. Of course this fact can be recognized without the creation of a fictitious division. Nothing more is necessary than the realization that there are certain corporate activities not directly related to the activities of the divisions.

However, any device which makes it easier to resist pressures (which exist in all companies) to allocate to operating divisions accounting quantities whose true significance requires that they be left unallocated is to be welcomed.

We shall probably see the device of the corporate division play a larger part in divisionalized companies in the future than it has done hitherto. One company already makes the corporate division responsible for launching new ventures so that the operating divisions do not have to bear the development costs and the resulting losses involved in establishing them. An operating division may be in too great a hurry to eliminate losses in the development period, whereas the corporate division, which theoretically is not expected to operate at a profit, can take a longer view. The corporate division has only limited production facilities of its own, and therefore subcontracts some production to one of the operating divisions. When the venture (a new group of products, for instance) has been successfully launched, it is handed over to an existing operating division. If of sufficient importance, it may be launched as a new division instead. This approach has considerable value. Its weakness in practice seems to be that the corporate division runs a risk of being short of the marketing skills necessary to make the new venture a success. Temporary assignment of suitable marketing personnel from an operating division is a possibility, but divisions do not welcome such loss of talent, even temporarily. In the company mentioned above, this problem has not yet been satisfactorily solved.

Just as there is no simple unique relationship between the legal entity and the responsibility center(s), so there are many possible relationships between responsibility centers and market entities. Since divisions are usually market-oriented, a responsibility center (Division A) will perhaps correspond to the market entity "agricultural chemicals," and in assessing the success of Division A's general manager, the value to the company of its agricultural chemicals business is also assessed. Because of the coincidence of the responsibility center with the market entity, the same figures are liable to be used to assess both the success of the one and the value of the other whereas, we shall see, different approaches may be necessary to these different tasks.

In other cases, responsibility centers and market entities may not coincide. For example, a company engaged both in retailing through stores and in mail order selling might organize these activities as separate responsibility centers appealing to the same markets. In other cases, a single responsibility center, which will itself be broken down into a number of subcenters, may contain several market entities. This occurs, for example, when a company which is for the most part engaged in mass production has a separate "special products" division to handle a variety of custom-built products. The special products division will represent a number of market entities—markets for a variety of products sold to many types of customers.

The significance of these distinctions, for us, lies in the fact that financial information collected for the purposes of one kind of entity may not necessarily be appropriate for another, and failure to recognize this fact will hinder effective financial control. We shall take up this point in the next chapter when we consider the methods to be used in assessing divisional results.

### *Enterprise continuity (going concern) concept*

This concept says that "in the absence of evidence to the contrary, the entity should be viewed as remaining in operation indefinitely. In the presence of evidence that the entity has a limited life, it should not be viewed as remaining in operation indefinitely."[4] We need not stay long to examine this, or to ask whether it is as applicable to internal as to external accounting, for it is a concept we can quite well do without. We do not need a "concept" to tell us that, depending on whether we are accounting for a continuing concern or for one which is expected to terminate in the foreseeable future, our accounting methods should be chosen appropriately. It is just worth noting that terminable entities do play a somewhat larger role in internal accounting (notably in considering abandonment decisions or replacement decisions) than in external accounting for the whole enterprise. But no more need be said than that it is important to recognize the difference between continuing and terminable entities and to account for them accordingly.

### *Money measurement concept*

Besides reminding us of the rather obvious point that "money is the common denominator in terms of which goods and services, in-

[4] Maurice Moonitz, *The Basic Postulates of Accounting,* Accounting Research Study No. 1, New York: American Institute of Certified Public Accountants, 1961.

cluding labor, natural resources and capital are measured,"[5] this concept raises a question of substance—is a monetary unit with a fluctuating purchasing power really a common denominator? And if it is not, should the accountant draw up financial statements in terms of a "constant dollar" either as substitutes for, or as supplements to, the conventional "fluctuating dollar" statements? These questions are relevant to both internal and external accounting. But whereas, on the external side, arguments can be brought forward to defend a "do nothing" attitude,[6] for internal accounting purposes the matter is entirely in the firm's own hands. It cannot, therefore, shift to anyone else the onus of deciding to what extent, if at all, it should recognize the instability of the dollar in the accounting statements it produces for its own guidance.

It would take us far beyond our present purpose to examine this question fully. Its relevance for divisional accounting lies principally in the impact which price-level adjustments would have on divisional depreciation charges and on the valuation of "capital employed" for rate of return calculations and on the effect on divisional profit measurement of the adoption of LIFO. These matters will occupy us further in Chapters III and IV.

The money measurement concept does not imply that measurements in nonmonetary terms have no place in accounting. We should expect to find more scope for nonmonetary ones in internal rather than in external accounting, for "the broader the scope of operations covered by a report, the less likely it is that a suitable common denominator, other than money, can be found as a means of expressing the results of business events."[7] In external accounting the totality of the company's operations has to be covered.

Since its scope is narrower than corporate accounting, we might suppose that divisional accounting would have developed and brought into widespread use a broad range of nonmonetary measures of divisional performance. The fact is, however, that little has been achieved in this area: but it has to be recognized that the supremacy of money as a measure of business results largely reflects the interconnection of the various parts of a business concern into a *system.*

---

[5] Moonitz, *op. cit.,* p. 52.

[6] Arguments such as that stockholders would be confused by a change, that the SEC would object, that the Internal Revenue Service would object, that the company's auditors would not certify the revised statements, and so on.

[7] AAA Management Accounting Committee, *loc. cit.,* page 528.

Only in money terms can we bring the results of several different functions together to see if the success of each of them has contributed to the success of the firm. For instance, a maintenance department may have been able to reduce the down time on machines in a particular operating department, and may rightly claim this as a success. But, if the operating department has excess capacity, the reduction in down time may simply run to waste. The success of the maintenance men, at least in the short run, will not have contributed to the success of the firm in that particular situation. Or, to take an example from quite a different field, the credit department may be able to point to a very low percentage loss from uncollectibles. For that department this is a success. But it is one that may have been achieved at the cost of turning away a large number of orders on which the profit would have more than compensated for any resulting increase in uncollectibles. It so happens that in this case the credit department, as well as the business as a whole, uses a money measure (or at least a ratio of two money measures to each other—credit losses as a percentage of sales) to assess its results. The point is that the success of the department is not a success for the firm. Whereas departmental successes may be scored in nonmonetary terms (in the case of the credit department, perhaps a reduction in the average length of credit allowed, measured in days) the firm as a whole, in the last analysis, can only use a monetary measure.

## *The cost, realization and matching concepts*

These three concepts together sum up the accounting approach to the measurement of profit, and it is therefore appropriate to consider them together. First, let us sum up what they say. Normally, on acquisition, an asset is brought into account at cost, i.e., at the value given up in exchange for it. If the asset was purchased for resale, or for incorporation in products for resale, it will continue to be carried at such cost until realized, unless there is reason to believe that the whole of its cost will not be recovered from the proceeds of realization. In that case, it will be revalued downwards to an amount equal to its expected realizable value.

Upon realization, whether previously revalued or not, the assets received in exchange for the realized asset (usually cash or receivables or, less commonly, securities) are substituted for it. The profit or loss on realization is arrived at by "matching" or offsetting the cost or revaluation of the asset disposed of against the value of the assets received in exchange.

In the case of assets purchased for use in the business, their costs will be progressively transferred as they are used up or otherwise lose expectation of life. If their use is directly associated with the manufacture of products for sale, a proportionate part of their costs will be transferred to the cost of those products. If their use is not so directly associated, a proportionate part of their costs will be transferred against the *period(s)* in which they are used up, as a part of the operating costs of those periods.

This is a very bald statement of the cost, realization and matching concepts.[8] Over the years these ideas have become much refined. There has been, for example, a proliferation of bases for ascertaining the costs of inventories leading to many different ways of arriving at the cost of sales. A great variety of depreciation methods have developed giving many ways of determining the cost of using up fixed assets. We have seen a tendency to move away somewhat from a narrow interpretation of "realization" and to recognize value changes in an asset even when they are evidenced by less than an actual legal transfer of ownership. The process of matching costs and revenues, apparently a simple idea, has taken on a controversial character in such issues as absorption costing versus direct costing and the treatment of R&D expenditure.

All these developments, and many more that could be cited, have somewhat blurred the outlines of the traditional idea of accounting profit as the excess of currently realized revenue over the cost of earning it. Nevertheless, the basic idea still holds sway.[9]

Traditionally, the accounting profit of a period means the realized profit on assets (the most important being inventory) sold during the

---

[8] A full recent statement of generally accepted accounting principles will be found in Paul Grady's *Inventory of Generally Accepted Accounting Principles for Business Enterprises,* Accounting Research Study No. 7, New York: American Institute of Certified Public Accountants, 1965.

[9] How strong that hold is has recently been strikingly demonstrated by the official reception given to Accounting Research Study No. 3 of the American Institute of Certified Public Accountants, *A Tentative Set of Broad Accounting Principles for Business Enterprises* by Robert T. Sprouse and Maurice Moonitz, 1962. Of the 12 members of the project's two advisory committees, nine appended comments to the report. Of these, seven were adverse, one was favorable, and one was neutral. The verdict of the AICPA Accounting Principles Board, in a statement dated April 13, 1962, was that "while these studies are a valuable contribution to accounting thinking, they are too radically different from present generally accepted accounting principles for acceptance at this time."—*Journal of Accountancy,* May 1962.

period less unrealized diminutions in the value of current assets held at the end of that same period. It is impossible to hold that such an amount corresponds to any fundamental notion of what the word "profit" should mean.

We can distinguish between two ideas of profit: (1) The profit resulting from a transaction or transactions, and (2) the profit of a business period. Taking the transaction idea first, it is initially necessary to decide whether a "transaction" means *either* a purchase *or* a sale, or, on the other hand, a purchase *and* its related sale. If the first interpretation is adopted, we should expect to take account of all changes in the value of an asset after it was purchased, whether these changes were up or down. But traditionally only downward changes are recognized. If we adopt the second interpretation, we should expect to recognize neither a profit nor a loss on a purchase so long as there had been no corresponding sale. Yet "generally acceptable accounting principles" do take account of unrealized losses on inventory. As a matter of fact, in a modern manufacturing business, with several successive conversions of material before it is finally sold, and with transfers of intermediates and other products between divisions, it becomes extremely difficult to isolate a purchase and its related sale. The idea of "profit on transactions" thus becomes quite a shadowy one.

If we turn to the idea of "profit of a period" as a way out of these difficulties, we shall be in no better shape. When we say that a business made a profit for a particular period, we presumably mean that it was better off at the end of the period than it was at the beginning (after correcting, of course, for any new capital put into the business, or dividends or capital withdrawals taken out). The meaning of "better off" is not easy to define. But presumably it would have to include all measurable changes in the value of the enterprise, whether they had resulted from transactions (however defined) which had taken place during the period, or had simply come about through changes in the value of the assets which the firm had held through the period. Also included would be changes in the value of goodwill resulting from alterations in its future prospects. It will be obvious that "better-off-ness," defined in this all-inclusive way, is quite a different thing from what we measure when we compute accounting profit.

If it is accepted that the fundamental idea of profit is better-off-ness even if, because of the practical difficulties, we cannot come at all close to measuring it, we do at least have an ideal standard against which to compare generally accepted bases of profit measurement and perhaps we shall be able to see their shortcomings more clearly. For internal accounting purposes, especially in divisionalized companies, those shortcomings are somewhat serious, especially when profit is used as a measure of success of the men responsible for directing a division. Over a series of years, the results will not misrepresent the facts at all seriously, so that if the same managers stay in the job year after year, the accounting results over the years will reflect their achievement reasonably well. But what generally accepted accounting principles purport to do is to measure profit a year at a time. We are entitled to judge them as if a different manager were in charge in each year in the series. The question we have a right to ask is: How well does each year's profit reflect the success of that year's manager?

To minimize the difficulties of the situation, let us assume that we have reached a period of stability in the purchasing power of the dollar. Of course, this does not rule out fluctuations in particular prices, either of the assets the firm buys and sells or uses or of the services it buys and uses. Then we can say that each year's profit, as conventionally measured, will accurately reflect that year's manager's success to the extent that the following conditions are satisfied:

1. There has been no appreciation during the year in inventories still held at the end of that year.
2. No inventories which had appreciated in a previous year were sold during the present year.
3. No fixed assets, for the location or selection of which the manager was responsible, had appreciated during the year, or had fallen in value more or less than was recognized in the year's depreciation charge.
4. There has been no change in the division's future business prospects except what would be needed to give an economic return on any additional capital invested in the division.

These four conditions correspond to the four elements of change in "well-off-ness" which accounting profit excludes from its purview. If these elements of change are absent or unimportant during the period in question, accounting profit will do well enough. If they are not absent, accounting profit will paint too rosy or too gloomy a picture of the manager's achievements. As will be seen, the exclusion of these value changes from accounting profit results from selecting the act of realization as the essential requirement for recognition of profit. This choice is made in order to link the recognition of profit with some specific and objectively verifiable event. But it has the unfortunate result of making the earning of a profit appear to be the result solely of the act of selling products, rather than of the whole process of production and marketing. Removing some of the emphasis from realization, with a consequential recognition of unrealized profits, would often fall foul of the requirement of objectivity, but it would also provide a more realistic measure of managerial performance.[10]

The fourth element of change listed above is probably the most important one that is left out of conventional profit measurements. It is quite possible for two managers to show identical profits for a year or two, or even identical rates of return on capital, and yet have quite different degrees of success as managers. One is building the foundations of a flourishing business, fostering good relations with customers, suppliers, and employees. The other is squandering the firm's goodwill. None of the former may show up in the current profit figures, nor may the frictions which the second manager is generating. But if profits really did measure better-off-ness, the two manager's results would look very different.[11]

## *Objectivity concept*

Objectivity is a property of accounting data to which most accountants attach the greatest importance. By objectivity is meant a factual quality of measurement in accounting which is void of personal opinion or bias, and which is capable of independent verification. This, it is generally agreed, is outstandingly a quality of his-

---

[10] Powerful support for the view that the emphasis on realization should be diminished, or at least that something less than an actual transaction of sale should be recognized as realization, is to be found in the Sprouse and Moonitz research study already referred to. The idea that holding gains and losses should be recognized, though separately from operating gains and losses, is developed in *The Theory and Measurement of Business Income* by Edgar O. Edwards and Philip W. Bell, University of California Press, 1961. Further support for these ideas has come from the American Accounting Association's Committee on the Realization Concept, the report of which appeared in the *Accounting Review,* April 1965, pp. 312-322, and in *A Statement of Basic Accounting Theory,* published by the Association in 1966.

[11] In none of the foregoing discussion has any attention been paid to the special problems of *divisional* profit measurement. These problems and a further look at the whole subject of measuring managerial success in financial terms are the subject of the next chapter.

torical cost, since this derives from a past transaction, the terms of which can be ascertained and verified.

An extended examination of this important concept would be inappropriate at this time.[12] However, a brief comment is, perhaps in order. First, objectivity is a secondary, not a primary quality of accounting data. The primary qualities are relevance and accuracy. If accounting information is accurate and is relevant to the needs of the user for whom it is prepared, we may hope that it has the additional and certainly desirable quality of objectivity. Unfortunately, historical cost is strong on objectivity but weak on relevance. If we have to choose between information which is relevant and accurate but not objective, or information which is objective but irrelevant or inaccurate, there can be no question as to which choice is the right one.

There can be even less question in the field of internal accounting than when reports to stockholders or the public are under discussion. In internal accounting, both those who prepare the figures and those for whom they are prepared are knowledgeable about the business. A follow-through on questions raised by the information is possible and, indeed, usually welcomed by the person preparing it. For all these reasons, the folly of choosing objectivity at the cost of relevance is even greater and less excusable in internal accounting than in external accounting. Fortunately, those responsible for preparing internal accounting information have been aware of this fact and have not been slow to adopt such tools as standards, budgets, forecasts, estimates and valuations wherever these have seemed useful. This has been done despite the fact that, in the nature of things, they cannot always have the objectivity which attaches to past transactions.

### *Consistency, materiality and full disclosure concepts*

These three concepts are so closely related to each other that, again, it seems best to consider them together. An item is considered "material" in accounting "if there is reason to believe that knowledge of it would influence the decisions of an informed investor"[13]—and, we may add, of any other informed reader of the accounts, such as a manager. It may be taken as a self-evident truth that accounting state-

---

[12] But see Harold Arnett, "What Does 'Objectivity' Mean to Accountants?" *Journal of Accountancy,* May 1961, pp. 63-68.

[13] "Accounting and Reporting Standards for Corporate Financial Statements," 1957 Revision, American Accounting Association, *Accounting Review,* October 1957, p. 543.

ments should fully disclose all material information relating to the purpose of the statement. It will be seen that the definition quoted above for "material" would serve equally well as a definition of "relevant." The importance of emphasizing the relevant in internal accounting, rather than other qualities to which, traditionally, more importance has been attached in the external accounting field, has already been sufficiently stressed.

The case for consistency has to be weighed in the light of what has just been noted about materiality and full disclosure. Inconsistency in the bases on which accounting information is prepared for an accounting entity from year to year may be deplored on one or both of two grounds. Most accounting measures, it is often pointed out, mean very little when taken by themselves. However, they take on significance when expressed as a trend over a period of time, or when related to other quantities by means of ratios or other types of comparison. These comparisons or trends may be vitiated, it is said, by inconsistencies of treatment and much useful information may be lost. This is one aspect of the case for consistency.

Another aspect is the argument that unscrupulous men may take advantage of inconsistently prepared figures to show results more favorable than they should be—for example, by inflating profits by means of a change in the basis of inventory valuation. A close look at these arguments will show, in both cases, that the real danger is not so much a lack of consistency as a lack of full disclosure. Only an *undisclosed* change in the basis of inventory valuation, for example, could seriously mislead anyone. Full disclosure would show not only that there had been a change of basis but also the effect of the change on the figures. This would also make it possible to dispose of the problem of comparisons between periods where consistency had not been preserved since all the information would be available to enable one or the other set of figures to be adjusted to restore comparability.

It hardly needs to be said that if consistency can be preserved without any loss of accuracy then, on the grounds of mere expediency and economy of effort, this should be done. A problem arises, however, when a possibility of improving accounting information presents itself at the cost of a break with the former basis of accounting. The solution in such cases, if it is practicable, is to take advantage of the improvement, disclose its effect fully, and go back and recompute past figures on the new basis to ensure an unbroken consistent series.

If such recomputation is not possible, then a judgment has to be reached as to whether the improvement in the information which the new method makes possible is more valuable than the comparability which will be lost. In most cases, the verdict should be in favor of change, for the loss of comparability will be only temporary while the loss from rejecting innovations will be permanent.

The foregoing is equally applicable to both internal and external accounting. However, whereas full disclosure to a stockholder involves the difficulty that data disclosed to him cannot be kept from competitors, the same objection cannot be raised against disclosure in internal accounting statements. Thus consistency becomes a less important virtue, and changes in accounting method can now be made more freely where there is good reason for them. So long as the requirement that all material information shall be fully and accurately disclosed is satisfied, consistency, it would seem, can be left to look after itself.

There is one aspect of consistency which might be thought to have special relevance for a divisionalized company, and that is consistency of accounting methods between divisions. Surprisingly or not, very little importance seems to be attached to this kind of consistency by most such companies. It is quite common to find, for example, that some divisions of a company use a LIFO basis of inventory valuation, while other divisions do not. Divisions may use a diversity of depreciation methods. It is less common, but not unknown, to find one or more divisions using direct costing while other divisions use absorption costing.

These inconsistencies reflect, in part, a desire of top management to leave as much room as possible for individuality on the part of divisions. They also imply recognition of the fact that different accounting methods may be appropriate to the diverse needs of the divisions. They further reflect a lack of interest in interdivisional comparisons of profitability. Such comparisons are generally regarded as of little value because of the differences in the nature of the businesses conducted by divisions. One division, perhaps because of patent protection, may have a near-monopoly in its field, another may be a new division in a rapidly expanding market. A third one may be an old division operating in a fiercely competitive field and facing a shrinking demand for its products. Few financial executives interviewed expressed much belief in the value of profit comparisons between divisions under such circumstances.

For the purpose of evaluating the performance of the men responsible for the divisions, this judgment is no doubt sound. But ventures, as well as men, have to be appraised. The fact that one division is earning a poor return, and has done so for several years, may not reflect adversely on the DGM or his men. Perhaps in the circumstances no one could have done better. But the question is whether the company should stay in that business at all. Here, interdivisional comparisons do have a part to play and they are certainly not facilitated by the kind of inconsistency referred to above.

Fortunately, it is not difficult to get the best of both worlds—to let divisions use the accounting methods best suited to their needs while still securing comparability of results. The solution lies in full disclosure by each division of all the information necessary to bring its results into line with those of other divisions. As an example, a division (A) using LIFO can easily be compared profit-wise with another (B) using FIFO if the LIFO adjustment (the valuation difference between FIFO and LIFO applicable to the *change* in inventory during the period) is shown separately on its statements, thus:

EXHIBIT I

| | Division A<br>$ | Division B<br>$ |
|---|---|---|
| Sales | 50,000 | 30,000 |
| Less | | |
| Cost of Sales (on FIFO basis) | 32,000 | 17,000 |
| Gross margin | 18,000 | 13,000 |
| Less | | |
| Division expenses | 10,000 | 8,000 |
| Net Profit (on FIFO basis) | 8,000 | 5,000 |
| Add (deduct) | | |
| LIFO valuation adjustment | (2,000) | |
| Net profit (on LIFO basis) | 6,000 | |

Many companies using LIFO for some divisions already utilize this technique and even go further by making the LIFO valuation adjustment entirely outside the divisional figures. This is charged or credited to the corporate division, for instance, where such a fictitious entity is recognized. Further discussion of this matter will be found on pages 95-100.

### *Conservatism concept*

This, the last of the concepts said to underlie accounting, is a curious bedfellow for such ideas as objectivity and consistency. It has been said that "the proper role of conservatism in accounting is to ensure that the uncertainties and risks inherent in any given business situation are given adequate consideration."[14] "Adequate consideration," in the hands of the conservatively minded, is apt to mean "excessive consideration." It has been pointed out many times that a conservative valuation of inventory (at the end of the period, for instance) is likely to result in an inflated profit when the inventory is sold in the next period. Accuracy and full disclosure are altogether better guides to practice in internal accounting (and probably in external accounting, too) than is conservatism. It is unlikely that we shall have any further use for this concept in this study.

## A Further Note on Responsibility Accounting

The scorekeeping function of accounting in divisionalized companies is very much concerned with the allocation of costs and revenues to the functions and persons responsible for them in the business. This accounting activity is concerned not only with the evaluation of past performance but also, importantly, with the motivation of managers to conduct their operations in a manner calculated to serve the best interests of the company as a whole. This will not be achieved by an accounting system which allows a department to escape the cost consequences of its actions by shifting the burden on to another department (as, for example, when service departments are able to pass on the cost of their inefficiencies by making inflated charges to the departments they serve). Nor will this goal be accomplished by a system which allows the cost of overtime in Department A to be escaped by Department B when Department A was forced to work overtime through bad planning or late deliveries on B's part. This is the first principle of responsibility accounting—*that*

---

[14] Moonitz, *The Basic Postulates of Accounting,* p. 47.

*costs should be borne by, and revenues should be credited to, the segments of the business responsible for them.*

The foregoing rule implies that, as far as possible, lines of responsibility should be drawn clearly and unambiguously. Although departments should be encouraged to consult together fully on matters of joint concern, no one section should be in any doubt as to where the final responsibility lies. A personnel department in a small business advertises employment vacancies in the press through the advertising department. The personnel department drafts the advertisement, the advertising department determines its size and layout and decides, in consultation with personnel, in which publications it shall appear. There need be no ambiguity as to how these responsibilities are to be divided. But what of the costs of the advertisement? Are they advertising or personnel costs?

It is generally accepted as a secondary principle of responsibility accounting that, in a situation such as the one described, *costs should be charged to the department which has the power to accept or reject the invoice or which pays for the labor required.* In the above illustration, this would be the advertising department. But to stop there would leave the cost with one department and the benefit with another. There must, therefore, be a further step. This will take the form of setting up two offsetting accounts, one in the advertising department (to which the charge to personnel will be credited), and the other in the personnel department (to take the debit). Both the gross debits and the amounts charged will be shown against advertising in the financial statements.

It will be clear from what has already been said that pinpointing "responsibility" for a cost is not a simple matter. Another aspect of the problem can be seen when one department does work for another for which it is agreed that the benefitting department should bear the cost. If the serving department is underemployed, or for any reason is working at less than normal efficiency, should the benefitting department be required to bear the resulting high cost of service? Common sense seems to demand that, if services are to be provided by one department for another at "cost," this must mean "standard cost." This leaves the responsibility for variances from standard with the department providing the service. But even this procedure does not insulate the benefitting department entirely from cost influences outside its control. Even standard cost, if it includes a proportion of the service department's fixed overhead, will depend in part on the scale on which it has been set up.

Responsibility accounting can be conceived of without budgets and standards, but its effectiveness has been greatly enhanced by the spread of these techniques since they contribute both to the scorekeeping and attention-directing capabilities of accounting. This would probably be true no matter how the standards and budgets were set. If, however, they can be set with the full cooperation and acceptance of those who are to be judged by them, the virtues of self-evaluation are added to the evaluation of the activities in question by an outside scorekeeper. This brings with it the possibility of self-correction by those controlled by the budgets and standards, a procedure which is always to be preferred to the imposition of correctives by higher echelons.

Even if budgets were never subsequently compared with actual results, there would still be great value in their preparation. The very act of formally putting plans down on paper forces the planner to think out his aims and procedures more carefully, and in greater detail. This becomes especially true if the job is done honestly and with the conviction that it is a worthwhile exercise. The value of the budget will be greatly enhanced if scorekeeping and attention-directing can be added to its planning aspect. This necessitates the preparation of information on actual results in a form permitting ready comparison with the budget—in fact the processes of budgeting and accounting may well be thought of as two parts of a single process. The marriage of accounts and budgets has become so much the central feature of a good system of responsibility accounting that many people think of the one as being synonymous with the other. They are not synonymous; but a system of responsibility accounting which relies on accounts without budgets or budgets without accounts is no more than half a system, and is, therefore, ineffectual.

## Summary

It may be helpful to summarize the conclusions already reached, some of which are important enough to merit further discussion in later chapters:

1. In internal accounting, as in external accounting, it is necessary to identify the accounting entities. Appropriate entities for internal accounting are:

a. Responsibility centers
b. Market entities
c. Projects

rather than legal entities. Each kind of entity has its own peculiar use in divisional accounting.

2. The important differences between a continuing enterprise and a terminable project must naturally be reflected in the methods of accounting. The facts of the situation, so far as they can be known, must dictate whether an accounting entity is to be treated as a continuing one or not. This applies to divisions as well as to other entities.

3. The smaller the segment of a business which accounting statements cover, the more scope there is likely to be for nonmonetary measures to supplement or even to replace money measures. Such measures are subject to the risk that they may signal successes in a limited field which are really defeats for the company as a whole.

4. Only in conditions of unusual stability will profit, as measured in accordance with generally accepted accounting principles, over a short period (such as a year) satisfactorily reflect managerial success or failure. This raises doubts as to the reliability of divisional profits as a measure of divisional success.

5. The primary qualities to be looked for in accounting information are relevance and accuracy. Objectivity is certainly desirable but is secondary. This is even more true in internal accounting than in connection with reports to stockholders.

6. So long as there is full disclosure of relevant accounting information to those for whom statements are prepared, a lack of consistency from period to period may be burdensome to the reader of the statements but it is not likely to mislead him. This is particularly true in internal accounting. Improvements in accounting methods should, in general, not be sacrificed to obtain consistency from period to period.

7. Comparisons of results of divisions are seldom made. It is true that the quality of managerial performance in different divisions cannot be compared by comparing profits: but comparisons of the profitability of *investments* should be fruitful, and for this purpose divisional figures need to be capable of adjustment to put them on a consistent basis as between divisions.

8. Conservatism, long considered a virtue in accounting, may con-

flict with objectivity and consistency. If wrongly understood, conservatism will certainly diminish the accuracy of accounting results. Accuracy and full disclosure, especially in internal accounting, are better guides than conservatism.

9. Costs should be borne by, and revenues should be credited to, the segments of the business responsible for them. Only if this is done with reasonable accuracy can these segments be fairly judged and helped towards better performance. Where responsibility for the incurrence of a cost is shared by two departments, it should be charged to the department which will accept the invoice or pay the labor. An offsetting charge to the benefitting department should also be made.

10. In judging who is responsible for a cost, it may be necessary to distinguish between responsibility for the standard cost and responsibility for the variance therefrom.

11. The ability to compare actual results with budgets greatly enhances a system of accounting for responsibilities. This calls for uniformity of budgets with accounts.

# PROFIT AS A MEASURE OF DIVISIONAL PERFORMANCE

CHAPTER III

A distinction was drawn in the last chapter between the success of a venture and the success of the men responsible for managing it. In the absence of evidence to the contrary, the presumption is that the success of one implies the success of the other. But, as has already been pointed out, circumstances outside a manager's control may dictate success or failure of the venture. Although the quality of management may heighten success or failure, conditions may be such that, within reasonable limits of ability, no management could reverse the trend.

This in itself does not imply that there has to be any difference between the figures used to measure the results of a venture and those used to measure the success of the manager. What it does imply is that there have to be different *standards* of success for judging both the venture and the manager. Thus, if the rate of return on investment is to be the criterion of success, four per cent before taxes might, because of the difficulties of the situation, represent a creditable performance by the manager, but could hardly represent a satisfactory result for the venture itself.

There may be no simple one-to-one relationship between a manager (or responsibility center) and a venture. A group executive may be responsible for several divisions, a DGM for several subdivisions. Ventures often comprise several responsibility centers, as when a large government defense contract calls in the services of several divisions, or when the market for a particular product is served by several plants. In such situations there can be no simple relationship between responsibility accounting and venture accounting.

Even where there is a one-to-one relationship between venture and manager, the accounting information necessary for reporting on the one may not be, and indeed usually is not, precisely the same as that necessary for reporting on the other. This is true at least where the venture under discussion is a complete division and the manager in question is the DGM in charge of it, for expenses outside the jurisdiction of the manager, and therefore not properly chargeable to *him,* may nevertheless clearly relate to the division's affairs and therefore be properly chargeable to *it.* A proportion of general administration expenses incurred at the head office is so treated by many divisionalized companies. Research work done in a central laboratory, and charged to a division against the wishes of a DGM, also falls into this category of expense. The distinction drawn here between the manager's performance and the venture's performance is an important one for all companies but especially, perhaps, for those organized divisionally.

## Measuring Managerial Success

Before exploring further the problem of measuring the success of divisional performance, let us first take up again the question of measuring managerial success in a general sense. We may simplify such measurement to start with, by taking a rather small venture with a manager separately responsible for it. In a case such as this, the success of the venture can be clearly identified with the success of the manager. In the interests of simplification, also, general changes in the purchasing power of the dollar will be ruled out.

What is success? Success in doing what? The obvious answer is success is earning a profit. According to this view, as between two managers running fairly similar businesses, the manager judged more successful will be the one who makes the larger profit. But there are two reasons for doubting the adequacy of this answer. In the first place, as has already been suggested, profit as measured in accordance with generally accepted accounting principles is a somewhat unsure gauge of success. Profits can be kept up for some years while the business is being "milked" by cutting down on research, maintenance, and certain kinds of advertising, or by realizing assets which have been steadily appreciating in value for several years even though the value of money in general has been steady. Conversely profits can be kept down by stepping up these expenditures and by declining to realize assets which have appreciated in value, but which accounting principles dictate shall continue to be carried at cost. Quite apart from these doubts about the adequacy of accounting profit, at least in the short run, as a measure of managerial success, what does "the larger profit" mean, when it is said that of two managers, the one who makes the larger profit is more successful? If it means simply the greater absolute number of dollars it is open to the criticism that if one of the managers has access to unlimited capital, either free of interest altogether or at a very low rate, he can probably increase the absolute profit he shows by pumping in more capital so long as he can show any return at all on it (if he gets it free), or any return in excess of his cost of capital.

If, in deference to this criticism, it is suggested that the relative success of the two managers should be measured, not by the absolute size of the profits they earn, but by the rate of return on the capital they employ, so that the more successful manager will be the one who shows the higher rate of return, a different but related difficulty confronts us. Is a high rate of return on a small capital better or worse than a lower but still satisfactory return on a larger capital? The simple figures in Exhibit II will illustrate the point.

### EXHIBIT II

| | Venture A | Venture B |
|---|---|---|
| Capital invested | $1,000 | $5,000 |
| Net annual return | $ 200 | $ 750 |
| Rate of return on capital | 20% | 15% |

Which is the more successful venture? If absolute profit is the test, Venture B is more successful; if rate of return is the test, then Venture A is better.

This is no mere academic question. The managers have to be given some instructions as to what their objective should be, what it is they should attempt to maximize. And if, as in so many companies, the instructions are to maximize the rate of return, a manager cannot be blamed if he restricts his investment, as in Venture A, for this, in effect, is what he has been told to do. The point has been well expressed in relation to the affairs of the General Electric Company as follows:

> It seems to us that the acid test of an index should be its effectiveness in guiding decentralized management to make decisions in the best interests of the company over all, since operating managers' efforts naturally will be to improve the performance of their businesses in terms of the index used for evaluation. This test points up the particular weakness of rate of return and of other ratio indexes, such as per cent profit to sales. This weakness is the tendency to encourage concentration on improvement of the *ratios* rather than improvement in dollar *profits*. . . . This tends to retard incentive to growth and expansion because it dampens the incentive of the more profitable businesses to grow.[1]

The fact is that the question whether Venture A or B is the more successful one cannot be answered correctly without taking account of the cost of capital. Suppose the cost of capital is 17½ per cent. Then Venture A alone can be called successful, while Venture B is misapplying capital which is costing more than it earns. But if it costs only 12 per cent, Venture B now becomes the more successful venture, for capital invested there is earning $150 more than it cost, whereas the capital in Venture A is earning only $80 more than it cost, as shown in Exhibit III.

**EXHIBIT III**

| | Venture A<br>$ | Venture B<br>$ |
|---|---|---|
| Net annual return | 200 | 750 |
| 12% on capital invested | 120 | 600 |
| Excess earnings over 12% | 80 | 150 |

Now suppose the cost of capital is 14 per cent. Venture B earns more than this, but Venture A can again be said to be more successful, for its excess over the cost of its capital is $60, whereas B's is only $50 (see Exhibit IV).

[1] Robert W. Lewis, "Measuring, Reporting and Appraising Results of Operations With Reference to Goals, Plans and Budgets"—Part V of *Planning, Managing, and Measuring the Business,* a Case Study of Management Planning and Control at General Electric Company, New York: Controllers Institute Research Foundation, 1955, p. 32.

EXHIBIT IV

| | Venture A | Venture B |
|---|---|---|
| | $ | $ |
| Net annual return | 200 | 750 |
| 14% on capital invested | 140 | 700 |
| Excess earnings over 14% | 60 | 50 |

Another way of expressing the point is to say that the $560 (which can be earned or saved at 14 per cent on the $4000 of capital freed by going into Venture A rather than Venture B) is then added to the return of $200, and the total return is $760. This is $10 more than can be earned by putting the whole of the $5000 into Venture B.

These comparisons of the two ventures can be summed up as in Exhibit V.

EXHIBIT V

| | Venture A | Venture B |
|---|---|---|
| Capital invested | $1,000 | $5,000 |
| Net annual return | $ 200 | $ 750 |
| Rate of return on capital | 20% | 15% |
| Excess of earnings over cost | | |
| of capital of 12% | $ 80 | $ 150 |
| 14% | $ 60 | $ 50 |
| 17½% | $ 25 | —$ 125 |

The exhibit shows that while the venture which gives the higher rate of return can be pointed to unequivocally, there is no simple answer to the question of which venture is more successful in terms of the excess of its earnings over the cost of the capital it employs. While Venture B is more successful at low rates of interest, A is more successful at high rates. A mere comparison of rates of return obscures this fact.

We arrive, then, at *the excess of net earnings over the cost of capital* as the measure of managerial success. The General Electric Company has given the name "residual income" to this quantity. It is a simple, descriptive name and we shall use it. This is the quantity which a manager should try to maximize. The cost of capital is deducted from the return after taxes to give residual income, and the rate used must, therefore, also be the after-tax rate.[2]

The reason for preferring to maximize residual income rather than to maximize the rate of return is that the latter may make a manager unwilling to expand investment in the enterprise if it will lower the average rate of return, even though the incremental return is still in excess of cost. This reasoning implies a situation in which the manager has the power to determine the amount of capital to be invested in his venture. In practice, in divisionalized companies, a DGM has only limited power to expand investment since approval of higher authority is needed for capital expenditures above a given limit. But the important thing is that the DGM has the power to *ask* for capital. Thus, there is an upper limit to his power to invest but no lower limit unless his powers of decision are to be very seriously curtailed. This is why the decision to maximize the *rate* of return will not do. If we were dealing with a situation in which the manager were given a specific amount of capital to use, without regard to his own wishes in the matter, then the problem of finding a criterion of success would be quite different. It would then be satisfactory to require him to maximize the rate of return on the capital entrusted to him, for this would be equivalent to requiring him to maximize his absolute dollar return as well.

## A Target for Residual Income

Instead of telling a manager to maximize something, it is more usual to set a standard or goal. He is then instructed to do his best to achieve or beat this standard, and will be judged by reference to it. Thus, commonly, a standard rate of return on investment is laid down. The basic weakness of this approach has already been explained, for the same reasoning applies to the achievement of a standard rate of return as to a maximum.

What target, then, should the DGM be given if, for the reasons already explained, residual income is preferred to a rate of return as a guide to action? The percentage of residual income to investment would be only a slight improvement on a rate of return. The best answer seems to be that *a target residual income should be set in dollars,* and the manager should be judged by his success in achieving

[2] The concept of residual income is further discussed in Chapter V. A method of determining the cost of capital is explained in pp. 156-159.

or bettering that figure. The reason for this conclusion can perhaps best be explained diagrammatically.

FIGURE 5
Setting a Residual Income Target

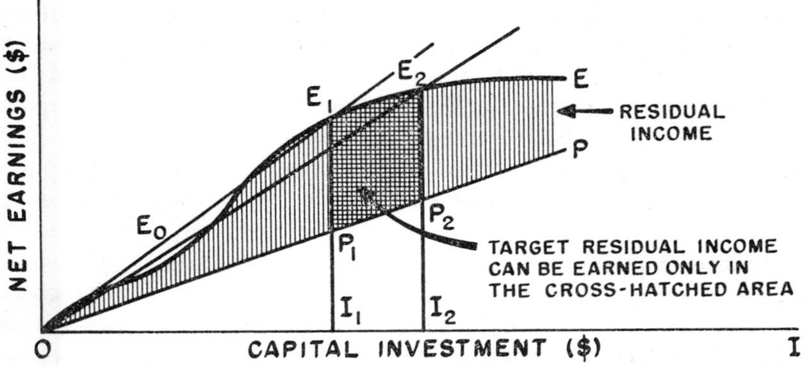


In Figure 5 the curve OE shows the net earnings of an enterprise rising as the amount of capital invested in it increases along the axis OI. There is a minimum amount of investment below which the business cannot be floated at all. Beyond this point, as we move to the right, the slope of the OE curve at first rises with increasing steepness, reflecting an *increasing* rate of return on investment secured by the economies of scale as the business grows. To the right of the point $E_0$ the increasing gradient gives way to a diminishing upward gradient (earnings continue to rise with increasing investment but not as fast as before), passes through a section of more or less constant gradient, and then begins to flatten out beyond $E_2$. The line OP shows the cost of capital. The line is straight because a single constant rate has been presumed (more will be said about this presumption later). As the amount of investment increases, the cost of capital increases in proportion. Residual income, the excess of net earnings over the cost of capital, is represented by the vertical distance between the curve and the line. As the amount of capital invested increases, residual income is seen to increase until it reaches a maximum somewhere around $E_1$, stays at or near this level until $E_2$, and then begins to diminish. The rate of return at any level of investment is given by the slope of a line drawn through the origin to the appropriate point on the E curve. Thus, the rate of return on an investment of $OI_1$ is given by the slope of $OE_1$ and on an investment of $OI_2$ by the slope of $OE_2$.

Now suppose the manager of the business is given a target rate of return to achieve. If this is set as high as possible, it will be a rate close to that represented by the slope of $OE_1$. The manager can achieve a rate only slightly less than this *at any level of operations less than* $OI_1$, whereas at these lower levels of operations, residual income is less than it is at $I_1$.

If the target rate of return is set somewhat lower—say a rate equal to that represented by the slope of $OE_2$—the manager can beat this rate *at almost any level of operations below* $I_2$, whereas residual income, at all lower levels except between $I_2$ and $I_1$, is less than it is at $I_2$.

Instead of giving the manager a target rate of return, let him now be given a target level of residual income, in dollars, roughly equal to the amounts $E_1P_1$ or $E_2P_2$ (these two amounts are approximately equal, so it does not matter which is chosen). At no level of operations much short of $I_1$, or much in excess of $I_2$, can this amount of residual income be earned. Thus, by setting the manager's target in terms of residual income, his freedom to manage his enterprise is preserved. He is not, however, left free to achieve his own target by sacrificing the interests of the company as a whole.

Residual income is the difference between two quantities, net earnings and the cost of capital. It is subject, therefore, to the shortcomings of net earnings (or profits) as a measure of the extent to which the enterprise has become "better off" during the accounting period. Most companies will, perhaps, be prepared to accept these shortcomings with no more than purely subjective corrections on the part of management whenever some recognition of them is thought to be necessary. It is a reflection on the art of accounting that these corrections have to be made in the form of mental reservations by managers rather than explicitly by accountants. However, for the present, this has to be accepted, and perhaps it will always be so.

## Rules for Determining Divisional Earnings

The foregoing discussion of the measurement of success was based on the explicit assumption that in small ventures the success of the manager and the success of his venture could be measured by the same set of figures, even though different *standards* of success might be looked for. In using the concept of residual income to measure the performance of divisions of a company, it is necessary to examine the problems of determining a division's net earnings and the cost of its capital, for only when these two quantities have been ascertained can its residual income be known. When it is known, there is still the problem of deciding what adjustments, if any, need to be made to convert it from a measure of enterprise success to a measure of management's success.

Shillinglaw suggests that there are three rules with which divisional profit measurements must comply before they can be regarded as acceptable. They are:

1. Divisional profit should not be increased by any action that reduces total company profit.
2. Each division's profit should be as independent as possible of performance efficiency and managerial decisions elsewhere in the company.
3. Each division's profit should reflect all items that are subject to any substantial degree of control by the division manager or his subordinates.[3]

### *The rule against profit conflict between division and corporation*

The implementation of the first of these rules is partly a matter of company organization and operating policy, and partly a matter of accounting policy. Thus, the rule may be broken if it is possible for two divisions of the company to compete with each other for the same business, and for one division to take business from the other by undercutting. Company directives always forbid this kind of conduct by divisions, and corporate management must have the power to discipline the management of a division which knowingly breaks this rule. Of course, it is possible that two divisions might not know that they are bidding for the same business. It is also possible that competitive bids might be quite legitimate, as where a customer is considering whether to package a liquid product in bottles or cans

[3] Gordon Shillinglaw, *Cost Accounting: Analysis and Control,* Homewood, Ill.: Richard D. Irwin, Inc., 1961, p. 688. See also his articles, "Guides to Internal Profit Measurement," *Harvard Business Review,* Vol. 35, No. 2, March-April 1957, pp. 82-94 and "Toward a Theory of Divisional Income Measurement," *Accounting Review,* Vol. XXXVII, No. 2, April 1962, pp. 208-216.

and both the ABC Container Company's glass and can divisions tender bids—to fail to do so might cause the company to lose the business entirely to a competitor. The rule would also be broken if a division, to cut its purchased materials costs a little, withdrew its business from a firm which is a good customer of another division. Many firms make a point of developing two-way relations with their suppliers, and have set up trade relation departments in the head office. Where such a department exists, it should be in a good position to advise on the unsatisfactory situation just described.

Interdivisional competition, and the refusal by one division to buy from another division's customer, are only two of many situations which can increase the profit of one division at the same time as they reduce the company's over-all profit. Situations such as this are beyond the power of mere accounting policy to prevent. The role of interdivisional transfer pricing can also be crucial in this connection, and we shall look at that problem carefully in Chapter VI. It is possible, however, that a company's rules of divisional profit measurement can themselves cause divisions to arrange their affairs so that *their* profits are increased while the company's are diminished. For example, any allocation of head office expenses based on divisional sales volume might cause a division to prefer a smaller volume of high-price sales yielding a slightly lower sales revenue and profit *before* expense allocation but a higher divisional net profit *after* expense allocation because the division's reduced sales revenue has attracted a reduced expense allocation. The company's total allocable expenses will not have fallen, but the divisional "contribution" will have, so the company as a whole will be worse off, yet the division will show a higher net profit.

Similar conflicts of interest may arise because of the way some companies charge for interest on capital. One company charged divisions interest only if it had to borrow to finance their capital expenditure projects. This meant that projects started early in the company's financial year could expect to be financed out of retained earnings, leaving the later ones to be financed by borrowing. This led all divisions to try to get their projects started in the first quarter of the year, with consequent pressure on the engineering department. There was a tendency to hang back on projects which "missed the boat." Another company charges divisions interest on their net investment, but at an unrealistically low rate. This encourages them to buy assets, even when they could lease them on favorable terms from the company's point of view, for the low interest charge on purchased assets will usually be less than the interest included in the rental paid on leased assets.

The treatment of depreciation is another fruitful source of conflict between divisional and company interests.[4] Dearden cites cases in which the assignment of fixed assets to divisions at their gross cost, while accounting for depreciation on groups of fixed assets at a composite rate, encourages divisions prematurely to scrap temporarily idle assets. Under this system, any particular asset, when retired, is regarded as fully depreciated whatever its age, so that divisions which scrap assets can escape the depreciation charge on them and yet show no loss on realization.

Where companies make no charge to divisions for interest on capital and use absorption costing methods, there is a real danger that divisions will improve their profit picture by producing for inventory when they cannot produce for sale. By doing so, a proportion of their overhead is carried forward into the cost of inventory, to the relief of the current operating statement. The division shows a better result than would otherwise be the case, even though the company's capital is being tied up to no good purpose.

These, then, are a few of the ways in which unwise rules of divisional profit measurement may cause a division to act against the best interests of the company. They are really all manifestations of a single defect. In every case there is a failure to make a division bear the true cost to the company of the division's action—the true cost of using capital, of administrative services, of scrapping equipment and so on. Once this common characteristic of these defective accounting methods is recognized, there is a good chance of keeping clear of them, and of others like them.

### *The rule of profit independence of divisions*

The second rule for divisional profit measurement proposed by Shillinglaw is that each division's profit should be as independent as possible of performance efficiency and managerial decisions elsewhere in the company. The point was made in Chapter I that a truly divisionalized company was something more than a closed-end in-

---

[4] See John Dearden, "Problem in Decentralized Profit Responsibility," *Harvard Business Review,* Vol. 38, No. 3, May-June 1960, pp. 79-86; for a discussion of related problems in the area of working capital see also his article, "Problem in Decentralized Financial Control," *ibid.,* Vol. 39, No. 3, May-June 1961, pp. 72-80.

vestment fund or collection of discrete investments. Though divisionalization is, more often than not, motivated by a desire for diversification, the divisions should be able to contribute something to each other as well as to the company. Most divisionalized companies achieve this to a greater or lesser degree, and the performance of one division, therefore, often has an impact on that of others. Most commonly this takes the form of interdivisional transfers of products and services. These transfers will be discussed at length later since, more than any other single factor, they differentiate the truly divisionalized company from others.

Interdivisional transfers are not the only feature of divisionalized companies which prevent a division's profit from being independent of the performance of other parts of the company. Another factor resulting in nonindependence is the existence of central service departments serving the divisions. Data-processing centers, market research departments, engineering departments, training schools and others have already been cited as examples. Since the costs of these service functions are usually passed on to divisions through the charges made for their services, any inefficiency on their part is a matter of concern to the divisions as well as to the company's central management.

Yet another way in which divisions can affect each other's profit is through the methods adopted by the company for the allocation of central administration costs, research costs, interest on capital, and any other central charges which eventually come to rest on the debit side of the divisions' profit statements. It has already been noted that these methods can cause a division to act in a manner prejudicial to the interests of the company as a whole. It is another drawback of bad methods of cost allocation that a division's costs can be increased, and its profit accordingly decreased, by events entirely outside its control which are happening in another division.

The most obvious case of this kind can be seen when some central expense is allocated among divisions in proportion to their sales. Division A's charge for the expense may go *up* simply because, all other things being equal, Division B's sales have gone *down*. The use of another common basis of allocation, property or fixed assets, can have a similar effect since an expansion project in one division, adding to its fixed assets, will reduce the charge to other divisions for, possibly, the central engineering department, the cost of which is frequently charged out on this basis. Where the total net investment in a division is the basis for charging it with some (and sometimes, all) of the central administration costs, the success of one or two divisions in reducing their net investment, perhaps by cutting down inventories or speeding up the collection of receivables, can push up the administration costs allocated to other divisions merely because an unchanged total fixed cost is being allocated in new proportions unfavorable to them.

In addition to the allocation methods used to charge out central administration expenses, the very level of these costs will also have an impact on divisional profits. Increased expenditure for institutional advertising, an expanded program of internal audit, increases in the salaries of top management, the costs of running the "company plane" (frequently a subject for ribaldry on the part of divisional personnel) are examples of costs not directly flowing from divisional activities. The charge made for them to divisions, though usually not a very material percentage of divisional revenue, does impair the independence of their profit performance.

### *Controllability as a desideratum of divisional profit measurements*

The third rule suggested by Shillinglaw for divisional profit measurement was that each division's profit should reflect all items subject to any substantial degree of control by the division manager or his subordinates. Stated positively in this way, it is easy to accept the rule, for divisional profit statements certainly *should* reflect all controllable items. More controversial is the view which Shillinglaw appears to hold—that the divisional profit measurement should reflect *only* controllable items. This goes beyond what the rule states, but there is no doubt that it is what he intends.

For purposes of discussion, we shall use his illustration[5] of three profit concepts from which a choice for divisional profit measurement may be made (see Exhibit VI).

Should we use net profit, contribution margin, or controllable profit in constructing our measure of divisional profit performance? The conclusion has already been reached, of course, that residual income is probably the best measure of performance we are likely to find. But we must still decide what is to be included in, and what ex-

---

[5] Shillinglaw, *Cost Accounting,* p. 689. The exhibit has been slightly adapted.

cluded from, the definition of "net earnings," the main constituent of residual income. There are many degrees of "net-ness" and the problem is to choose the one that suits our purpose best.

EXHIBIT VI

| | $ | $ |
|---|---|---|
| Sales | | xxx |
| Less: | | |
| Variable cost of goods sold | xxx | |
| Variable divisional selling and administrative expenses | xxx | xxx |
| Variable profit | | xxx |
| Less: | | |
| Controllable divisional overhead | | xxx |
| Controllable profit | | xxx |
| Less: | | |
| Fixed noncontrollable divisional overhead | | xxx |
| Contribution margin | | xxx |
| Less: | | |
| Allocation of extradivisional fixed expenses—noncontrollable | | xxx |
| Net profit before taxes | | xxx |
| Taxes | | xxx |
| Net profit after taxes | | xxx |

### *Limitations of net profits as a measure of divisional earnings*

Some of the principal objections to the use of net profit have already been mentioned. To measure divisional performance by means of a profit figure arrived at after deducting items which are neither controllable at divisional level nor directly related to divisional activity is to use a measure which is arbitrary to the extent that the allocations are arbitrary. It is not independent of conditions outside the division, and may lead divisions into courses of action detrimental to the company. It could, moreover, mislead head office executives into thinking that a division was making a loss or a very small profit, and that therefore it should be liquidated. This could happen even though the facts were that, while the division was failing to make an adequate contribution to the head office expenses and profit, it was making *some* contribution, sufficient perhaps to keep it operating in the hope of eventual recovery.

Most company executives are aware of these arguments against expense allocations but are not always convinced by them. The counterargument most commonly used is that divisions must be made aware that there are nondivisional costs to be covered out of their earnings before the company as a whole can show a profit. Unless this awareness is sharpened by showing the central expense allocations on the divisional profit statements each month, the division may, in pricing policies and other marketing decisions, plan to contribute less than its due share of the company's net income. Moreover, it is argued, if the division were an independent company it would have a top administration of its own.

These counterarguments are not convincing. It is true that some methods of overhead allocation (e.g., allocations based on divisional sales) create possibilities for a division to diminish its contribution to the company's over-all profitability while increasing its own apparent net profit. But such aberrations result simply from the fact of allocation itself. Apart from such allocation practices, *so long as corporate (i.e., nondivisional) expenses are independent of divisional activity,*[6] whatever policies maximize divisional net profits will also maximize divisional contributions to corporate profits before the allocation of corporate expenses. In the general case, in other words, corporate net profits will not suffer if corporate fixed expenses are left unallocated. If, on the other hand, the division's objective is not to maximize net income, but only to achieve some target level of income laid down for it, it is just as easy to have this target fixed at a somewhat higher level in terms of contribution margin than would be done if it were

---

[6] Incremental corporate expenses resulting from divisional activity are in a different category. Their treatment is discussed below.

set in terms of divisional net profit. If all divisions attain their target contribution margins, there will be sufficient total contribution to cover the central expenses, and to leave as much in excess thereof as the company plans to have.

Where a division is subject to a state income tax, the argument for making it bear a proportion of the head office expenses is obviously unanswerable. The same is true where a division is engaged on government contracts and the contract price is, in part, cost-determined. All that need be said here is that, while for these special purposes it is clearly to the corporation's advantage to allocate as much expense as it reasonably can to the division in question, it should be possible to ignore these allocations for other purposes such as the evaluation of performance.

It should be understood that the allocated expenses which are the subject of this argument do not include the charges made by service or staff departments located at corporate headquarters and providing services (such as data processing, engineering plans, marketing information, or advertising) which divisions would be prepared to buy outside if they were not provided centrally. Although clumsy methods of charging for these services are sometimes used, so that the charges take on the nature of semiarbitrary allocations (for example, if data processing or advertising were charged to divisions in proportion to the book value of their fixed assets) usually methods can be found that will roughly equate the charge made either with the cost or the value of the services provided.

The basis of charging for services will be taken up in a later chapter, as a special aspect of the transfer-pricing problem. But the matter cannot altogether be bypassed at this point, for the question arises whether the costs of services furnished to divisions by central service departments are "controllable" costs from the division's point of view. No simple answer to this question is possible, for every conceivable nuance in the degree of independence enjoyed by divisions can be found in some company somewhere. To divide expenses neatly into two categories, controllable and noncontrollable, is to draw a picture in black and white and to ignore all the shades of grey in between. However, we can at least distinguish the following three situations:

1. The division is completely free to "shop around" for the service, and only "buy" from the central service department if this is the most advantageous arrangement it can make. Where this situation

applies, the cost of the service is as controllable as any other cost directly incurred by the division.

2. The division is not free to choose an outside source of supply for the service in question, but is free to decide how much of the service it will take. In this case, the quantity factor in the cost of the service to the division is controllable, but the price factor is not. A good example here is centralized purchasing of basic materials. The division says what quantity and quality it needs, the central purchasing organization does the buying and therefore determines the price, usually under a long-term contract. The procedure adopted by one company which buys base metals this way is to charge divisions with the market price of the metal at the time of shipment to the division. Differences between the contract price paid by the company and the fluctuating market prices charged to divisions are accumulated at headquarters through the year, and passed on to divisions, in proportion to their annual purchases, at the end of the year. It would be more logical, perhaps, since buying is a head office function, to leave the price variance as a head office gain or loss, but the example suggests how quantity variances can be included in the division's controllable costs while excluding price variances therefrom.

3. The division is not free to decide either the quantity of the service it takes or the price it will be charged. Industrial relations may fall into this category, where divisions have no choice but to use the services of the headquarters department. In a situation such as this, the cost charged to the division for the service can only be regarded as a noncontrollable element of divisional overhead.

A glance at Exhibit VI will suggest the possibility of a statement that may satisfy both those who emphasize the importance of divisional net profit and those who prefer to look to contributory margin. Most companies are careful, in their divisional profit statements, to charge head office allocations for general administration and interest, at least, "below the line" and not merge them with divisional charges proper. There is an educational job here which is likely to be neglected as a result of this compromise procedure. If the foregoing analysis is sound, it points to the conclusion that the allocation of central fixed charges, while it may have to be done for special institutional purposes, cannot contribute to the making of right decisions and may lead to wrong ones. There is, then, a strong argument for educating nonfinancial executives not to look for divisional net profit figures. Perhaps the best way to do that is not to show them in divisional operating statements prepared for general managerial use.[7]

### *Controllable versus noncontrollable expenses*

If the divisional net profit, either before or after taxes, is to be rejected for the role of "net earnings" in the computation of residual income, the choice must presumably lie between contribution margin and controllable profit. Which one is to be preferred will depend on what the function of the measure is thought to be. Shillinglaw's preference is for controllable profit, because he believes that "the primary purposes of routine profit reporting are to guide and appraise the performance of division executives, not to say whether the investment entrusted to them is profitable or unprofitable."[8] On this basis, he would exclude from the expenses charged against divisional revenue those costs, like the DGM's own salary or the data-processing costs in the circumstances discussed above, which are fixed costs of carrying on the division's operations, but which are not controllable by the DGM or his subordinates.

Before the soundness of this view can be judged, it is necessary to look rather closely at the make-up of the "fixed noncontrollable divisional overhead" which constitutes the difference between controllable profit and contribution margin in Exhibit VI and also at the purposes of routine profit reporting by divisions.

Taking up the first of these points, it quickly becomes apparent that the distinction between what is, and what is not, controllable at divisional level will differ in detail from company to company according to the degree of autonomy enjoyed by divisions and the way in which functions are divided between the divisions and head office.

---

[7] Methods of allocation have been surveyed many times in the literature, and will not be further examined here. Any good cost accounting text may be referred to, and several references to periodical literature will be found in the bibliography at the end of this book. The following studies will be found useful:

*Allocating Corporate Expense,* Study in Business Policy No. 108, National Industrial Conference Board, 1963.

"Assignment of Nonmanufacturing Costs for Managerial Decisions," Research Series No. 19, *NAA Bulletin,* Vol. 32, No. 9, May 1951.

Survey of parent administration or corporate expense and methods of allocation presented by E. A. Weberling at the Electrical Manufacturing Institute of America, Annual Conference, November 6, 1961.

[8] Shillinglaw, *Cost Accounting,* p. 690.

Some remarks about the classification of central service department costs charged to divisions, depending on the amount of freedom the divisions have, have already been made above.

One of the most difficult groups of costs to classify satisfactorily as between controllable and noncontrollable is the group consisting of the costs of capital other than interest (depreciation, taxes and insurance on property). But the difficulty is substantially reduced as soon as it is recognized that, corresponding to the distinction between controllable and noncontrollable expenses, we need to distinguish between controllable and noncontrollable investment; for divisions have a much greater degree of control over important segments of their total investment than, for instance, a plant manager has in a centralized company. In distinguishing between what costs the plant manager is, and is not, responsible for, depreciation and property taxes and insurance would clearly fall into the noncontrollable category. The plant manager is entrusted with certain capital assets, and he is responsible for their use, but not for their amount and not to any material extent for their composition. The cost of capital, therefore, is a cost of his operations but not one for which he is in any way responsible. To carry this reasoning over to the situation of a division is unwarranted. Though a new DGM inherits from his predecessor a collection of assets measurable in amount and composition, he has wide latitude to change both, given time. This applies especially, but not only, if the change in amount is downward. The choice of replacement equipment, the extent to which the division mechanizes or automates its processes, the expansion plans presented by the division (to the extent that the company is able and willing to finance them) —these factors determine the asset base on which depreciation will be charged. Subject to the choice of depreciation rate and method, an important matter which will be taken up shortly, depreciation as a cost is much more within the control of a division than of a plant. The same is true of property taxes. Although the rate of tax is outside the control of the division, in this respect it is not different from the market prices and wage rates which confront the division in the market for its factors of production. If lack of control over the prices paid for the resources it buys makes their costs noncontrollable, then virtually all costs are noncontrollable. This is surely not what the term means.

It is true, too, that the age structure and composition of a division's fixed assets cannot be changed overnight. It is, indeed, the slower rate of turnover of fixed equipment which principally distinguishes fixed from current assets. But this fact limits the division's power to alter fixed assets only a little more than it limits the power of the president or the board of directors. It would be unrealistic to suppose that they are likely, in normal circumstances, to make sweeping changes in the asset structure except at the request of, or with the concurrence of, the DGM and his staff. We are, of course, speaking of divisions having genuine profit responsibility, in fact as well as in name.

This is not to say that all divisional fixed investment is controllable by divisions. A division may find that one of its buildings has become redundant and would like to sell it but cannot because the company thinks that a different use may eventually be found for it, perhaps by a different division or by corporate headquarters. The best procedure, in such a situation, is to transfer the asset from the division previously using it to the corporate or general division. But even if this is not done and the building continues to be regarded as a divisional asset, it should certainly be excluded from the category of controllable investment.

Many companies allocate corporate fixed assets, such as research laboratories and the head office building, to divisions to ensure that all the company's assets, of whatever kind, are accounted for somewhere in the divisional capital computations. This practice will be discussed further in Chapter V. It is only necessary to point out here that such allocated assets have no place in the category of controllable investment.

The discussion of whether depreciation, taxes and property insurance are, or are not, controllable expenses has led, then, to the not unreasonable conclusion that the cost of using controllable investment is a controllable expense, and the cost of using noncontrollable investment is a noncontrollable expense. The same distinction between controllable and noncontrollable investment, extended into the field of current as well as fixed investment, will be useful in determining that other element of the cost of capital, interest, which must be deducted from net earnings to give residual income. The consideration of interest on capital, how capital should be computed and what interest rate should be used will be taken up in Chapter V. Many of the questions which arise there are similar to those pertaining to the use of the rate of return on capital as a criterion of managerial success. It will therefore be convenient to discuss them together.

Before proceeding, it is worth noting that to reach any other conclusion than the one just arrived at—that the cost of operating controllable investment should be deducted in arriving at controllable profit—would produce one unfortunate result. A division which progressively substituted capital equipment for labor over the years would show a steady rise in controllable profit, other things being equal. The reduction in labor costs would push controllable profit up, but the compensating increase in depreciation would show up only below the controllable profit line. If this were the figure by which the division was to be judged, it would be easy to show an improvement where no real improvement had been effectuated, simply by substituting so-called noncontrollable inputs for controllable inputs.

### *Nonoperating income and expense*

Many nonoperating items of income and expense, such as profits and losses on the realization of investments and interest on long-term debt, are more likely to be encountered in the accounts of the corporate division or head office of the corporation than in those of a domestic operating division. Likewise, gains and losses on foreign exchange transactions are more likely to be found in an international division. But not all items of a nonoperating nature can be kept out of a division's statements without falsifying results. Royalty income on processes developed within the division, rentals and other income from divisional assets, short-term interest payments and the like are appropriately brought into the division's income statements as a separate nonoperating group of items to be included in controllable residual income but not in controllable operating profit. Even domestic divisions sometimes have dealings in foreign exchange, the gains and losses on which should also be brought into this nonoperating group of items.

The most important transactions of a nonoperating nature entered into by a division are likely to be disposals of fixed assets with some resulting gain or loss. If the asset disposal was the result of a divisional decision, or of a corporate decision in which the division concurred, there is every reason to include such gains or losses in any assessment of the division's long-term performance. To do otherwise is to insulate a division from one of the consequences of an abandonment decision, or of a decision to curtail operations. This will invite irresponsibility in making, or in recommending, such decisions. To treat these gains or losses as additions to, or deductions from, the income of the year in which an asset happens to be disposed of, however, is to allow the accident of realization to distort the results of a single year. The gain or loss, to the extent that it is not the result of the instability of the dollar,[9] may be no more than a recognition of past errors in depreciation policy. It may be due, also, to an ill-advised asset purchase. Such gain or loss ought properly to be attributed to the year in which the asset was bought, not the year in which it was sold. If it were possible to reopen past income statements, it would be appropriate to allocate the gain or loss to the year or years in which it arose. However, such a procedure is not possible, and if it were, it would not be managerially useful. All that can be done is to hold the division accountable for this belated recognition of past mistakes, without allowing those same mistakes to distort the results of the year in which they came to light. To attribute errors wholly to the year in which they are discovered is not a fair reflection of the performance of that year.

Gains and losses on any disposal of divisional assets effectuated without approval of the division's management are in a different category from those just discussed. Since they are not controllable gains and losses, and are likely to be extraordinary in nature, it will usually be best to transfer the assets in question out of the division's charge and into the charge of the corporate division at book value. Thereafter, the financial results of disposal will not be reflected in the operating division's statements.

### *Chargeable noncontrollable expenses*

Although certain expenses incurred by a division may not be controllable by the division they may, for the purpose of computing contributory margin, be quite appropriately chargeable to it. Thus, there is a strong case for charging divisions with any increments in central administration as well as with other expenses for which they can be held responsible. This is not the same thing as charging divisions with an allocated proportion of these expenses so that the sums allocated to all divisions together will, in the aggregate, exhaust the total central expenses. It has already been argued that such a procedure is more likely to mislead than to conduce to sound decisions. The incremental central expenses which should be charged to divisions would *not,* in the aggregate, exhaust the total of these expenses,

[9] The accounting consequences of such instability are discussed briefly below.

nor would they be intended to do so. A substantial proportion of these costs would be left unallocated, representing the cost of maintaining the central headquarters even if it were shorn, for a short time, of all its divisions. The unallocated residue is not particularly significant. The allocated *increments* of central expenses chargeable to divisions are, however, since divisions are held responsible for them. Only when these incremental expenses have been charged to divisions can their true contribution margins be ascertained.

The principal objection likely to be raised against this procedure is the difficulty, perhaps the impossibility, of estimating to what extent central administration costs would be reduced if any one division were discontinued. To be sure, it is useless to look for precision and complete objectivity in arriving at such a figure; but neither are these qualities present in the more usual "exhaustive" allocations of central expenses to divisions. Indeed, they are less in evidence in these allocations. If the calculations of cost increments are made, expense by expense, by those head office personnel most familiar with each one (as is commonly done now with existing allocations) there is no reason to doubt that the results would be close enough to have much practical value.

## A Form of Divisional Income Statement

A form of divisional income statement which would give effect to the conclusions reached in the foregoing discussion is shown in Exhibit VII. It introduces a distinction between controllable residual income and net residual income. Controllable residual income is what is left out of the divisional revenue after meeting variable costs, controllable fixed costs, and interest on controllable investment. If, from controllable residual income, we deduct noncontrollable costs directly attributable to the division, either by the division itself or by the corporate head office, the result is net residual income before taxes. The treatment of interdivisional transfers in the statement is in accordance with the recommendations about transfer prices made in Chapter VI and which are fully explained there. It should be noted that the statement does not provide for the allocation of central company overhead to divisions.

## The Choice of Financial Criteria

There are three important purposes of routine profit reporting by divisions:

## EXHIBIT VII

### A Form of Divisional Income Statement

| | $ | $ |
|---|---|---|
| Sales to outside customers | xxx | |
| Transfers to other divisions at market value | xxx | |
| Variable charges to other divisions for transfers not priced at market value | xxx | |
| | | xxx |
| Less: | | |
| Variable cost of goods sold and transferred | xxx | |
| Variable divisional expenses | xxx | |
| | | xxx |
| Variable profit | | xxx |
| Add (deduct): | | |
| Fixed charges made to (by) other divisions for transfers not priced at market value | | xxx |
| | | xxx |
| Less: | | |
| Controllable divisional overhead | xxx | |
| Depreciation on controllable fixed assets | xxx | |
| Property taxes and insurance on controllable fixed assets | xxx | xxx |
| Controllable operating profit | | xxx |
| Add (deduct): | | |
| Nonoperating gains and losses | | xxx |
| | | xxx |
| Less: | | |
| Interest on controllable investment | | xxx |
| Controllable residual income before taxes | | xxx |
| Less: | | |
| Noncontrollable divisional overhead | xxx | |
| Incremental central expenses chargeable to division | xxx | |
| Interest on noncontrollable investment | xxx | xxx |
| Net residual income before taxes | | xxx |
| Less: | | |
| Taxes on income | | xxx |
| Net residual income after taxes | | xxx |

1. To guide divisional executives in making decisions.
2. To guide top management in making decisions.
3. To enable top management to appraise the performance of divisional management.

There is, of course, a fundamental distinction between the use of profit figures to guide decisions and their use to appraise management. Decision-making looks to the future, appraisal looks to the past. Decision-making can, therefore, at its best, make only limited use of profit figures. Expected earnings are really of interest to the decision-maker and reported earnings are only helpful to the extent that they have predictive value. Appraisal of past performance is quite a different matter, for reported earnings have more direct relevance here. Other reasons for scepticism in the use of reported profit figures even for appraisal purposes have, however, been suggested earlier. Whatever can be said to indicate that any one variant of reported earnings is better than another for decision-making or appraisal purposes must be accepted subject to all these important reservations.

With this point established, it will be argued that the most suitable income figure for use in appraising the performance of divisional management, and also for use by divisional executives in guiding their decisions, is *controllable residual income before taxes,* arrived at in the manner indicated in Exhibit VII. To guide top management in its decisions relating to a division, the most appropriate figure seems to be *net residual income.* Whether this should be taken before or after taxes depends very much on how the tax charge to divisions is computed. More will be said about this shortly.

It is almost a self-evident proposition that, in appraising the performance of divisional management, no account should be taken of matters outside the division's control. These executives are to be judged on *their* conduct of affairs, not on the conduct of others, even when the latter has a bearing on the success of the divisional enterprise. It is mainly for this reason that, in spite of the difficulties involved, it is worth while to try to measure controllable residual income, free of all cost elements which are completely beyond the division's control.

The same figure is also the most appropriate one for use by divisional management to guide its decisions, as far as historical information ever can be used to guide decisions. Indeed, as between controllable residual income and net residual income, the first is the only one which could sensibly be used at the divisional level. Net residual income is arrived at after deducting noncontrollable items which, for the most part, will have been incurred by the head office for the division—advertising expenditure, where divisions do not handle their own advertising, will serve as an example. Although these expenditures will be reported to the division for inclusion in its statements, the division may know little about the way the figures were arrived at. This would certainly be true, too, of incremental central expenses where these were charged to a division. It follows that divisional managers would know little about how these noncontrollable expenses might react to any decisions they might take. For that reason, net residual income is less useful as a guide to divisional decision-making than is controllable residual income.

Turning now to corporate as distinct from divisional decisions, it must be noted that some corporate decisions relating to a division are concerned with men—the promotion or transfer of a DGM, for example. The principle so far established applies to those decisions which follow, in part, from an appraisal of managerial performance. In these cases, only controllable performance should be taken into account. For other corporate decisions, such as new investment or a withdrawal of funds from the division, the important thing is the success or failure of the divisional venture, not of the men who run it. All information relating to the venture, whether it refers to matters within the control of the division or to matters handled by the head office for the division, should be taken into account. This requires that top management examine net residual income even though this figure may provide only background information for most of the decisions with which top management will be concerned. New investment decisions will be based on *forecasts* relating to *projects,* as will abandonment decisions. These forecasts call for special studies rather than routine reports of the earnings of a whole division. The function of the routine reports in the area of decision-making will most likely be to stimulate questions, as a result of which the special studies will be made. Routine reports can never take the place of special studies: indeed, the principal value of the reports will often be to suggest the need for such studies.

# SOME SPECIFIC PROBLEMS OF DIVISIONAL PROFIT MEASUREMENT

CHAPTER IV

Now that we have a clearer idea of the kind of profit figure best adapted to the needs of divisional control, it will be worth while to consider some of the situations and factors in business life giving rise to accounting procedures which, at best, are not conducive to effective managerial control and, at worst, are in direct conflict with it. By far the most important of such factors is the federal income tax. In their desire to minimize tax payments within the limits allowed by the law, companies naturally adopt accounting methods which, if they cannot ultimately reduce the profits subject to taxation, can at least defer these profits as long as possible, thus postponing the payment of taxes on them.

Some of the more important deferment provisions of the tax code have been made available to taxpayers as devices for mitigating the deficiencies of generally accepted accounting principles in a period of monetary instability. The use of the last-in-first-out basis of inventory valuation (LIFO) and accelerated methods of depreciation accounting are the most familiar examples. Usually, though not always, these valuation methods are used by companies seeking to defer profits for tax purposes without necessarily deferring them for internal or external reporting purposes. A surprisingly large number of companies choose not to use different methods of profit measurement for different purposes, with the result that their taxable profits and their reported profits are substantially identical. There appear to be two important reasons for this state of affairs. One is the purely practical point, that in the view of these companies it is more expedient and economical to have one set of profit calculations rather than two. The other reason is primarily concerned with business philosophy. Many business men believe that, if business wants to retain the tax advantages which a liberalized tax code has brought in recent years, it will do well to show its belief in the liberalized methods of profit measurement by adopting them for reporting purposes as well as for tax purposes.

The requirements of tax accounting have a negative influence also. Because the Internal Revenue Service has, in all but a few cases, refused to countenance direct costing as a method of arriving at the cost of manufactured inventories, many manufacturing businesses which might otherwise have adopted this approach have been discouraged from doing so. Business has allowed the rulings of the tax authorities, therefore, to deprive it of the possible benefits of direct costing in fields such as profit planning and price determination, fields quite removed from that of taxation. These firms have also been denied the use of direct costing for internal profit measurement unaccompanied by its concomitant use for tax reporting.

This study is not directly concerned with taxation, but to discuss and prescribe methods of divisional profit measurement as if the disturbing factor of taxation were not ever-present would be hopelessly unrealistic. The impact of taxation on divisional accounting, therefore, calls for a closer look, especially as it affects the treatment of depreciation and inventories.

## Depreciation Accounting

It was argued earlier, in discussing where the line should be drawn between those expenses controllable at divisional level and those which are not, that depreciation is really a controllable expense. This conclusion is based on the view that the nature and the amount of capital equipment and other fixed assets employed by a division are matters over which it has a large degree of control, if not in the immediate sense, at least in the longer view. Underlying this statement is the supposition that, when a decision is taken to acquire or to scrap divisional fixed assets, the decision will be *appropriately* reflected on the debit side of future divisional income statements through the depreciation charge for such assets. If the depreciation charges are inappropriately calculated for reasons unconnected with the circumstances of the division itself—and corporate tax requirements are the most likely cause of such inappropriate calculations—the status of depreciation as a controllable expense of a division has to be seriously questioned.

But what is an "appropriate" charge for depreciation? The answer must depend on what the role of depreciation is presumed to be. Broadly speaking, an operating asset bought under competitive conditions will have cost the purchaser a sum roughly equal to the discounted present value of the future stream of benefits expected to accrue to the purchaser from the asset. In money terms, this is equivalent to the discounted present value of the asset's expected contribution to net profit. As the asset renders services over the years, the asset's expectation of life diminishes, and the present value of its remaining services therefore falls. The position will be taken here that, ideally, depreciation reflects this periodic fall of present value.

If the time-pattern of the depreciation charges for a particular asset is to match, broadly speaking, the time-pattern of its net earnings, it follows that a firm with a varied collection of fixed assets should have a depreciation policy employing many different depreciation methods, each of which is appropriate to a different type of asset. It would be strange indeed if the multitudinous earnings patterns of the firm's many assets could be, except in the crudest possible manner, reflected by any single depreciation method. It would be stranger still if the patterns were reflected by a method which was chosen, not because it approximately matched the earnings pattern of a substantial proportion of the firm's assets, but because it brought the firm the advantage of tax deferment.[1]

A depreciation method chosen for any reason except that it results in write-offs roughly reflecting the diminution in the discounted present value of the asset's expected earnings must impair the effectiveness of the divisional income statements for performance evaluation purposes. If the asset were expected to have *equal* annual net

---

[1] Yet the majority of firms do use the same depreciation methods in their accounts and tax returns. In NAA Research Report No. 33, April 1958, on *Current Practice in Accounting for Depreciation* it is reported, p. 20, that 49 out of 55 companies questioned used the same methods for accounts and tax. In a survey of 1325 companies by Financial Executives Research Foundation in 1960, 78 per cent did so (see "Depreciation Allowances Not Fully Utilized" by W. Joseph Littlefield, *The Controller,* July 1960, p. 325). In the present study about four fifths of the companies participating did so.

earnings through its life, the loss of present value in the first yea would be less than in the second. In each subsequent year the loss i present value would increase by reason of the interest factor originall used in the process of arriving at the *discounted* present value. Th annuity method is the theoretically correct technique of depreciatio with a flat time-pattern of net earnings. If it is not desired to tak account of the interest factor, then the straight-line method is ac ceptable. If a declining pattern of net earnings is expected from th asset the diminishing balance (or the sum-of-the-years-digits) meth ods will be suitable. However, rates must be used which are dictate by the facts of the asset's expected performance and not by any ta regulation. All these methods, however, are simplifications or ap proximations. For the majority of firms it is only expediency whic precludes the use of more complicated write-off patterns for financia reporting and internal accounting purposes. There are, howeve many firms in this country of which this is not true as, for exampl those companies having whole divisions engaged exclusively on wor for the Federal Government under the defense or space program At least for pricing purposes, these divisions have no alternative bu to accept the depreciation allowances laid down in the Government' procurement regulations. Such firms should recognize, so far as thes divisions are concerned, *three* depreciation figures, one for tax pur poses, one for government contract pricing, and a third for thei own costing and profit reporting. Anything less than this, while i may be pardonable and even justifiable on grounds of accountin expense, must involve some loss of useful data on true operating cost and profit.

It may be noted that many companies using accelerated methods o depreciation for accounting purposes justify them on the ground tha annual diminishing depreciation charges are offset by rising mainte nance costs on aging assets. Other things being equal, if the cost o maintaining an asset increases as it gets older, then it follows that it *net* earnings (after deducting maintenance costs) must fall. Thus th rising maintenance costs justification for accelerated depreciation i really a falling net earnings justification: and where an asset's ne earnings really do fall over its life, depreciation methods which mak diminishing charges from year to year are entirely appropriate.

It can also be shown that there is no substance to the claim tha accelerated depreciation methods upset cost comparability from yea to year, or between one plant and another, because pieces of equip ment identical in all respects except age give rise to different depreciation charges. Nor is there substance, for the same reason, to the claim that a firm's price policy may be distorted. These distortions *can* result when accelerated depreciation is applied in circumstances where it is not appropriate, i.e., where the asset's net earnings do not diminish as it gets older. Where earnings do diminish, however, the cause must be rising operating costs, diminishing physical productivity, diminishing acceptability of the asset's products, or increased competition from newer and more efficient equipment. All these reasons involve either increased costs other than depreciation, or reduced gross earnings for the asset as it gets older. In these circumstances, reduced depreciation charges either stabilize total operating costs (including depreciation), or match falling gross earnings. Neither comparability of costs nor price policy need be distorted, therefore.

Once the shackles of tax regulations are removed from a company's internal accounting procedures it becomes easier to recognize that each division in a divisionalized company should be free to adopt the depreciation method best suited to it. What is important is not that there should be uniformity between divisions, but that each division's reported income each period should, as accurately as possible, reflect its performance during that period. Only to the extent that this goal is achieved will divisional results be truly comparable, however diverse the depreciation methods used by divisions may be.

Fortunately, in large divisions which have reached full growth, the choice of depreciation methods will generally make less difference to reported earnings than might be supposed. This happily robs the question we have been discussing of some of its importance. The underlying cause is that divisions reaching maturity will normally have a collection of assets of varying ages. So long as depreciation is calculated on each asset separately, and the more evenly distributed the ages of the assets of a particular type are, the less difference will the choice of depreciation method make to the magnitude of the total depreciation charge.[2] This is not true, it must be noted, of firms or divisions in the process of expansion, since such businesses will have a disproportionately large amount of capital invested in new assets.

[2] For a fuller demonstration of this point, and a discussion of its relevance to the argument about providing for deferred income tax, see Sidney Davidson's article, "Accelerated Depreciation and the Allocation of Income Taxes," *Accounting Review*, Vol. XXXIII, No. 2, April 1958, pp. 173-180.

Accelerated depreciation will diminish their reported profits below what would be reported with straight-line depreciation. The converse of this is true, of course, of declining and contracting businesses.

## Depreciation and the Price Level

The foregoing remarks on depreciation policy have been based on a tacit assumption of stability in the value of the monetary unit. For some time now this has not been an unrealistic assumption so far as the United States, Canada, and most of Western Europe is concerned. However, the substantial decline which took place in the monetary units of these countries, in some much more than others, during the period between 1940 and 1957 (in the United States, the level of wholesale prices for all commodities taken together increased about two and one-third times during that period) has left most businesses with long-lived assets acquired in the past at much lower price levels than those now ruling.

The application of the cost principle in its traditional form results in depreciation charges based on those low acquisition costs, while the revenues currently being produced by these older assets are, of course, measured in monetary units of today's diminished purchasing power. Though the assets, therefore, appear to be earning an abnormally large profit, it may be questioned whether this is indeed a true profit, if profit is thought of in real (nonmonetary) terms. The problem arises from the time-lag between inputs and outputs, the inputs being valued in dollars of higher purchasing power than the outputs. The time-lag between inputs which take the form of fixed assets and their final outputs (at the end of their lives) is particularly marked. It is different only in degree, not in kind, from the time-lag between the input of inventories, and the output, or sale, which later results.

Is management likely to be misled by the effects of this time-lag coupled with fluctuations in the purchasing power of the dollar? It is more than possible. Suppose a division has to decide which of two plants to scrap, one of them bought years ago, for perhaps $500,000, and the other bought more recently, when prices in general were higher, for twice as much. Suppose also that, in spite of the difference in age, the newer plant is only slightly more efficient than the older one. As against its slight efficiency advantage over the older plant, the newer one will save the division twice as much in depreciation if it is scrapped than will the older one. It is likely, therefore, to be chosen for scrapping. Yet if the costs of the two plants were reduced to truly comparable terms, it would probably be seen at once that the older one was the truly high-cost plant.

What is to be done about it? The answer lies in expressing inputs and outputs in truly comparable dollars—"stabilized accounting," or "common dollar reporting," as it has been called. Stabilized accounting involves the use of index numbers to re-express costs or revenues in terms of any desired level of prices—the current level or any other. The simplest use of this idea is to apply it to fixed assets and depreciation only. Thus, if a fixed asset was bought for $16,500 when the index of wholesale prices, say, was 110, and today the index stands at 120, and the asset is being written off at 10 per cent per annum straight line, the asset's cost would be re-expressed in current dollars as $16,500 x 120/110, or $18,000, and the year's depreciation would be 10 per cent of that figure, or $1800 and not $1650.

This is the simplest possible explanation of an important idea which has produced a greater volume of accounting literature since the end of World War II than any other single topic. There are many questions to be answered by any company wishing to use stabilized accounting, which, in its full expression, reduces all the figures in the financial statements, not just fixed assets and depreciation thereon, to common dollars. Some of these questions can, perhaps, be briefly indicated:

- Is stabilization to be applied fully to all items in the accounts, or only partially to fixed assets or otherwise?
- Are all values to be expressed in current dollars or those of some other date? If the latter, which date?
- Which series of index numbers is to be used and, in particular, should it be an index of general purchasing power (e.g., wholesale or retail prices) or of the prices of the specific assets which the company owns?
- Should the stabilized data be made public in the annual report to stockholders or should it be used for internal purposes only?

The first of these questions is worth a brief comment, for it has been argued that price-level adjustments in accounts should be made completely across the board or not at all. One form of this argument is that it is wrong to eliminate the "inflationary" element in business profits unless, at the same time, the gains resulting from inflation are also recognized. One of these unrecognized gains is the reduction in the real burden of bonds and other long-term debt which accrues to a company when debts are incurred at one price level and repaid at a higher price level with the same number of dollars. Each dollar has lost some purchasing power since it was borrowed and the lender's loss is the borrower's gain. Offsetting this is the unrecognized loss from holding cash and other "money assets" in a time of rising prices.

There is merit in this argument in that it draws attention to the fact that inflation cuts both ways. But the logic is at fault in lumping together two different kinds of inflationary distortion. The inflationary profits arising from depreciation and inventories are the result of the time-lag between inputs and outputs: the *same real* events have *different money* values attached to them because of the time-lag between the input event (the purchase of a machine, for instance), and the output event (the yielding of its services and the depreciation which reflects it). With the gain from the diminished burden of debt through inflation, or the loss from the diminished purchasing power of a cash balance there are, on the other hand, no *real* events, only monetary phenomena. There is a time-lag here too—between borrowing money and repaying it, or between receiving cash and using it. But it is a time-lag between two *monetary* events, whereas in the other case it is a time-lag between two *real* events—the receipt of goods and services and their use. It is possible to distinguish between these two kinds of distortion if we wish to do so. No doubt we ought to correct both. But accounting opinion has some way to go on this yet, and one kind of correction is surely better than none at all. An astigmatic myope would do well to correct his myopia, even if he had to learn to live with his astigmatism.

Some companies defend the failure to put fixed assets acquired at different price levels onto a truly comparable basis on the ground that the higher cost of more recently acquired assets is offset by their greater efficiency. This argument is a *non sequitur,* as can be seen if it is applied to a deflationary situation. In such a situation, the last acquired assets would still presumably be the most efficient but would have a *lower* cost than the older, less efficient ones. In a period of price stability, technical progress may be expected to produce improved equipment, generally speaking, without any increase in its cost. The correlation between rising efficiency of equipment and rising prices of equipment in a period of inflation is accidental. It provides no argument for failing to recognize that dollars of different dates, having different purchasing powers, should not be compared or aggregated but should, first, be reduced to common purchasing power terms. Only then can conclusions properly be drawn from the relationships disclosed.

As the period of price stability lengthens, the problem we have been discussing diminishes in importance since, as old assets are retired and replaced by new ones bought at current price-levels, the legacy of depreciation based on out-of-date costs diminishes. If the present stability can be maintained for a few more years, the urgent need for accounting to recognize price fluctuations will perhaps have passed for the present. No one can know, however, when the problem of instability will return. A period of comparative calm is, perhaps, not a bad time to install methods which can cope with the more serious fluctuations which may again be encountered in the future.

### *Rules for depreciation accounting*

Let us now try to formulate some rules for depreciation accounting which will promote rather than hinder the purposes both of the company and of its divisions. The rules we need will be found to stem from a single simple principle—that the accounting methods adopted should reflect the facts of the situation facing management as they see it, not as the U.S. Treasury or some other government agency sees it. In accordance with this principle the following rules are suggested:

1. Each division should be allowed to choose its own depreciation methods, subject only to the requirement that it must satisfy the corporate financial executives. The policy chosen must be appropriate to the needs of the division in the sense that it does, as accurately as possible, reflect the facts of divisional asset life expectancies. There is no reason why all divisions should follow a uniform policy if their needs are not uniform.

2. In selecting its depreciation methods, each division should classify assets into as many groups as may be necessary to make each group reasonably homogeneous. In the light of the expected pattern of net receipts to be generated by the assets in each group, the method and rate of depreciation should be chosen for each asset group. No attention should be paid, at this stage, to the regulations of outside

agencies except where the law requires these regulations to be observed for internal accounting, as it does for public utilities.

3. Though the depreciation methods and rates must, for practical reasons, be chosen for groups of assets rather than for individual assets, a separate record should be set up for each asset having a cost in excess of some modest amount (possibly $250, though some companies use a figure as low as $100). A separate calculation of the annual depreciation charge and the total accumulated depreciation in respect of each asset should be made. Though this involves a great amount of record-keeping, *some* detailed asset records are necessary for nonaccounting purposes, and the additional work involved in providing the needed accounting information is not great, especially when a computer is available to handle it.

4. Divisions should be required to account only for fixed assets under their control. Corporate (as distinct from divisional) assets should be held by a corporate division, and should not be allocated to divisions for the purpose of computing capital employed by the divisions or for any other purpose.

5. As far as possible, because of the considerable time-lag normally occurring between the acquisition of a fixed asset and its ultimate consumption, steps should be taken to put fixed asset records on a stable dollar basis. This may be done by applying index number adjustments to the asset accounts, with corresponding adjustments to a revaluation reserve, depreciation then being computed on the revised book figure of fixed assets. A second method is through periodic revaluations of the fixed assets with corresponding revisions of the depreciation charges.[3]

6. Decisions to replace assets, or otherwise to dispose of them, should be taken in the light of *ad hoc* computations, not on the basis of the figures used for routine reporting. In reaching such decisions, it is normally the disposal value of the old asset, rather than its book value, which is relevant.

7. Divisions should be given considerable autonomy in the matter of asset disposals. They should, however, be required to offer surplus assets to other divisions (or to the corporate division) at the price

---

[3] It may be noted that Moonitz and Sprouse, *op. cit.* p. 34, suggest periodic fixed asset revaluations, in implementation of their restatement of accounting principles. They suggest once every five years as a reasonable frequency of revaluation, but what is reasonable must clearly depend on the degree of monetary instability which is being experienced.

they propose to accept from outside purchasers prior to selling the asset outside. If corporate headquarters thinks an asset up for disposal is worth more than the division is ready to accept for it, the asset should be transferred to the corporate division at the price acceptable to the disposing division, pending final sale or other disposition.

8. Depreciation figures for tax purposes should be kept separate from those used for managerial purposes, though a single set of asset records might incorporate both sets of computations. While, as recommended above, divisions should be given a large degree of freedom to choose their own depreciation methods for internal accounting purposes, the choice of income tax depreciation method should be made at corporate level without reference to the divisions.

9. Similarly, for pricing government contracts and other special purposes, a different set of depreciation computations should normally be used rather than those applied to internal reporting. Government procurement regulations are designed to meet the purchasing needs of government agencies, not the managerial needs of the firms with whom the Government does business. However, it is appropriate to take the incremental cost of extra record-keeping into account in deciding whether, in a particular situation, one set of records may be required to serve more than one purpose.

## LIFO and Divisional Profit Measurement

Divisional use of an accelerated depreciation method for internal profit reporting, not because it is appropriate to the circumstances of the division, but because of the tax advantages accruing from it, must be judged to be a distortion of the accounting information needed by management. When a company adopts a last-in-first-out method of inventory valuation for one or more of its divisions because this approach withholds from taxation some portion of the divisional profits, must this, too, be looked on as a distortion of managerially useful information tolerated for the sake of the tax advantages it brings?

It is clear that some companies think it is, for they take steps to insulate the divisional profit results from the effects of LIFO by reporting divisional figures internally on a first-in-first-out basis (FIFO), leaving the so-called "LIFO valuation adjustment" to be brought in as a nondivisional addition or deduction (as the case may be in a particular year) to corporate profits on consolidation of the divisional results. This procedure effectively preserves the tax advantages of LIFO for the company while allowing the division to report its profit on a FIFO basis.

Does LIFO distort profits, or does it reveal the true profits of a division? Is it perhaps FIFO which is really guilty of distortion? These questions have to be answered before we can say whether the LIFO adjustment properly belongs in the divisional profit statement, or whether it is best treated as a corporate adjustment. The questions, unfortunately, are not easy to answer in a simple, unequivocal manner, for the answers depend in part on the circumstances, and in part on what the nature of profit is held to be.

The circumstances referred to here relate to changes in the volume of physical inventory. It will be assumed that LIFO is being used by divisions which can readily compare their raw material inventory levels at different dates by means of some common measurement unit, in tons of tin plate or raw cotton or wood pulp, for example. So long as the physical volume of inventory is substantially unchanged over the period, it is easy to make sense of what LIFO does. It achieves a comparison, in the income statement, of the period's sales with the cost of replacing the goods sold, for with constant inventory levels the cost of current purchases *is* the replacement cost of sales. The same thing is true under LIFO when there is an *increase* in the inventory level. The excess of purchases over consumption goes into stock at cost, while the remaining purchases, the materials bought and currently consumed, again constitute the replacement cost of sales, which is compared with sales revenue to determine current profit.

It is when there is a *decline* in the level of inventory that the results produced by LIFO are less easily acceptable. In this situation the goods being sold are coming partially from current purchases and partially from stock. To the extent that they are coming out of current purchases, sales revenues are being compared with replacement costs. But to the extent that the goods being sold are coming out of stock, current sales revenue may have to be compared with costs incurred in a previous period, perhaps long past. If the reduction in inventory follows a lengthy period in which inventories have been maintained at a more or less constant level, the LIFO costs attaching to the goods taken out of stock may bear little relation to current cost levels. This fact has caused LIFO to produce some surprising results in the form of unexpectedly high profits at such times as the 1960 steel strike when, even with curtailed production, firms were eating deeply into stocks of steel which had been carried for years at low inventory values. In normal circumstances, these same companies which had adopted LIFO would have taken steps to replenish their inventories before the end of the fiscal year, to prevent profit fluctuations of this kind. If circumstances make such replenishment impossible, then high profits result. They will result, also, if a permanent reduction in the level of inventory becomes possible. One company, using operations research methods, was able to cut its inventory of basic raw material quite substantially, and the tax on the nonrecurrent profit, caused by the low LIFO value at which the inventory had been carried, looked like a poor reward for this striking managerial success.

To judge the managerial value of LIFO as an accounting (as distinct from a tax) device, we must ask how effectively it achieves what it sets out to do. How effectively does it insulate profits from the disturbing effects of changes in the value of money? To test this, it will be useful to set up a simple, if somewhat exaggerated, model:

During Year I, the Gay Corporation maintained a constant level of inventory, starting with 8500 units bought at $1.00 a unit. It purchased 73,000 units during the year in even monthly instalments, at prices starting at $1.00 and rising steadily to $1.20 at the end of the year, at which figure the closing inventory may be supposed to have been bought. The corporation sold 73,000 units for $82,500, also in even monthly instalments. During the year, the level of wholesale prices rose from an index number at the beginning of the year of 100 to a closing figure of 120. All expenses other than the cost of goods sold will be ignored.

In a situation such as this, LIFO will show a much lower profit than FIFO. But that comparison does not tell us which figure is "right." A further comparison with a stabilized or common-dollar profit statement will throw some light on the relative merits of the two sets of figures. The comparative statement is shown in Exhibit VIII.

The LIFO profit is $1,700 less than under FIFO. This is equal to $0.20 a unit (the difference between the opening inventory price of $1.00 and the closing FIFO price of $1.20) on 8,500 units. But it is quite close to the stabilized profit figure, the $200 difference between them being due to the conversion of the purchases and sales figures from their midyear value (for their even monthly spread through the year can be equated with a single midyear value, taking the index at 110) to its year-end equivalent. In this situation, LIFO gives us a profit figure which approximates quite well to the stabilized results.

At the end of Year I the price rise stopped and prices remained constant through Year II at an index of 120. During this year, the com-

## EXHIBIT VIII

### PROFIT STATEMENTS—YEAR I

| | UNITS | FIFO $ | | STABILIZED* $ | LIFO $ |
|---|---|---|---|---|---|
| Sales | 73,000 | 82,500 | $\times\frac{120}{110}$ | 90,000 | 82,500 |
| Cost of sales | | | | | |
| Opening inventory | 8,500 | 8,500 | $\times\frac{120}{100}$ | 10,200 | 8,500 |
| Purchases | 73,000 | 80,300 | $\times\frac{120}{110}$ | 87,600 | 80,300 |
| | 81,500 | 88,800 | | 97,800 | 88,800 |
| Closing inventory | 8,500 | 10,200 | $\times\frac{120}{120}$ | 10,200 | 8,500 |
| | 73,000 | 78,600 | | 87,600 | 80,300 |
| Profit | | 3,900 | | 2,400 | 2,200 |

* The year-end dollar (price index = 120) has been chosen for stabilization purposes.

## EXHIBIT VIII (Continued)

### PROFIT STATEMENTS—YEAR II

| | UNITS | FIFO $ | LIFO $ |
|---|---|---|---|
| Sales | 73,000 | 90,000 | 90,000 |
| Cost of sales | | | |
| Opening inventory | 8,500 | 10,200 | 8,500 |
| Purchases | 70,000 | 84,000 | 84,000 |
| | 78,500 | 94,200 | 92,500 |
| Closing inventory | 5,500 | 6,600 | 5,500 |
| | 73,000 | 87,600 | 87,000 |
| Profit | | 2,400 | 3,000 |

pany was unable to replace its inventory as it used it up, and finished the year with 3,000 units fewer than it had on January 1. It sold exactly the same quantity as in Year I, 73,000 units, for $90,000.

In this situation, since prices are constant throughout the year, the income statement stabilized in terms of year-end prices (=120) will be identical with the unstabilized FIFO statement. In the comparative statement for Year II set out above, therefore, the stabilized figures have been omitted.

In this year, because low-priced inventory has been drawn down, LIFO shows a larger profit than FIFO, even though prices have remained stable. The stabilized statement would have shown a profit of $2,400 (using end-of-Year-II dollars as the stabilization unit). In a situation like this, FIFO does a better job than LIFO in removing the distortions caused by price level instability.

Our model shows up the most glaring deficiency of LIFO, its liability, in periods of inventory reduction, to backfire. Uncomfortable as this is from the tax standpoint, it also suggests two related objections to the use of LIFO for divisional profit measurement when, as will usually be the case, the management of the division is likely to be judged on its profit performance. The first is that in periods of fluctuating prices the use of LIFO lends itself to profit manipulation through changes in inventory levels, since a decision by a division merely to replace or not to replace low-cost inventories will affect its profit. The second and related objection is that, for tax reasons outside its purview, a division may be discouraged from doing what it ought to be encouraged to do, namely to cut its investment in inventory to the minimum amount consistent with fully efficient operations.

The motive which has led so many companies to adopt LIFO during a period of rising prices is easy to understand. Setting aside the tax implications which, in practice, are all-important, the device can be viewed as an attempt by accountants to do what they are always being told to do—to recognize the changing purchasing power of the dollar, and to give effect to this recognition in the accounts they prepare. The trouble with LIFO is that it is a half-hearted attempt at such recognition which, taken on its own, has some undesirable side effects. The best hope is that a continuance of the present era of price stability will make such devices unnecessary in the future. The legacy of LIFO's existing low-cost inventories will doubtless be with us for a long time to come, however. In the meantime, there is much to be said for the practice of making inventory adjustments in divisional income statements on a FIFO basis. This leaves changes in valuation adjustments, necessary to raise or lower inventories to a LIFO valuation, to be made in the corporate profit consolidation only. If, for managerial purposes, it is thought to be desirable to move in the direction of common-dollar reporting, something much more consistent and thoroughgoing in its approach than LIFO seems to be called for.

## Direct Costing

Something approximating a direct cost approach has already been adopted in the treatment advocated here for central overhead, namely, only that increment of central overhead which can be more or less directly attributed to the activities of a division should be allocated to it. The full direct cost approach goes further along the same line, and argues that units of product, as well as divisions, should be charged only with those costs for which they can be said to be directly responsible. "Direct" responsibility is not always easy to establish, but direct costs normally include materials which enter into the product, the labor which works directly on it, and any *variable* factory overhead associated with the production of the product. The indirect costs (not charged to products) are regarded as "period costs," and are charged against the net revenue of the period in which they were incurred. It is the distinction between product costs and period costs that distinguishes direct costing from absorption costing. The latter regards all costs as product costs, to be allocated to products by the best available method even where this involves an element of the arbitrary, as it usually must. By a logical step, direct costing identifies product costs with variable costs, and period costs with fixed costs. Direct costing permits a proportion of the direct costs only to be attached to unsold output and hence carried into inventory. Absorption costing attaches a proportion of all costs to products going into inventory. Direct costing naturally results in a lower inventory valuation than does absorption costing.

The division of costs into fixed and variable elements is not a simple matter, for costs which are variable in one set of circumstances may be fixed in another. The length of time given for adaptation and the area of operations under consideration (a section of a shop, a whole shop, or a plant) may determine whether a particular cost is fixed or variable with output. A cost can be directly allocable to a segment of the business and yet be a fixed cost of that segment, like a department manager's salary. Nevertheless, so-called direct costs are used as a rough-and-ready approximation to variable costs. They exclude fixed factory overhead as well as administrative and selling overhead, both at divisional and corporate levels.

The pros and cons of direct costing[4] gave rise to a vast literature even before the practice had become at all widespread. Even now it is practiced by a small minority of companies.[5] There is no doubt that a powerful force preventing its more widespread use has been the refusal of the Internal Revenue authorities to accept it, except in a few isolated instances, as a legitimate method of inventory valuation and therefore of income determination. There does seem to be evidence, however, that more and more firms are likely to adopt direct costing for internal accounting purposes, even though they revert to an absorption costing basis of income determination for external reporting and for their tax returns.

---

[4] The pro and con positions are argued in a two-part article, "The Concept of Direct Costing" by Wilmer Wright (pro) and Felix P. Kollaritsch (con) in *The Controller,* Vol. XXX, No. 7, July 1962, starting on p. 322. See also NAA Research Reports No. 23, April 1953, entitled *Direct Costing,* and No. 37, January 1961, *Current Application of Direct Costing.*

[5] In the article by Mr. Wright cited above, he quotes the March 24, 1962 issue of *Business Week* as saying that direct costing was in use by nearly 250 companies at that time. Of the 25 companies participating in the present study, only two and some divisions of a third are using direct costing for measuring divisional profits.

### *Why use direct costing?*

In the brief discussion of direct costing which follows, attention will be directed mainly to its control aspects. Its use as an aid to decision-making, notably in the area of price-determination and in connection with decisions about output levels, selection of products and optimization of the use of resources, important as these all are, lies for the most part outside the domain of this study. However, they cannot be completely disregarded, for in the choice of accounting methods all the uses of accounting data have to be kept in mind.

The use of direct costing for control has two aspects which are of particular importance to decentralized companies. One is that direct costing will cause a division to report different profits from those it would report under absorption costing, different both from year to year and from month to month. The division's performance will therefore look different. The second important aspect is that, since under direct costing fixed costs are not "unitized" by allocation over the units of products produced, control of them is exercised through budgets and standards, rather than by examining the level of unit costs.

The first of these two points, though a familiar one, still gives rise to keen controversy. A simple illustration is given in Exhibit IX. The division in question has a seasonal business which reaches a low level in the summer and recovers in the fall. Goods are produced in August for stock, to even out fluctuations in production. As the exhibit shows, though the total profit for the two months together is the same, $20,000 under both methods, August, the month of low sales, looks more profitable under absorption costing than under direct costing. The reason for this, of course, is that under absorption costing, as one-fifth of the month's output was added to inventory, the income statement was relieved of one-fifth of the month's period costs, or $4000, and this sum was added to the value of inventory in the balance sheet.

The results shown in the two parts of Exhibit IX pose at least three questions for us, and we shall examine them in turn.

1. *Can one set of figures be described as right and the other as wrong?*

The two statements reflect different views as to what is meant by "matching costs and revenues." The absorption costing school argues that costs are only incurred in order to procure a supply of goods and

## EXHIBIT IX

**(a) Divisional income statement for August and September under absorption costing**

| | August | September |
|---|---|---|
| Sales (units) | 8,000 | 12,000 |
| Output (units) | 10,000 | 10,000 |
| Sales (value) @ $6.00 a unit | $48,000 | $72,000 |
| Cost of sales | | |
| Direct cost of output @ $3.00 | 30,000 | 30,000 |
| Period costs | 20,000 | 20,000 |
| | 50,000 | 50,000 |
| Inventory change at full cost of $5.00 a unit | (10,000) | 10,000 |
| Cost of sales | 40,000 | 60,000 |
| Profit for month | $ 8,000 | $12,000 |

**(b) Divisional income statement for August and September under direct costing**

| | August | September |
|---|---|---|
| Sales (value) @ $6.00 a unit | $48,000 | $72,000 |
| Direct cost of sales @ $3.00 | 24,000 | 36,000 |
| Contribution | 24,000 | 36,000 |
| Period costs | 20,000 | 20,000 |
| Profit for month | $ 4,000 | $16,000 |

that this is true of the fixed costs as well as of the direct costs. They are all, therefore, equally "product costs." There is no more reason to exclude the cost of the services rendered by machinery (i.e., depreciation, maintenance, etc.) than there is to exclude the cost of direct labor. As labor is progressively replaced by machinery this point will become more and more important. In Exhibit IX (a), the goods, which sell for $6.00 a unit, cost $5.00 a unit to make. The profits shown for the two months properly represent $1.00 a unit on the quantities sold each month.

The direct costing school, on the other hand, argues that costs which would be incurred in the short run, whether products were produced or not, ought not to be capitalized as inventoriable costs. In the case of fixed assets, so long as the assets which are the result of capital expenditures remain in existence, the expenditures do not normally have to be incurred all over again. But this, they point out, is not true of period costs such as factory rent, supervision and maintenance and depreciation of equipment. Producing for inventory one month will not prevent these costs from recurring the following month. Hence it is theoretically wrong, the direct costing school argues, to capitalize period costs or any part of them by including them in the balance sheet value of inventory.

This last argument is a powerful one as long as profit measurement is thought of (as it normally is) as a process of matching costs and revenues. A different view of profit hinted at earlier looks to the "better-off-ness" of the firm as a measure of profit. From this perspective, direct costing fails to give full credit, in Exhibit IX, for the 2,000 units of output by which the firm is better off at the end of August, assuming, of course, that these units can eventually be sold for close to the present selling price. The inventory valuation method which comes closest to reflecting "the increase in well-off-ness" in the profit figures is that method which comes nearest to valuing inventory at net realizable value at the balance sheet date, even though this would involve the recognition of unrealized profits. Therefore, unless inventory has declined in value since manufacture, absorption costing would normally come closer to this ideal than would direct costing.

We shall leave the question, "Which profit figure is right?" without a definite answer. The traditional view that profit is the result of a matching process implies that neither of them is clearly wrong, while the alternative view, that profit is the result of a valuation process, suggests that neither of them is right. Generally, in normal circumstances, absorption costing gives a better answer.

The same conflict of opinion about the fundamental nature of profit again besets us when we turn to the second question.

2. *Which figures, those under absorption costing or those under direct costing, best reflect divisional performance?*

We cannot answer this question, either, without some prior consensus as to what constitutes the best measure of performance. At least we must define the ideal, if unattainable, measure at which we are aiming. If we adhere to the view that the manager should, ideally, be judged by the contribution which he makes to the "well-off-ness" of the firm within the limitations imposed on him by higher authority, then absorption costing seems to be preferable simply because in normal circumstances it gives an inventory valuation closer to the dollar value it will sell for.[6] This second question turns out, on inspection, to be the first question expressed slightly differently, and the prior discussion need not be repeated. Unless selling prices have fallen below the level expected when the products were made and put into inventory, absorption cost methods will give a profit figure for the division which will better reflect divisional performance according to the "better-off-ness" criterion which has been adopted as our ideal. It must be emphasized, though, that use of this criterion involves the abandonment of the act of realization as the all-important test of when a profit is made, and the adoption of the view that it is the whole process of production and sale that produces a profit, not just the sale alone.

This defense of absorption costing, namely that absorption costing more nearly reflects a division's contribution to the increase in net worth of the firm because manufactured inventory is valued at a figure closer to its realizable value than it would be under direct costing, is subject to a serious criticism which the choice of figures in Exhibit IX has, until now, averted. In that exhibit, the two months of August and September showed no change in either volume of output or the level of period costs. Thus, the period costs per unit of output were constant, and the absorption costs per unit of output were accordingly also constant. In these circumstances, absorption cost can, perhaps with reason, claim to be a better approximation to realizable value than can direct cost. Had output fallen, say, from August to September, the period costs per unit would have risen, and the absorption cost of inventory would accordingly also have risen. It is impossible to justify this rise in inventory valuation by pretending that it reflects a true rise in the value of inventory when, in fact, it is actually caused by a *fall* in the level of output.

[6] There is much confusion, in discussions of inventory valuation, between cost and value. Cost does not create value, it is value which creates cost, in the sense that it is only because a product is expected to have a sale value that anyone will be willing to incur costs to produce it. This is why arguments about what inventory is "really worth" which are conducted in terms of cost are and must always be futile.

A situation such as the one just described is illustrated in Exhibit X. Shown here, at the end of the second quarter, is an inventory as great in volume as that at the end of the first quarter. It has, however, considerably more value, simply because the second quarter shows a drop in output. This high-cost inventory has its impact on the third quarter which, though it is a good period in both sales and output, shows only about the same profit as the first quarter, when both sales and output were lower.

There is a significant conclusion to be drawn from this situation. If net profit arrived at by absorption costing methods is to have any claim to reflect more fairly the over-all performance of a division in producing and selling than does net profit arrived at by direct costing methods (which treat the moment of realization as alone the decisive moment in the long drawn-out process of earning a profit), then the value of inventory under absorption costing must not be allowed to go up and down merely by reason of fluctuations in volume of output. The implementation of this idea leads, of course, to the use of "normal output" to give normal period costs per unit for inventory valuation purposes. This, in turn, requires the recognition of a volume variance representing the over- or underabsorption of period costs in periods of high or low output. This variance is treated wholly as a current expense (or gain). No part of it is allowed to enter into inventory. The same figures used in Exhibit X are used in Exhibit XI to show what profits are attributed to each of the four quarters when period costs are allocated between cost of sales and inventory on the basis of the unit period cost of normal output.

The profits for the four quarters shown in Exhibit XI do seem to reflect the total activity of producing and selling in each quarter much better than those in Exhibit X. The third quarter is the most active and shows the largest profit, while the second quarter is the least active and shows the smallest profit. The fourth quarter has the largest sales, but only the third largest profit. This reflects the substantial idle productive capacity in that quarter.

It will be illuminating, before finally leaving this topic, to see what profits would be shown, applying direct costing methods to the same facts. The figures are shown in Exhibit XII and it is at once apparent that the quarterly profits now exclusively reflect the quarterly sales. With three sets of profit figures to choose from (as set out in Exhibits X, XI, and XII) it is hardly surprising that managers who are

| | First Quarter | Second Quarter | Third Quarter | Fourth Quarter | Annual Total |
|---|---|---|---|---|---|
| Output (units) | 12,000 | 8,000 | 13,000 | 7,000 | 40,000 |
| Sales (units) | 8,000 | 8,000 | 10,000 | 12,000 | 38,000 |
| Sales (value) | $48,000 | $48,000 | $60,000 | $72,000 | $228,000 |
| Opening inventory (units) | — | 4,000 | 4,000 | 7,000 | — |
| Closing inventory (units) | 4,000 | 4,000 | 7,000 | 2,000 | 2,000 |
| Period costs (total) | $20,000 | $20,000 | $20,000 | $20,000 | $ 80,000 |
| Direct costs per unit | $3.00 | $3.00 | $3.00 | $3.00 | $3.00 |
| Selling price per unit | $6.00 | $6.00 | $6.00 | $6.00 | $6.00 |

OPERATING STATEMENTS
WITH INVENTORY VALUED AT "ACTUAL" FULL COST

| | $ | $ | $ | $ | $ |
|---|---|---|---|---|---|
| Sales revenue | 48,000 | 48,000 | 60,000 | 72,000 | 228,000 |
| Cost of sales | | | | | |
| Opening inventory | — | 18,666 | 22,000 | 31,769 | — |
| Direct cost of output | 36,000 | 24,000 | 39,000 | 21,000 | 120,000 |
| Period cost | 20,000 | 20,000 | 20,000 | 20,000 | 80,000 |
| | 56,000 | 62,666 | 81,000 | 72,769 | 200,000 |
| Less: | | | | | |
| Closing inventory | | | | | |
| $56,000 × 4,000/12,000 | 18,666 | | | | |
| $44,000 × 4,000/ 8,000 | | 22,000 | | | |
| $59,000 × 7,000/13,000 | | | 31,769 | | |
| $41,000 × 2,000/ 7,000 | | | | 11,714 | 11,714 |
| | 37,334 | 40,666 | 49,231 | 61,055 | 188,286 |
| Profit | 10,666 | 7,334 | 10,769 | 10,945 | 39,714 |

## EXHIBIT XI

OPERATING STATEMENTS
WITH INVENTORY VALUED AT NORMAL FULL COST

(NORMAL OUTPUT = 10,000 UNITS)

| | First Quarter $ | Second Quarter $ | Third Quarter $ | Fourth Quarter $ | Annual Total $ |
|---|---|---|---|---|---|
| Sales revenue | 48,000 | 48,000 | 60,000 | 72,000 | 228,000 |
| Cost of sales | | | | | |
| Opening inventory | – | 20,000 | 20,000 | 35,000 | – |
| Direct cost of output | 36,000 | 24,000 | 39,000 | 21,000 | 120,000 |
| Absorbed period expense | 24,000 | 16,000 | 26,000 | 14,000 | 80,000 |
| | 60,000 | 60,000 | 85,000 | 70,000 | 200,000 |
| Closing inventory | | | | | |
| $60,000 × 4,000/12,000 | 20,000 | | | | |
| $40,000 × 4,000/ 8,000 | | 20,000 | | | |
| $65,000 × 7,000/13,000 | | | 35,000 | | |
| $35,000 × 2,000/ 7,000 | | | | 10,000 | 10,000 |
| | 40,000 | 40,000 | 50,000 | 60,000 | 190,000 |
| Profit over normal cost | 8,000 | 8,000 | 10,000 | 12,000 | 38,000 |
| Volume variance—over- or (under-) absorbed expense | 4,000 | (4,000) | 6,000 | (6,000) | – |
| Net profit | 12,000 | 4,000 | 16,000 | 6,000 | 38,000 |

## EXHIBIT XII

### OPERATING STATEMENTS WITH INVENTORY VALUED AT DIRECT COST

| | First Quarter $ | Second Quarter $ | Third Quarter $ | Fourth Quarter $ | Annual Total $ |
|---|---|---|---|---|---|
| Sales revenue | 48,000 | 48,000 | 60,000 | 72,000 | 228,000 |
| Direct cost of sales | 24,000 | 24,000 | 30,000 | 36,000 | 114,000 |
| Contribution | 24,000 | 24,000 | 30,000 | 36,000 | 114,000 |
| Period costs | 20,000 | 20,000 | 20,000 | 20,000 | 80,000 |
| Profit | 4,000 | 4,000 | 10,000 | 16,000 | 34,000 |

not accountants are apt to be confused. Fortunately, as will be explained shortly, a compromise solution is possible.

3. *Which figures are best for decision-making purposes?*

When we turn from the evaluation of performance to the provision of data for decision-making, the advantages on the whole lie heavily in favor of direct costing for the reason that operating statements prepared along the lines of Exhibit XII lend themselves readily to extrapolation. Thus, suppose we want to know what is likely to be the result, profit-wise, of adding $1000 to the fixed processing costs in the first quarter, if this extra expenditure, by improving the quality of the product, can be expected to increase sales by 10 per cent or 800 units, with a corresponding increase in output, everything else remaining unchanged. It is easy to see that, on the direct costing view that period costs should not be carried into inventory, this would increase net profit by $1400, for the total contribution would increase by 10 per cent or $2400, from which $1000 would be deducted for additional period costs. This answer does, however, depend on our acceptance of the $4000 as the "right" absolute amount of profit for the quarter. Profit will go up by $1400 if $1000 more is spent on processing, so long as all period costs are currently written off.

Nothing like this simple projection can be made if an "actual full cost" system is used. In fact, all the figures must virtually be recalculated. With a "normal full cost" system the difficulties of projection are not so great, though even there a permanent change in the level of fixed costs necessitates a recalculation of normal cost. Also the necessity of recalculating the volume variance every time there is a change in the level of output is something of a stumbling block to the uninitiated. There is no doubt at all that, for purposes of prediction, direct costing has a simplicity that other costing methods cannot match.

The impact of direct costing on the inventory policy of divisions is another matter usually considered important by companies using it. They point out that, under absorption costing, divisions are encouraged to accumulate inventory since, by producing for stock, they can charge off to the inventory account a proportion of their fixed overhead. On the other hand, if the productive capacity not needed to replace goods currently sold were left idle, this fixed overhead would have to be recognized as a current expense, either by adding it to the cost of sales or by writing it off separately as a volume variance. By the same reasoning, they argue, divisions may be discouraged from liquidating inventories when prices are sagging since the fixed overheads previously charged to inventory will depress profits when sales are made from inventory. This latter argument, it must be said, is a good deal less convincing than the previous one, for the "cost or market" rule of inventory valuation would require depreciating inventory to be marked down at least to replacement cost, with consequent inventory losses being suffered in place of losses on sales. Whatever absorption costing's effect may be as a deterrent to inventory decumulation, impressive successes are claimed for direct costing as a deterrent to its accumulation.

There is an implication in the foregoing argument that inventory accumulation is always undesirable. That this is not so is particularly obvious in seasonal trades where inventory fluctuations are the means of achieving smooth production with uneven sales. Direct costing does nothing to promote this smoothing of production. Moreover, because of the low inventory values which it sets, direct costing may lead managers to think themselves immune from losses when prices begin to decline. It may thereby encourage them to hold on to inventories longer than is wise. Once more, the arguments do not point unequivocally in one direction or the other.

## The Reconciliation of Direct Costing and Absorption Costing

As we have seen, some of the arguments for and against direct costing are evenly balanced. Some of the arguments for it are very strong, particularly the ease with which certain decisions, superimposed on past results, can be projected into the future to give the probable results of these decisions. The real objections of auditors to its use for external reporting reinforce the conclusion to be drawn that a combination method which gives the best of both worlds has much to commend it. This is the way in which direct costing is coming to be used, and the way in which its use is likely to spread.

The combination method requires that, after the profit for the period has been ascertained by direct cost methods, an adjustment for period cost be made in the divisional income statement to the book value of the manufactured inventory. It is unnecessary to make a detailed allocation of actual period costs to products for the purpose of this adjustment. All that is required for the determination of profit is to calculate what proportion of the period expense in total is applicable to the change in inventory which occurred during the period. Two simplifications in the procedure make this a relatively straightforward calculation:

1. The use of budgeted rather than actual period expense in the calculation.
2. Since aggregate inventory and aggregate output cannot be expressed in physical terms in any but a single product firm, these aggregates are expressed in terms of their direct costs.

The inventory period cost adjustment is then given by the formula:

$$\text{Budgeted period expense} \times \frac{\text{Direct cost of inventory change}}{\text{Total budgeted direct cost for the period}}$$

If inventory has increased, the adjustment is an addition to profits as determined by direct cost methods. If inventory has decreased it is a deduction.

This calculation implies, of course, that all products should attract overhead in proportion to their direct costs. If all products follow much the same production pattern through the various processes, no great error will result from this assumption. Where, however, the production pattern of different products varies greatly, and the proportion of period costs to direct costs varies materially from shop to shop, then the calculation can be refined by making the inventory period cost adjustment separately for each shop and aggregating the adjustments. Thus in a plant which has a machine shop and an assembly shop, there would be two period cost adjustments to inventory as follows:

(a) $$\text{Budgeted machine shop period expense} \times \frac{\text{Total direct machine shop cost of inventory change}}{\text{Total budgeted direct machine shop costs for the period}}$$

(b) $$\text{Budgeted assembly shop period expense} \times \frac{\text{Total direct assembly shop cost of inventory change}}{\text{Total budgeted direct assembly shop costs for the period}}$$

The aggregate period cost adjustment would, of course, be the aggregate of (a) and (b) above.

Again using the data from Exhibit X, the way in which both profit

## EXHIBIT XIII

### RECONCILIATION OF OPERATING PROFITS UNDER DIRECT COSTING AND ABSORPTION COSTING

| | First Quarter $ | Second Quarter $ | Third Quarter $ | Fourth Quarter $ | Annual Total $ |
|---|---|---|---|---|---|
| Profit under direct costing (per Exhibit XII) | 4,000 | 4,000 | 10,000 | 16,000 | 34,000 |
| Inventory period cost adjustment | | | | | |
| (1) $\$20{,}000 \times \frac{\$12{,}000}{\$30{,}000}$ | 8,000 | | | | |
| (2) No inventory change | | — | | | |
| (3) $\$20{,}000 \times \frac{\$\ 9{,}000}{\$30{,}000}$ | | | 6,000 | | |
| (4) $\$20{,}000 \times \frac{(\$15{,}000)}{\$30{,}000}$ | | | | (10,000) | |
| (5) $\$80{,}000 \times \frac{\$\ 6{,}000}{\$120{,}000}$ | | | | | 4,000 |
| Profit under absorption costing (per Exhibit XI) | 12,000 | 4,000 | 16,000 | 6,000 | 38,000 |

Note: Negative figures shown in parentheses.

figures, that calculated by direct cost methods and that calculated by absorption costing, can be combined in a single statement is demonstrated in Exhibit XIII where the adjustments have been calculated by means of the first formula given above. The budgeted direct cost is $30,000, because the normal output each quarter was 10,000 units, and the budgeted direct cost was $3.00 a unit.

Should this inventory period cost adjustment be made in the division's own income statement, or as a consolidation adjustment in the corporate statements? The answer must clearly depend on what purpose the adjustment is thought to serve. The more common practice seems to be to regard it as a corporate, rather than a divisional, matter. Therefore, the adjustment is made in the corporate statements only. This implies that it is made primarily to bring the corporate results into line with the demands of the tax authorities and of the auditors, rather than to reflect more properly the division's operating results.

Indeed, the implication is that these results are best revealed by the techniques of direct costing and that, but for external pressures, no adjustment would be necessary. The alternative view, which has been favored here, is that absorption costing is to be preferred for measuring performance while direct costing does a better job in the planning area. In accordance with this view, it is recommended that a combination of both methods should be used. This procedure requires that the inventory period cost adjustment be left in the division's own operating statement so that both profit figures may be shown there. Each in its own way has its use.

## Other Conflicts Between Accounting for Tax Purposes and Accounting for Management

Financial executives are only too well aware of the conflict existing between the accounting procedures which may legitimately be used to minimize a company's tax liabilities and those which would, if adopted, maximize the flow of accurate and managerially useful information about the company's affairs. In certain circumstances, as has been suggested above, both LIFO and accelerated depreciation are manifestations of this conflict. Many others could be cited. The almost universal practice of writing off research and development expenditures as they are incurred, rather than as the benefits from the expenditures are received, must be explained for the most part by the desire to get the earliest possible tax relief. There is also a very real difficulty, at the time R&D expenses are incurred, of knowing whether future benefits will, in fact, accrue from them or not. The lack of refinement in the treatment by American business of these expenses (costing, in 1962, about $11.6 billion according to an estimate by the National Science Foundation) constitutes one of accounting's most notable failures.

The only consideration which can be relevant in deciding how particular expenditures should be accounted for, for managerial purposes, is that the accounting method chosen should reflect the facts of the situation as accurately as possible. Thus a division of one company, which had spent a considerable sum on moving certain production facilities and setting them up elsewhere, was allowed, in its internal accounting, to recognize that the benefits of the move would accrue over several years, the cost being written off over a period, though for tax purposes the company's consolidated figures wrote the cost off at once. Had the tax treatment prevailed internally, the division's profit performance in the year of the move would have suffered even more than it did. It is worth pointing out that if the company had had accumulated and continuing losses, perhaps even in other divisions, tax considerations might have prompted the carrying forward of the expenditure to some future period when there were profits to be taxed and taxes seeking relief, even though such deferment of the expenditure might have had little or no managerial justification. The conflict between tax accounting and management accounting does not work in only one direction.

It makes very little sense from the managerial point of view that a change in the tax law should cause accounting methods to alter even though there has been no alteration in the underlying facts of the situation, except where a liberalization of the tax code removes an impediment which previously had prevented the abandonment of an inappropriate accounting method. Yet there have been several instances of tax changes which have led to accounting alterations in circumstances which made it very difficult to regard the latter as changes for the better. One was a change in the law a few years ago which enabled employers having an agreement with a union to give their workers a paid vacation in the following year to accrue and charge for tax purposes a reasonable estimate of the vacation pay at the end of the tax year prior to the vacation. It is, of course, only the profits of the first year of accrual which are seriously affected by this change in procedure (for that year has to bear the charge for two vacations, that year's and the next's); subsequent years' profits are only affected to the extent of any difference between the opening and closing accrual. Nevertheless, the reported profits of companies which changed their *accounting* methods because of this change in the law did suffer in one year for a reason in no way connected with managerial performance.

A large company which acquired a smaller one (and ran it as a division under its former management) allocated a substantially greater part of the purchase price to the acquired company's equipment than the amount at which the equipment stood in the old company's books. The equipment was written up to the new figure in the division's books, and the divisional manager could never be persuaded that his division was not being short-changed through the increased depreciation which it had to carry. The equipment was the same as it was before the merger, he argued, why should the depreciation on it go up? This looks like another conflict between accounting and the needs of management, but it may not have been. If the write-up of the equipment did no more than recognize its true current value, it was the old depreciation figure which constituted the distortion, not the increased charge. If the re-appraisal was no more than a tax-saving device, on the other hand, the division manager was right to complain.

It is not difficult to insulate divisional results, by which divisional management is so largely judged, from distortions which have their justification in the tax code. All that needs to be done is to bring any special tax-saving adjustments into the consolidated company figures while excluding them from the divisional figures. Neither the divisions nor the company can suffer from such a procedure. To be sure, a special problem exists where a division is a separate corporation filing a separate tax return. In such a case, while it may be necessary to leave the special tax-saving adjustment in the division's (subsidiary's) accounts it should be reported as a "below the line" item which is not to be taken into account in judging the performance of the subsidiary's management.

## The Allocation of Income Taxes to Divisions

Divisions as such (unless they happen to be organized as separate corporations) do not pay income taxes since the tax is levied on the legal entity. Nevertheless, a majority of divisionalized companies do allocate back to each of their divisions a part of the company's tax assessment proportional to the share of the company's taxable profit deemed to have been earned by each division. This raises certain questions, namely:

Is the tax allocation a controllable expense of the division?
Should negative tax allocations be made to divisions making losses?
How, if at all, should taxes be allocated to divisions, where the company chooses not to allocate central company overhead and therefore does not report divisional *net* profits?

In answering the first question, it is necessary to take note of the fact that the taxes allocated to a division typically have two sets of determinants. One is the actual controllable contribution which the division makes to the company's profitability, whether the divisional profit statements ever show that figure or not. The other is made up of all those other items (or, at least, such of them as are allocable to the division) which account for the difference between this "actual controllable divisional profit" and the division's share of the company's taxable profit. These items include any difference between the division's true depreciation and the depreciation actually charged on its assets for tax purposes. They also include any LIFO valuation adjustment in those circumstances where LIFO results in a distortion of true profits. Finally, they include any other accounting quantity introduced into the division's profit computation for tax-saving reasons rather than because it properly reflects the division's profitability. None of this group of tax-saving items can be said to be controllable by the division, since tax policy is invariably a corporate, not a divisional matter. It is conceivable that in a rare case there might be no such tax-saving items, true profit and taxable profit consequently being identical; but this situation is so unusual that we can dismiss it. If, then, the divisional tax allocation is the resultant of two sets of forces, one controllable and the other noncontrollable at the divisional level, the net result must be declared to be noncontrollable; and if the tax allocation is noncontrollable, the division's after-tax profit must be noncontrollable also.

This means that after-tax profit is not an appropriate figure to use in evaluating the performance of the division's management. It does not mean, however, that the allocation of income taxes to divisions serves no purpose whatever. Following the distinction advocated earlier between the appraisal of the performance of a division's *management* and the appraisal of the performance of its *business,* though a divisional tax allocation may not be useful for the first purpose it would seem to be essential to the second so long as it represents, at least approximately, the increment in the company's tax liability which results from the division's operations. This is likely to be particularly important where the company's various divisions are not at all uniformly placed tax-wise, e.g., where some of them are engaged in manufacturing activities subject to the normal tax rules relating to depreciation while one or two are engaged in mining or other extractive operations and therefore enjoy special depletion allowances. The relative profitability of these different kinds of divisions in after-tax terms will probably be much more favorable to the extractive divisions than if the comparison is made in before-tax terms. To use before-tax profits as a basis for decisions about investment policy, say, would be sure to lead to unsound decisions.

Turning now to the treatment of divisions making losses, the question was raised whether they should receive negative tax allocations. Most companies do give such tax relief to loss-making divisions on the ground, presumably, that the company's tax liability is reduced by reason of a division's loss. The correctness of this procedure is not entirely self-evident. It may be argued that, if the loss division were a separate corporation, except for carry-backs and carry-forwards against its own past or future profits, it would not *recover* taxes on its losses. To give a loss division a negative tax allocation is to credit it with part of the taxes which have been borne by the profit divisions. If all divisions were making prolonged losses, there would eventually be no tax savings to allocate. The rule of divisional profit independence would seem, therefore, to veto negative tax allocations to loss divisions except to the extent that a separate company making losses could recover taxes it had previously paid.

On the other hand, it may also be argued that the rule of divisional profit independence does not require that divisions should be treated as if they were separate companies (which they usually are not), but that they should be credited with revenue which they produce for the company, and charged with costs which they cause the company to incur. On this basis, it is perfectly correct that profit-making divisions should be charged with tax on their profits, and loss divisions should get credit for tax which their losses save the company. Of course, the loss division may be a separate subsidiary company. If it is, and the parent company has exercised its right to file a consolidated return, the loss division's legal identity can be ignored. In the event that the subsidiary files separately, there seems to be no reason why it should bear more (or less) in taxes than its separate legal identity obligates it to pay.

Suppose a company has only two divisions. Division A makes a profit for the year, Division B makes a loss in excess of A's profit. The company pays no tax for that year and carries the net loss forward to the following year. In that year Division B breaks even, A makes a profit and the loss carry-forward is used up by setting it off against that profit. Two possibilities seem to be open here. One is to give Division B a negative tax allocation in the year of the loss equal only to the tax saved on A's profit, and crediting it with the balance of the tax it saves the company only in the following year when the further relief in respect of the loss is obtained. The second possibility is to give Division B the full negative tax allocation on its loss in the year it was incurred, debiting the amount by which this exceeds the tax on Division A's profit, for internal reporting purposes, to a tax recoverable account. Using some simple illustrative figures, suppose in Year 1 A made a profit of $100 (thousands) and B made a loss of $180 (thousands). In Year 2, A makes a profit of $90, B breaks even. Under the first of the above schemes, assuming a 50 per cent tax rate, in Year 1 A would be charged with tax of $50, B would receive a negative allocation of $50. In Year 2, A would be charged $45, B would be credited with $40, and the company would make a net payment of $5 in tax. Under the second scheme the charges to A in both years would again be $50 and $45, B would receive a credit of $90 in Year 1 instead of $50 and the difference of $40, the future tax recovery, would be carried forward as an asset to make up, with the $5 cash payment for tax in Year 2, the $45 charged to A in that year. There would be no credit or debit to B for tax in Year 2.

The principal objection to the second scheme is the uncertainty that the company will make sufficient profits in the second and subsequent years to use up the unexhausted loss left over at the end of Year 1. It is for this reason that, for external reporting purposes, the "official" view is that "where taxpayers are permitted to carry forward losses or unused excess-profit credits, . . . as a practical matter, in the preparation of annual income statements the resulting tax reduction should be reflected in the year to which such losses or unused credits are carried."[7] We have here an interesting example o the conflict between generally accepted accounting principles and th accounting needs of management. If after-tax profit figures have an significance at all as guides to managerial action, so, presumably, d after-tax loss figures. If management is confident that future profit will more than wipe out past losses, then whatever the requirement of external reporting may be, it makes more sense, for management' own purposes, to show the expected tax benefits from loss carry forwards as a reduction of the loss of any loss-making division i the year in which the loss occurs.[8]

The company pays income tax on its aggregate taxable net profit which is arrived at, of course, after charging all head office adminis trative expenses, central research costs, and similar items. How shoul tax be allocated to divisions if the company chooses not to charg these central expenses to divisions, or only allocates to them those ex pense increments for which they can be held responsible, as wa recommended in the previous chapter? The answer to this questio will be clear as soon as the purpose of tax allocation is restated. Th purpose of allocating income tax to divisions is to ascertain how mucl the division "contributes" (negatively) to the company's tax burden as a step on the way to determining how much it contributes (posi tively) to the company's after-tax income. To do this it is not neces sary to allocate the whole of the central expenses if, as has been ar gued earlier, for other reasons such allocations are thought to b undesirable. All that is necessary is to:

1. Determine the taxable income of each division, giving effect i the computation to any special tax treatment (such as depletio allowances) which the company enjoys by reason of that divi sion's activities. In arriving at these divisional taxable incomes unallocated central expenses will be ignored.

---

[7] Accounting Research Bulletin No. 43, Chapter 10, Section B, American Institut of Certified Public Accountants.

[8] Some support for this view is to be found in the view of Arthur Andersen & Co., *Accounting and Reporting Problems of the Accounting Profession,* 1960, p. 37 that "a proper matching of costs and revenues requires that the federal income ta reductions from the carry-forward of operating losses be related to the years i which the losses occurred." However, they are apparently prepared to honor thi principle only when the tax reductions are realized, by crediting the reduction t earned surplus and applying it retroactively to the year or years in which the los was suffered. This compromise position has little merit from a managerial point o view, for though retroactive adjustments may correct the historical record, they wil not provide management with the information it needs when it needs it.

2. Compute the nondivisional or corporate division's taxable income, if any, such as income from corporate investments.

The aggregate of (1) and (2) will exceed the *company's* taxable income by the amount of the unallocated central expenses. Nevertheless, the company's tax liability should be allocated to divisions (including the corporate division) *in proportion to* the taxable incomes arrived at in (1) and (2). By so doing, the divisions will be charged with the relative burden of taxation which they attract to the company. The resulting net residual income after taxes of each division will properly reflect its investment performance. The method of allocating taxes advocated above is illustrated in Exhibit XIV.

## EXHIBIT XIV

(Zeros omitted)

| | Division A $ | Division B $ | Corporate Division $ | Total $ |
|---|---|---|---|---|
| Divisions' taxable income (before charging unallocated central expenses) | 16 | 11 | — | 27 |
| Nondivisional taxable income | | | 2 | 2 |
| | 16 | 11 | 2 | 29 |
| Central expenses charged in company's tax computation but not charged to divisions | | | | 4 |
| Company taxable income | | | | 25 |

The company's tax assessment should be allocated to Divisions A and B and the corporate division in the ratio of 16:11:2.

Some companies, instead of allocating income taxes by reference to divisional *taxable* incomes, do so by making a flat-rate deduction from a division's accounting profits. Though possessing the virtue of simplicity, this practice cannot be commended on any other ground since it fails to take account of the different tax treatments which divisions may enjoy. Even if divisions are similar enough for all to enjoy much the same treatment, the practice does not seem a useful one, for 50 per cent of a division's profit has no more interpretive significance than 100 per cent. It may be that comparison with some standard level of after-tax earnings is being sought. If a realistic tax allocation is not to be made, however, it seems better to adopt a before-tax standard of earnings as a criterion against which to judge the division's before-tax earnings.

# EVALUATING DIVISIONAL PERFORMANCE BY RETURN ON INVESTMENT AND RESIDUAL INCOME

CHAPTER V

A great increase in the attention devoted to the rate of return on investment, viewed both as the expected return on future investment and as the attained return on past investment, has been observed in the past few years. The developing interest in the prospective rate of return has revolutionized methods of capital budgeting, thus largely but not entirely displacing less sophisticated methods of assessing the probable value of alternative investment plans. In this chapter, however, it will be the use of the rate of return as a measure of past performance which will occupy our attention. Its use by decentralized businesses as a gauge of the success of their several segments will receive special emphasis.

Though almost all the companies participating in this study make some use of the concept of return on investment, the nature and extent of its use are by no means uniform. In this respect, these companies are probably typical of the rest of American industry. At one end of the spectrum are those firms which use the rate of return concept least. For these organizations "profit as a percentage of sales" still plays the largest role in the apparatus of control. Then there are those companies which use the rate of return primarily as a measure of corporate success and publish the corporate earnings rate for the information of the stockholders. They, however, take relatively little interest in divisional rates of return viewed as control data. Finally, there are some companies which have placed the rate of return right in the center of their thinking about both planning and control, and never make a decision (or judge a past decision or the achievement of a past period) without relating earnings to the capital investment needed to generate them.

Some companies, or some divisions of companies, have only a limited interest in the rate of return on investment because of their special circumstances. For example, those which do most of their business with departments or agencies of the United States Government (so that their prices and earnings are subject to the Government's procurement regulations rather than to the ordinary market forces) do not seem to attach much importance to the rate of return, at least as a control figure for judging segments of the business. Regulated utilities have a special kind of interest in their return on investment, for it is normally the basis on which their prices are regulated by public utility commissions. But the very fact of regulation causes the figure to have a great deal less significance as a gauge of success than it has for companies operating in competitive industries. A third category of firms for which the return on capital has less than normal significance is made up of those using relatively little capital, and whose ability to make profits is much more a function of technical skill or research than of the capital investment they command. Such industries as publishing and pharmaceuticals may perhaps be taken as representative of this group.

The existence of this last class, which relies less on its physical equipment than on its technical skill, serves to remind us of what is, perhaps, the most serious deficiency in rate of return calculations—namely, that most computations of "capital employed" or "investment" limit themselves to tangible investment. Because expenditure on research is not usually capitalized (even when its results are evidenced by patents), no intangible assets are deemed to result from it. The same thing is true of the initial expenditures which a company makes to bring itself into existence, and to get itself organized to do business. Similarly, money spent over the years in developing harmonious relations with customers, suppliers and employees—the constituents of valuable goodwill—does not enter into investment computations.

The result, then, is that "investment" as shown in a balance sheet at best means "tangible investment" only. Indeed, it may be questioned how well it represents even that. The tendency to favor a conservative policy towards the capitalization of expenditures, writing off at once or as rapidly as possible all outlays for which such treatment is at all defensible, must often lead to a more or less serious understatement of even tangible investment (let alone total investment) in the accounts of most companies.

It is obvious that the policies causing an understatement of investment also result in an understatement of net income (at least in certain accounting periods) through unduly heavy write-offs. Though the numerator and denominator of the rate of return calculation are both depressed in consequence, the rate of return is by no means unaffected. A profit of $170,000 on an investment of $1,000,000 will show a 17 per cent return. If $30,000 of expenditure charged off in these figures had instead been capitalized, the profit would have been $200,000, the investment $1,030,000, and the rate of return 19.4 per cent. Expenditures capitalized today have to be written off sooner or later, of course. But the rate of return as a short-period analytical tool can be badly blunted in the meantime.[1]

It is sometimes argued that the omission of leased assets from an investment computation gives rise to a similar distortion of the investment figure used in calculating the rate of return. However, the use of assets held under lease is not at all comparable with the situation just discussed. Their treatment will be taken up shortly.

The reservations expressed earlier about the significance of the rate of return as customarily computed do not seem to bulk large in the thinking of most companies. It is widely regarded as a simple and effective measure of the efficiency with which a division or other profit-earning segment of the business is using the capital entrusted to it. That such a computation is not, in fact, particularly simple is clear from the great number of variants of the concept which are found in common use. How effective it actually is, quite apart from the doubts just expressed about the possibility of calculating it accurately, depends on whether the amount of capital employed by a division is a variable the magnitude of which can, within limits, be determined by the division itself—or whether it is a fixed quantity (from the division's point of view) determined by higher authority.

On the latter view, which implies that the division is given a certain amount of capital to use as best it can, the rate of return is a

---

[1] The sceptical view of the rate of return is well put by Prof. William J. Vatter in his article "Does the Rate of Return Measure Business Efficiency?" in *NAA Bulletin,* January 1959, pp. 33-48.

useful tool. If the *rate* of return is maximized on a fixed quantity of capital, the absolute return itself is maximized. A "fixed quantity of capital" here means simply that the quantity is outside the power of the division to determine, not that it may not vary from time to time as the result of decisions taken at corporate level. However, if the division can determine, to any material extent, how much capital it uses, then the rate of return is greatly weakened as an instrument of control. In these circumstances, maximizing the rate of return need not be the same as maximizing the absolute dollar return. A division might achieve the target set for it—if this target were expressed in terms of a rate of return—while making a quite unsatisfactory contribution to the corporation's total profits.

Most companies do have small operations, almost hidden away among their complex of activities, which earn a good rate of return and yet which never, so to speak, grow to manhood. This can be the result of paying too much attention to the *rate* of return, rather than to the return itself. The *rate* of return, taken by itself, ignores the *scale* of operations and emphasizes a secondary rather than a primary magnitude.

Companies paying attention to the rate of return do, of course, regard it as more than an *ex post* measure of performance. They look to it also to provide an incentive to divisions to economize in their use of capital for, other things being equal, the less capital divisions use, the higher will be their return on it. This is an important aspect of the matter, but in this context also the rate of return as commonly used must be judged to be a blunt tool. The mere fact that many divisional investment computations mix up controllable and noncontrollable components of investment can mean that a division's success in economizing in controllable investment may be more than offset by an increase in a noncontrollable item. This possibility cannot but diminish the effectiveness of the rate of return as an incentive to cut down the use of capital by divisions.

A means of resolving these difficulties has already been put forward in Chapter III, where it was suggested that the best way to express a division's objective is to require it either to maximize its residual income or to attain some budgeted level of residual income set by agreement between the divisional and corporate managements. The residual income, by which divisional management was to be judged, was then somewhat more precisely defined as the controllable profit less interest on the division's controllable investment. This quantity we have called controllable residual income before taxes. To judge the results of the investment in the division, as distinct from the results achieved by its managers, certain deductions of noncontrollable costs have to be made from controllable residual income before taxes to yield net residual income before and after taxes. One of these noncontrollable costs is the interest on the noncontrollable investment in the division. Although these statements define residual income, both controllable and noncontrollable, at least three major questions have to be answered before residual income can be determined with any precision. These questions are:

1. How is controllable investment to be determined?
2. How is noncontrollable investment to be determined?
3. What rate of interest is to be charged on these amounts of capital?

The first two of these three questions have to be faced even if a rate of return rather than residual income is being used as a criterion of success. Whatever is the best way of quantifying the "investment" to which the interest charge is to be applied in arriving at residual income will presumably also be the best way of quantifying it when computing the rate of return. It is true that the distinction between controllable and noncontrollable investment is not often found in practice at the present time. That, however, is simply a weakness in present-day practice, the recognition and removal of which would usefully refine the rate of return computations on which many companies now place such reliance. The first two questions above can, therefore, be considered without specific reference either to the rate of return or to residual income, but rather with reference to both together.

Not so the third question. Deciding on the rate of interest to charge does not arise where a rate of return is to be calculated—at least it should not, though there are some companies which do compute a divisional rate of return after making an interest charge. When residual income is to be measured, however, the rate of interest to be used is one of the determinants and not, as in the other case, the variable which is to be determined. This is perhaps a disadvantage of using residual income as compared with using the rate of return. It is, nevertheless, one which must be accepted, for it is small when compared with the advantages to be obtained.

## Computing Divisional Investment

The problems of computing a division's total investment, and of separating this total into its controllable and noncontrollable components, cannot be examined separately without a great deal of repetition. We shall therefore try to discuss these matters more or less simultaneously. We want the "best" way of defining and determining the investment in a division. A mere examination of current practice will not get us far along the road towards finding it. However, in the course of the analysis which follows, reference to practice will be made where this seems useful. Fortunately, there is substantial agreement between the findings of this study and those drawn from a smaller sample of decentralized companies which submitted information in the same general study area to the NAA[2] so that there is no difficulty in determining what the dominant current practices are.

Some of the questions to which answers must be found are:

1. Should investment in a division be interpreted to mean the division's total assets, net assets (total assets minus total liabilities), or fixed assets plus net current assets?

2. Whichever of these definitions of investment is used, should fixed assets be included at cost, or net book value (i.e., after making a deduction for accumulated depreciation), or at an appraised value?

3. How should assets shared by two or more divisions, or held by the company as corporate assets (e.g., a central research laboratory), be treated in computing the investment in one of the divisions? Where divisions do not hold separate cash balances of their own, should any part of the central cash balance be imputed to divisions for inclusion in their capital computations? Where receivables are not recorded divisionally, how, if at all, should receivables be included in the division's capital computation?

4. Where inventories of some or all divisions are valued on a LIFO basis, is any adjustment to this valuation necessary when computing the investment in a division?

5. Should the investment base for the rate of return calculation be taken at the beginning of the period, at the end, at some intermediate point, or should it be an average for the period?

---

[2] See *NAA Bulletin*, Vol. XLIII, No. 6, February 1962, Accounting Practice Report No. 14, *Experience With Return on Capital To Appraise Management Performance.* For an earlier, more general study by the NAA, see its Research Report No. 35, *Return on Capital as a Guide to Managerial Decisions*, December 1959.

6. What should be included in net income for rate of returr poses?

7. Should divisional return on investment be calculated befc after tax?

Answers to at least some of these questions wait on the answer to another. When we talk about the investment in a division, we may mean the amount that was put in. Conversely, we could mean the amount that could now be taken out. These are seldom equal to each other, for the value of what can be salvaged on a liquidation is usually only a part, and perhaps no more than a small part, of the amount originally invested. The choice between these two concepts of "amount of investment" must depend on the purpose which is to be served.

For the most important purpose here, the evaluation of the performance of a division or of its management in terms of a rate of return, it is necessary to have the relationship between the division's earnings, or of that part of them subject to the control of the divisional management, and the amount of capital historically sunk in the division. For this purpose, therefore, it is the amount of capital put in, rather than the amount that can be taken out, which is relevant. For the more forward-looking purpose of guiding the division's investment policy, the reported earnings, however used and to whatever ratios they are reduced, can never be as useful as a budget. There are, to be sure, decisions in connection with which it is relevant to ask how much capital can be disinvested from a division, such as, for example, decisions about the abandonment of a complete division or a substantial part of one. Such decisions, when they have to be made, call for *ad hoc* computations. They are far removed from the more routine problems of control with which we are here concerned.

In the light of this discussion, we can now take up the questions posed above concerning a computation of divisional capital.

## 1. *Total assets, net assets or fixed assets plus net current assets?*

The predominant practice, as disclosed both by the NAA study and by our own, is to use total assets as the measure of investment. If the different ways that companies express their measures of investment are listed, there appears to be a bewildering variety of different definitions of it. Thus, each of the following has its adherents:

Net worth plus intercompany loans
Equity plus long-term loans
Total assets less current liabilities
Fixed assets, receivables and inventory
Total equity

and this list is not complete. Yet on closer inspection, all these reduce to or approximate to one or another of the principal contenders referred to in the question above. These are, namely, total assets, net assets or fixed assets plus net current assets. Which one will give the best measure of investment?

The adoption of total assets as a measure of investment is tantamount to saying that, when all we want to know is how much capital is being used, there is no need to worry about where it comes from. The essential question is how effectively the division is using the capital entrusted to it regardless of what its source may be. Moreover, it can be argued, long-term indebtedness (at least where this takes the form of bonds) is a matter which is almost always handled at the corporate level. Whether new investment in a particular division is financed out of the proceeds of a corporate issue of bonds or of stock is of no significance to the division. Unless the division is a separate subsidiary corporation, therefore, it is seldom argued (and it is not recommended) that corporate bond issues should be allocated to divisions and deducted in arriving at divisional investment.

The matter is not quite so clear where the division is separately incorporated as a subsidiary and has issued its own bonds, or where the division has taken on a long-term obligation by mortgaging one of its assets. However, consistency and common sense demand that all long-term debt be treated as a liability of the parent company. If a subsidiary, instead of issuing its own bonds, were to be financed out of the proceeds of bonds issued by the parent, the recommendation made above, that finance so provided should be treated as part of the subsidiary's capital, would apply. There seems to be no reason to reach a different conclusion when the subsidary issues its own long-term debt. The same reasoning can be applied to divisional mortgages.

To what extent can the investment in its fixed assets be regarded as "controllable investment" from the point of view of a division? The answer to this question must depend on the degree of autonomy which the division enjoys. It was pointed out earlier that increases in investment in a division's fixed assets usually result from proposals which originate with the division, or at the least with head office suggestions which the division takes over and adopts as its own. Seldom is a decision to invest in a division made over the determined opposition of the divisional management. The same is true of a decision to dispose of any of a division's assets. The percentage change in the volume of investment in a division's fixed assets, once the division is firmly established, is likely to be relatively small in any one year, but this is just as true of a business managed by a sole owner as it is for a division of a large business, so that this point throws little light on the question of controllability. It is not the speed of adaptation which is in question here but, rather, the seat of the authority to make the adaptation. Where divisional autonomy is at a minimum, investment in fixed assets is likely to be one of the things least under divisional control; but in such a situation, the whole question of controllability loses most of its significance. Where divisional autonomy is substantial, we shall regard investment in fixed assets as controllable by the division, subject to an upper limit set by corporate executives or by the board of directors.

We cannot overlook the possibility that a division may have idle buildings and equipment. The question arises whether such idle assets should be included in the division's investment base. It is not usually in a company's interest that one of its divisions should retain idle assets, and the best reason for continuing to include them in the investment base is to provide an incentive for their employment or disposal. Disposal should always first be cleared with a central staff department in case there are possibilities of using the assets elsewhere within the company. If disposal does not seem to the staff department to be in the company's best interests whereas the division concerned is confident that it has no further use for the assets, it should be open to the division to relieve itself of them by transfer to the corporate division, thus removing them from its investment base.

Will a change from ownership of fixed assets to leasing distort the rate of return computation by eroding the investment base? If an asset is leased, not owned, the rental paid for it will represent the depreciation on the asset plus an interest charge on its capital value. The nearer the lessor's interest rate approximates the rate of return which the asset can earn in operation, the less difference will the substitution of leased assets for owned assets (or vice versa) make to the calculated rate of return. This is illustrated in Exhibit XV. In the illustration, the rental of $70,000 charged for the leased asset is made up of $40,000 for depreciation plus interest at 15 per cent on the initial value of the asset ($200,000).[3] Since the rate of interest charged and the rate of return earned are the same, the results of the two divisions remain comparable.

EXHIBIT XV

| | Division A $'000 | Division B $'000 |
|---|---|---|
| Investment in sundry assets | 1000 | 1000 |
| Equipment owned and used by Division A, leased and used by Division B | 200 | — |
| Total investment | 1200 | 1000 |
| Profit before charging equipment costs | 220 | 220 |
| Depreciation on equipment | 40 | |
| Rental of leased equipment | | 70 |
| Net profit | 180 | 150 |
| Rate of return on investment | 15% | 15% |

Let us assume that the rate of interest charged by the lessor is substantially different from the rate of return earned by the leased equipment. In that case, comparison of the two divisions' results will be upset. Instead of reflecting simply the relative efficiency with which assets are operated, the comparison will reflect in part the methods used to finance them. It has already been argued that the sources of finance should not be allowed to affect the rate of return. To correct this situation, it appears necessary to go behind the lease arrangement and to bring the capital value of the leased equipment into the investment base of the leasing division, arriving at this value by direct appraisal. The alternative method of arriving at a value of the equipment by capitalizing the lease payments is only acceptable if

[3] It is recognized that, realistically, the interest portion of the lease payment will diminish and the amortization portion will increase in successive periods, the total remaining constant. However, to keep the illustration simple, Division A's investment base has been taken at asset cost. It is quite consistent, therefore, to calculate Division B's interest charge on the initial cost of the leased asset.

the period of the lease is equal to the expected life of the equipment. With the capital value of the equipment included in the investment base, depreciation should be substituted for the annual rental under the lease. The excess of the rental over the depreciation figure represents the finance charge paid for the use of the capital provided by the lessor. Like other interest payments, this is properly excluded from the rate of return calculation. This procedure could be adopted, equally, in the situation represented in Exhibit XV, but because the interest charge and the rate of return were equal, increasing the investment base of Division B and increasing the net profit (by eliminating the interest portion of the rental) would have left the rate of return unaffected.

What about current liabilities, and especially accounts payable? Should the argument that the source of capital does not matter for our present purpose be pushed to the point of making no deduction for payables in computing (a) a division's total investment, or (b) its controllable investment?

In computing total investment, it does not seem necessary to distinguish between different kinds of liability. As for long-term debt, no deduction need be made, therefore, for current liabilities. But a different treatment seems appropriate in computing controllable investment.

The "controllable" status of accounts payable is presently undergoing change. So long as the rapid settlement or deferment of payables remains within a division's competence, there is good reason to deduct them from the division's assets in arriving at its capital. An increase in divisional inventory will, other things being equal, penalize the division by increasing total investment. If the increased inventory is financed by the supplier, through a corresponding increase in credit, it seems reasonable that this should offset the inventory increase, leaving the divisional investment unchanged. Where divisions still handle their own payables, therefore, it seems most appropriate to treat them as a deduction in arriving at controllable investment. But, with the spread of centralized data processing, many companies are relieving their divisions of responsibility for keeping or paying their accounts payable. This considerably weakens the argument for treating them as a deduction from the divisional investment; they take on, in fact, more of the character of general company liabilities. On the other hand, so long as divisions do their own purchasing, they may be able to influence the credit terms which suppliers give. It is desirable that favorable terms so obtained should be reflected in the capital computation. This leads to the conclusion that in this situation, too, accounts payable should be deducted in computing the division's controllable investment.

Other current liabilities should be treated in the same way. If the question of payment or nonpayment of a liability or the terms on which credit is obtained are controllable at divisional level, the liabilities should reduce controllable divisional investment. Taxes payable (if shown in a divisional balance sheet at all) would normally not be controllable and should, therefore, not be so treated.

## 2. *Fixed assets at cost, net book value or appraised value?*

To judge from the results of both the present investigation and the NAA's enquiries, about 70 per cent of the companies which calculate rates of return on investment include fixed assets in the capital computation at their net book value (i.e., after deducting accumulated depreciation). Of the remaining 30 per cent, the great majority value fixed assets at cost for this purpose. The remainder, a small number, use some estimate of current value.

Companies which include fixed assets at cost, without making any deduction for accumulated depreciation written off to date, do so on the ground that the contribution a piece of equipment, as it gets older, makes to the division's earnings from year to year bears little relation to its declining book value. Apart from such special considerations as the increasing burden of maintenance expenditure as an asset gets older, it seems illogical that the asset's rate of return on book value should rise steadily as book value falls, if its ability to contribute to net income is unimpaired. These companies, therefore, ignore accumulated depreciation on fixed assets. One of the strongest advocates of this view is E. I. du Pont de Nemours & Co., Inc., one of the pioneers in the use of rate of return analysis. Their position on this question is explained in the following quotation:

> Gross operating investment represents all the plant, tools, equipment and working capital made available to operating management for its use; no deduction is made for current or other liabilities or for the reserve for depreciation. Since plant facilities are maintained in virtually top productive order during their working life, the depreciation reserve being considered primarily to provide for obsolescence, it would be inappropriate to consider that operating management was responsible for earning a return on only the net operating

> investment. Furthermore, if depreciable assets were stated at net depreciated values, earnings in each succeeding period would be related to an ever-decreasing investment; even with stable earnings, return on investment would continually rise, so that comparative return on investment ratios would fail to reveal the extent or trend of management performance. Relating earnings to investment that is stable and uniformly compiled provides a sound basis for comparing the profitability of assets employed as between years and between investments.[4]

There is something inherently strange about the view that it is right to include fixed assets in a balance sheet at their depreciated value, but wrong to include them in a computation of capital at that value. The only reason for holding such a view is the irrational behavior of the rate of return on investment when fixed assets are taken at book value rather than at cost. The proper remedy is to be found in the use of a compound interest method of depreciation, not in the abandonment of book value as a basis for valuing investment. If depreciation were handled in a theoretically correct manner (i.e., by the compound interest method) the decline in the book value of depreciating assets would not of itself disturb the stability of the rate of return on investment.

Let us assume that we have a machine which generates a constant level of net earnings throughout its life. It costs $1000, has a life of five years, and has no scrap value. Let us also assume that the compound interest method of depreciation is used, and the amounts set aside for depreciation each year are reinvested in "other assets" which earn the same percentage return as the machine itself. If we want the total investment to earn 10 per cent per annum (i.e., if earnings after depreciation are to be $100 a year), then the machine's earnings (before depreciation) must be $264 a year. Exhibit XVI sets out fully what the results of the investment will be in these circumstances. In order to avoid complications arising out of the reinvestment of retained earnings, it will be assumed that all profits are disbursed, either by way of taxation or dividends.

Exhibit XVI shows a constant return of 10 per cent, when net profit is related to total investment, the machine being included therein at depreciated book value. We get this result because of the

---

[4] *Executive Committee Control Charts,* E. I. du Pont de Nemours & Co., Inc., 1959.

that depreciation has been calculated. The charge for the first year computed by using the formula $A/s_n$ where $A =$ cost of the asset o be depreciated and $s_n =$ the sum to which an annual sinking fund installment of 1 will accumulate in n years. We find from interest tables that $s_n = 6.105$ when $n = 5$ and the rate of interest is 10 per cent, and dividing $1000, the cost of the asset, by 6.105, we get $164 as the first year's depreciation.[5] Each subsequent year's depreciation is obtained by adding interest at 10 per cent to the previous year's charge, as shown in Exhibit XVII.

The rise in the depreciation charge year by year is just offset by the additional earnings of the "other assets" retained in the business as a result of the depreciation charges. At the same time, the rise in these other assets in the balance sheet just offsets the decline in the book value of the depreciating asset. Thus, total net income (from the machine and from other assets) is constant from year to year, as is the total book value of all assets combined. Consequently, if investment is defined as "total assets at book value" (since in this case there are no liabilities to worry about) the ratio of net income to investment must also be constant.

## EXHIBIT XVI

### INCOME STATEMENTS, YEARS 1-5

| | Year 1 $ | Year 2 $ | Year 3 $ | Year 4 $ | Year 5 $ |
|---|---|---|---|---|---|
| Earnings of machine | 264 | 264 | 264 | 264 | 264 |
| Earnings of other assets | — | 16 | 34 | 54 | 76 |
| | 264 | 280 | 298 | 318 | 340 |
| Depreciation on machine | 164 | 180 | 198 | 218 | 240 |
| Net profit | 100 | 100 | 100 | 100 | 100 |
| Dividends and taxes | 100 | 100 | 100 | 100 | 100 |

[5] We can also get the same result by formula, dividing the cost of the asset by $\frac{(1+i)^n - 1}{i}$, where i is the rate of interest and n the life of the asset in years. In the above example this becomes $\frac{(1.10)^5 - 1}{.10}$, or again 6.105.

## EXHIBIT XVI (continued)

### BALANCE SHEETS

| | Beginning of Year 1 $ | End of Year 1 $ | End of Year 2 $ | End of Year 3 $ | End of Year 4 $ | End of Year 5 $ |
|---|---|---|---|---|---|---|
| Machine at cost | 1000 | 1000 | 1000 | 1000 | 1000 | 1000 |
| Less: accumulated depreciation | – | 164 | 344 | 542 | 760 | 1000 |
| Machine, at book value | 1000 | 836 | 656 | 458 | 240 | – |
| Other assets | – | 164 | 344 | 542 | 760 | 1000 |
| | 1000 | 1000 | 1000 | 1000 | 1000 | 1000 |
| Capital | 1000 | 1000 | 1000 | 1000 | 1000 | 1000 |
| Return on investment | | 10% | 10% | 10% | 10% | 10% |

The essential point is that the operation of a depreciable asset results (if all goes well) in two income streams, not one. The asset itself produces income, and so do the other assets which are accumulated in the business as the result of the firm's depreciation policy. The conclusion to which Exhibit XVI points is clear enough. If depreciation is correctly calculated, the inclusion of assets in the computation of total investment at their depreciated book values will not cause a shrinkage in the investment base, and will not, therefore, cause the rate of return to rise continually.

## EXHIBIT XVII

| | |
|---|---|
| Depreciation charge for year 1 | $164 |
| Interest thereon at 10% | 16 |
| Depreciation charge for year 2 | 180 |
| Interest thereon at 10% | 18 |
| Depreciation charge for year 3 | 198 |
| Interest thereon at 10% | 20 |
| Depreciation charge for year 4 | 218 |
| Interest thereon at 10% | 22 |
| Depreciation charge for year 5 | 240 |

This conclusion is not upset if the asset is of the kind which shows declining earnings as it gets older (perhaps because of rising maintenance costs). In such a case, net earnings (after depreciation) may be stabilized by a modification of the depreciation policy which charges heavier write offs in the early years of the asset's life; or, if the net earnings (after depreciation) of the asset decline through its life, then the rate of return which it shows should decline also, and the procedure recommended above will show it as doing so.

Unfortunately, compound interest methods of depreciation are quite uncommon in practice, and the use of simpler methods greatly weakens the case for taking fixed assets at book value in investment computations. This will easily be seen if we rework Exhibit XVI, using straight-line depreciation of $200 a year, instead of the annually increasing depreciation charges which the compound interest method gives us (this has been done in Exhibit XVIII). Now the return on investment does indeed more than double, from 6.4 per cent to 14.4 per cent, over the five-year life of the machine. But the reason why this happens is not the reason given in the du Pont statement, that the investment base falls as the machine's book value falls. As can be seen, the *total* investment base (the machine plus the other assets set aside by way of depreciation) remains constant at $1000. It is the mounting earnings of these other assets which, when added to the constant income generated by the machine, swell the net profit from year to year. This causes the rate of return on investment to rise steadily. If straight-line depreciation is to be used, a constant rate of return cannot be expected if fixed assets are included in the investment base at depreciated values, precisely because total investment stays constant while earnings rise.

Since the cause of this phenomenon is a theoretically unsatisfactory depreciation policy, it is for those who use such policies (which means practically everyone) to decide whether an unsatisfactory method of determining profit (so far as depreciation is concerned) should lead them to compensate for it by adopting an unsatisfactory basis for evaluating investment; or whether it is better to have half of the return on investment calculation soundly based even though the other half is not. Fortunately, for most businesses the dilemma can be avoided since firms generally do not have a single fixed asset (as in the exhibits) but possess a large number of units of all ages

## EXHIBIT XVIII

### INCOME STATEMENTS, YEARS 1-5

| | Year 1<br>$ | Year 2<br>$ | Year 3<br>$ | Year 4<br>$ | Year 5<br>$ |
|---|---|---|---|---|---|
| Earnings of machine | 264 | 264 | 264 | 264 | 264 |
| Earnings of other assets (assumed 10%) | — | 20 | 40 | 60 | 80 |
| | 264 | 284 | 304 | 324 | 344 |
| Depreciation | 200 | 200 | 200 | 200 | 200 |
| Net profit | 64 | 84 | 104 | 124 | 144 |
| Dividends and taxes | 64 | 84 | 104 | 124 | 144 |

## EXHIBIT XVIII (continued)

### BALANCE SHEETS

| | Beginning of year 1 $ | End of Year 1 $ | End of Year 2 $ | End of Year 3 $ | End of Year 4 $ | End of Year 5 $ |
|---|---|---|---|---|---|---|
| Machine, at cost | 1000 | 1000 | 1000 | 1000 | 1000 | 1000 |
| Less: accumulated depreciation | — | 200 | 400 | 600 | 800 | 1000 |
| Machine at book value | 1000 | 800 | 600 | 400 | 200 | — |
| Other assets | — | 200 | 400 | 600 | 800 | 1000 |
| | 1000 | 1000 | 1000 | 1000 | 1000 | 1000 |
| Capital | 1000 | 1000 | 1000 | 1000 | 1000 | 1000 |
| Return on investment | | 6.4% | 8.4% | 10.4% | 12.4% | 14.4% |

ranging from the practically new to the almost exhausted. When the business has reached a stable size, therefore, its total fixed asset valuation will remain fairly constant (apart from disturbances caused by fluctuating price levels), whether the assets are valued at cost or at net book value. There will not be an "ever-decreasing investment" as is threatened in the du Pont quotation if net book value is used instead of cost, even apart from the balancing effect of other assets accumulated as a result of depreciation policy. For companies which have reached a stable size, therefore, with fixed assets being discarded and replaced evenly over time, a constant rate of return on investment can be shown, whether the assets are valued at cost or at a depreciated book value, though it will not be the same in the two cases.

There is one important respect in which the position of the company shown in Exhibit XVI would be different if it were a division of a multidivisional company. In the case of a self-contained company the other assets which accumulate in preparation for fixed asset replacement cannot "get out" of the balance sheet unless the company suffers operating losses. In the case of a division, however, they can get out, for it is always within the power of the corporate headquarters to transfer capital resources from one division to another. This procedure is made particularly easy when, as is now usually the case, the cash balances and other liquid assets of all divisions are centralized. In the "single asset" case discussed, this constitutes an argument for including fixed assets in the investment base at cost rather than book value. As already explained, the main counterargument in favor of book value, in such a case, is that the diminution in book value of the fixed asset is offset by the increasing amount of other assets retained for fixed asset replacement. For that reason, the total asset value remains constant even though the value of the depreciating fixed asset declines. As a result, a constant rate of return is maintained. But though this counterargument is sound for companies as a whole, given appropriate depreciation policies, it is not applicable to divisions whose funds for replacement may be withdrawn for use elsewhere within the corporation.

Neither book value nor cost as a basis for including fixed assets in total investment will prevent distortions in the rate of return resulting from fluctuations in the price level. If such fluctuations are serious, the need to recognize them by a revaluation of fixed assets, or by some other means, ought to be considered. The problem arises here because of the distortion in the relationship between profits and capital which takes place in a period of unstable money by reason of the fact that accounting figures are, generally speaking, tied to historical cost. This phenomenon has been discussed more fully in the previous chapter in connection with depreciation accounting. What is significant in the present context is that, because of the time-lag effect already discussed, profits rise somewhat rapidly with rising prices, while the investment base, on the other hand, rises more slowly since recently purchased assets bought at or near current prices usually constitute only a small proportion of the total complex of fixed assets. Hence, the percentage of profits to capital appears to rise in a period of rising prices. When the price rise stops and prices tend to stabilize, an opposite trend in the return on investment may be expected. As new assets are added each year into the investment base at current price-levels, after prices have stabilized at the new high level, the investment continues to increase long after profits have ceased to do so.[6] Neither the upward nor the downward trend in the rate of return in such circumstances is really genuine, for it results from a comparison of inputs and outputs measured in dollars of different purchasing power.

It is worth noting that divisionalized companies are afflicted in a particular way by these effects of monetary instability on rate of return calculations. Comparisons of the rates earned by different divisions are likely to be distorted, and even completely vitiated, by differences in the age structure and method of acquisition of their assets (e.g., pooling of interest versus purchase), for the level of fixed asset costs and the depreciation charges thereon will be affected accordingly.

The solution to this problem has already been indicated. It is to apply a "stabilization" technique, reducing the accounting data to a common price-level by means of index numbers. The valuation of assets at replacement cost is a step in this direction. Such methods are presently used by only a very small number of companies. A periodic reappraisal of fixed assets, and the substitution of the appraised values for book values, is not an altogether satisfactory substitute for genuine stabilization. The adjustment of an asset value by the application of an index number corrects for changes in the value of money, and for

---

[6] Indeed, investment may continue to rise after profits have begun to fall, because so long as investment is rising so, probably, is the charge for depreciation. So if, by then, revenue has stabilized itself, rising depreciation will, other things being equal, cause profits to decline.

nothing else. Appraised values, however, reflect many other influences, and in particular they reflect changes in the *relative* values of the assets in question. The appraised value of a revenue-earning asset represents, predominantly, the capitalized (expected) earning power of the asset. To the extent that the appraised value of an asset reflects the asset's earning power, the calculation of a rate of return by relating earnings to asset valuation can only arrive back at the capitalization rate which was used to determine the appraised value of the asset in the first place. So far as rate of return calculations are concerned, then, asset reappraisals in periods of monetary instability are likely to replace one kind of distortion by another. This is not to decry the value of reappraisals for other purposes.

### 3. *The treatment of shared or corporate assets*

Because a divisionalized business is more in total than the sum of its parts, the assets directly traceable to one or another of the divisions of the business will not, when aggregated, account for the whole of the capital invested in the business. Sometimes, because of the thorough decentralization which has been achieved, the nondivisional assets may be of little importance. Whether or not they are included in the computations of divisional investment makes little difference to the rate of return calculations. More generally, however, it is not so easy to side-step the issue. It is not the existence of what we may call "pure corporate assets," such as minority holdings in other companies or holdings of government securities, which presents difficulty. Such assets, with the income which they produce, clearly belong in a corporate division, if such a thing is recognized. At least it is clear enough that there is no case for including any part of such assets in the computation of the amounts invested in the operating divisions, for no purpose can possibly be served by such inclusion.

What is not so clear is the proper treatment to be given to corporate assets which serve the divisions or which are used in connection with the central administration of them. Typically, two of the most important nondivisional fixed assets will be the company research laboratory and the head office. There may also be service departments which are shared by all divisions or by a group of divisions, especially where the main establishments are located close together. The divisions may also share sales offices.

The question, therefore, arises as to how, if at all, the company investment in these nondivisional activities shall be allocated to divisions for inclusion in the figures of divisional investment. Moreover, cash collected by divisions, or for divisions by a central collection department, will almost always be held centrally, and the centralization of collections may mean that receivables are held centrally also. The question, therefore, also arises as to whether and how these centrally held current assets should be allocated to divisions.

Taking up the treatment of fixed assets first, it will be argued here that no purpose can be served by allocating a centrally held and centrally used asset, such as a head office building, between the divisions to foster an illusion that some part of the capital invested in the building is really invested in each of the divisions. If such central administrative assets are significant in amount, the result of nonallocation will be that the corporate return on investment will be somewhat lower than the weighted average of the divisional returns. However, that is not important. The target rates of return set for the divisions will have to be a point or two higher than they would otherwise be. It is much better to face up to the fact that the aggregate of divisional investment is not equal to the company's total investment, just as the aggregate of divisional costs is not equal to the total costs borne by the corporation.

Sometimes a group of divisions will share a single location, including the buildings, and use services such as power, steam, catering services, etc., which are provided for all the divisions on a group basis, rather than separately by each division. There may also be a group laboratory and sales offices serving all the divisions in the group. Some of these assets, such as shared buildings, can usually be allocated more or less accurately, for the parts of the buildings occupied by each division can normally be identified without difficulty and the total value of the asset can be allocated accordingly. In other cases, such as shared service departments, the only way to allocate the common assets may be on the basis of the proportionate usage, enjoyed by each division, of the facilities. The investment so allocated would become part of the total divisional investment, though not part of controllable divisional investment. However, an alternative procedure is worth considering. The charge made to operating departments or divisions for the services of laboratories and service departments (e.g., power or steam generation, or maintenance) could be made to cover a return on the investment in the laboratory or service department. This could be done whether the charge for services were made on the basis of cost of service or on some other basis of charging. It would then be unnecessary to include any part of the service department investment in the investment computations of the operating divisions, for the divisions' net returns would have already made allowance for a return on the extradivisional investment which provides the services they use.

The sharing of sales offices is perhaps easier to handle. If they are rented premises, it is only the rent which has to be allocated between divisions, not the capital investment. Where the premises are owned, it is probably best that they should be held by a corporate property department, which can then make a rent charge to each division sharing the premises. This rent charge, like the service charges discussed above, can include a return on the investment of the corporate property department. Again, therefore, the pretense that a nondivisional asset forms part of a division's investment can be avoided.

Among the current assets, cash is almost always held as a corporate asset. In such circumstances no process of allocation, however refined, can make it part of a division's controllable investment. It is not unreasonable, however, to include some cash in a division's total investment. The abandonment or sale of a complete division might reduce the amount of cash the corporation needed to hold and an estimate of this potential reduction is the measure of the portion of the corporate cash balance which may reasonably be regarded as being invested in the division.

Some companies use a simple rule of thumb to allocate the corporate cash balance to divisions, e.g., allocation in proportion to their annual sales to outside customers. This is open to two objections. First, it is costs, not sales, which make a cash balance a necessity. Second, it ought to be recognized that some transactions make greater demands on cash resources than others, per dollar of sales value. One company participating in this study attempts to meet these objections by using *cost of sales* figures, and applying different percentages in the case of sales of manufactured products to customers, sales of factored products which the division actually handles, and sales of factored products shipped direct from a division's supplier to its customer. This computation is made only once a year so that the cash figure in a division's investment computation does not change from month to month, whereas the figures in it for other assets do.

While this attempt to obtain a more sophisticated allocation of cash to divisions is to be applauded, it is doubtful whether the difference between manufactured and factored products, which the company recognizes in its divisional cash allocation, is as important as differences in the *timing* and the certainty of demands for cash, which it does not recognize. To illustrate, a division with certain and regular cash collections of $100,000 a day and equally certain and regular payments of $90,000 a day would make no demands on the corporate cash resources at all; each day's payments could, with certainty, be met out of that day's receipts, and the holding of a cash balance would in these circumstances be unnecessary.

Cash balances are necessitated by two factors only:

1. Phasing of receipts and payments.
2. The uncertainty of receipts and payments.

This implies that the more even and the more predictable a division's cash flows are, the smaller would be the cash balance which it would have to hold if it were a separate self-contained business. But there is the further point that, if the minimum cash needs of two divisions occur simultaneously, the needs of the corporation must at least equal the sum of these divisional needs, whereas, if they occur at different times they need not be additive, for the same cash can do duty for both divisions.

The implication of this analysis is that the burden of a division's cash needs cannot be looked on as a simple function of its sales or cost of sales. What is needed is a careful and complete analysis of the day-by-day fluctuations in the cash flows of each division to see how closely, within each division, the timing of heavy receipts and payments coincide. It must also be determined how predictable the fluctuations are and, as between divisions, whether or not the maximum cash needs of any division avoid coinciding in time with those of other divisions. In the light of such an analysis, it should be possible to discover the main factors which determine the size of the corporate cash balance so far as the divisions are concerned, although nondivisional factors play their part too. Something more equitable in the way of an allocation of cash to divisions should then be possible.

Whether accounts receivable are a controllable constituent of divisional capital depends on whether credit control and collections are handled centrally or by the divisions themselves. Even if they are handled centrally, so that they must be excluded from a division's controllable investment, there is good reason for including some portion of the receivables in a division's total investment. With the abandonment of a division the capital needed to finance receivables would be reduced, so that even though the receivables generated by a division's sales may be handled centrally, they may still properly be attributed to the division when computing the investment in it. For any division, the amount to be so attributed will depend on the credit terms taken by the division's customers. Credit terms may differ from division to division and between different categories of customers within a division. Thus, in the absence of "actual" figures of receivables for each division, a fairly detailed analysis of sales within divisions (as well as between divisions) will have to be used to give a satisfactory approximation of a division's true receivables. An appropriate number of weeks of each category of sales must be taken to build up the required total. Of course, if "actual" totals of receivables by division can be ascertained readily, then they become direct divisional assets rather than "shared" assets. They do not, on that account, become part of the division's controllable investment unless the credit and collection activity is a direct responsibility of the division.

There is seldom any question of omitting inventories, either of products or of materials, from a division's total investment, for inventories usually clearly belong to some division or other. Nor will there usually be any doubt about the propriety of including inventories of products in a division's controllable investment, for a division usually has a substantial degree of control over the level of product inventory which it carries. The same is true of the inventory of materials when a division does its own purchasing. The point is not so clear when some of the purchasing is done by a central purchasing department. If the central department makes purchases strictly on the orders of a division, then inventory levels will be controllable by the division. The same is true where a division is left to call forward shipments against a centrally negotiated purchase contract. The price at which the inventory is acquired will not be controllable by the division although the quantity acquired will be. It is, therefore, not strictly correct to say that the value (at cost) of the inventory held is within the control of the division, for it is the product of two factors, one controllable, and one not. However, unless price fluctuations are very severe, few would object to the inclusion of a materials inventory, in these circumstances, in the category of divisional controllable investment.

## 4. *The treatment of LIFO inventory*

In the discussion of LIFO in Chapter IV it was recommended that, because of the disturbing effects on divisional results of a reduction in inventory carried at LIFO, the best course was consistently to make inventory adjustments in divisional income statements on a FIFO basis. Any changes in the adjustment required to bring inventory to a LIFO valuation would be passed through the consolidated corporate profit statement only. It is a corollary of this view that inventory should be included in a computation of divisional investment also at a FIFO valuation. This will approximate current replacement cost of the inventory, and will therefore represent realistically the present investment in inventory. This could not be said of a LIFO valuation.

## 5. *Opening, closing or average investment?*

In view of the inevitable and more or less serious shortcomings of any measures of investment and of net income, the precise choice of an investment base from among several closely related possibilities is not of major importance. Where the rate of return is computed quarterly or more often, the opening investment for the period should normally be an acceptable figure. This implies that investment added during the period is not expected to earn anything until the beginning of the next period, not an altogether unrealistic expectation where accounting periods are short. The longer the period for which the rate of return is calculated, the more desirable is the use of an average. Thus, if it is calculated only once a year, there is no single date at which the investment can be taken to be representative of the level of the investment throughout the year (unless, of course, there was no fluctuation in investment during the year) and an average for the year becomes a necessity. This may be an average of the beginning-of-year and the 12 month-end investment figures, a common method, or some variation of this. It is doubtful whether this is an area in which greater sophistication is likely to pay high dividends.

## 6. *What should be included in net income for rate of return purposes?*

There can be no single answer to this question, since it must depend on what the rate of return is intended to measure. One of the most useful figures for evaluating managerial performance will be the percentage of controllable operating profit (see Exhibit VII on page 83) to controllable investment. This figure is unaffected both by noncontrollable items and by nonrecurrent items such as gains and losses on sales of assets which may be included in nonoperating gains and losses. It does, therefore, reflect the management's success in conducting the division's routine operations, so far as they are within its control. If we are interested, however, in the success of the division's business rather than of its management, subject to what is said in the next section about the treatment of taxes, the appropriate relationship would seem to be the percentage of net residual income plus interest on total investment to total investment. This is an all-embracing figure, as seems fitting for the purpose of evaluating the over-all results of the division for the period.

### 7. *Divisional return on investment—before tax or after tax?*

The answer to this question is again really dictated by what was said in the last chapter about the value of divisional tax allocations. The view put forward was that so many things were done in the process of measuring a division's taxable profit, solely for reasons of corporate tax policy, that the amount of tax allocable to a division could not be regarded as controllable by the division. Therefore, the division's after-tax profit could also not be so regarded.

It follows that, for the purpose of assessing the performance of the division's management, the rate of return before tax will be more suitable than the after-tax rate. It was also argued in Chapter IV that, for the purpose of assessing the success of the division's business, as distinct from its management, the after-tax profit was more significant than the profit before tax; and again it follows that the after-tax rate of return will be a better gauge of investment success than will the pre-tax rate. It is again assumed here that by "after-tax profit" is meant the divisional profit after making a careful calculation of the additional tax the corporation will pay by reason of the division's profits, with any special exemptions or privileges which the corporation enjoys by reason of its ownership of the division being credited to the division in computing its income tax allocation.

## Rate of Return on What? A Summary

Before proceeding to consider how the rate of return may be used as an instrument of financial control of divisions, it may be worth while to summarize the conclusions just reached concerning the best way of quantifying the investment in a division. We need thes conclusions to help answer the question: Rate of return on what Alternatively, if residual income is adopted as a criterion in prefe ence to the rate of return, it is equally necessary to quantify the in vestment on which an interest charge is to be made in arriving a residual income.

The conclusions reached above require that for the purpose c rate of return analysis, "investment" shall be defined in accordanc with the following rules:

1. Total investment is best defined in most situations as tot assets. To determine controllable investment, a deduction mu be made for controllable liabilities. The extent to which invest ment in fixed assets can be regarded as controllable by division must depend on the degree of autonomy which divisions enjoy
2. Fixed assets should be included in the computation of invest ment, for the present purpose, at cost. The recognition, b means of index number adjustments, of the effect of changes i the value of the dollar on asset values is desirable but is seldor practiced.
3. Fixed assets held as corporate assets should not be allocated be tween divisions for inclusion in their computations of invest ment. The allocation of portions of a centrally held ban balance to divisions is appropriate, if a basis which really re flects their incremental cash demands can be found. The alloca tion of centrally held receivables, on the basis of a number o days sales where direct allocation to divisions is not possible, i also appropriate in recognition of the additional financing division's receivables require. These allocated assets form pa of a division's total investment but not of its controllable in vestment.
4. The investment in a division's inventory is generally controllabl investment. It should be valued on a FIFO basis, any adjust ment to bring it to a LIFO basis being treated as a nondivisiona adjustment.
5. In calculating the rate of return for a quarter, or for an shorter period, the investment at the beginning of that period i suitable as the base. For a longer span of time, an average in vestment figure should be used.
6. For evaluating managerial performance, if the rate of return i

to be used, the percentage of controllable operating profit to controllable investment is the most appropriate way of defining it. For evaluating the over-all performance of the division's business, the relationship between net residual income plus interest and the total investment in the division is more suitable.

7. The before-tax rate of return is more appropriate for judging the performance of the division's management, whereas the after-tax rate is more appropriate for judging the results of the division's business.

## Using the Rate of Return

It has already been argued that a division's rate of return is less effective than residual income, both as a target for divisional management and as a means of judging its performance. This applies in circumstances where the amount of investment in the division can be controlled or at least strongly influenced by the division's management. The use of the rate of return for these purposes should be confined to situations where the division has little or no control over the level of its investment. It follows, of course, that in such a situation the idea of controllable investment is virtually meaningless, and that only total investment is significant. Suppose that the division's total investment has been arrived at in accordance with the foregoing rules. This has to be related to the division's net profit after taxes, defined by reference to Exhibit VII as net residual income after taxes plus interest on investment, to give the after-tax rate of return on the division's investment. How, when it has been determined, can this figure be used for control purposes?

Enquiry of firms which attach importance to the rate of return suggests that few of these firms use it at all systematically. The rate of return is calculated for each division either monthly or quarterly, and is reported on the division's earnings statement. Its change from month to month is recorded, and it will probably be compared with a forecast rate of return. The above reference to its systematic use was meant to imply something more than this; when used systematically, it is its application as the first link in a chain of ratios, or other magnitudes, which enables any unsatisfactory movement to be diagnosed, explained, and eventually corrected. The beginning of the chain shows the rate of return on investment as the product of earnings as a percentage of sales and the rate of turnover of investment, or

$$\frac{\text{Earnings}}{\text{Investment}} \times 100 = \left(\frac{\text{Earnings}}{\text{Sales}} \times 100\right) \times \left(\frac{\text{Sales}}{\text{Investment}}\right)$$

Then each of the factors which enters into the rate of return is further analyzed. Earnings are the difference between sales and cost of sales: sales are the product of quantities and prices. Cost of sales is the aggregate of production costs and other costs, production costs are the product of quantities and unit costs, and so on. Investment is made up of fixed investment and working capital and each of these elements can be further broken down into its constituents and the rate of turnover of each constituent examined. This idea is, in part, represented schematically in Figure 6.

E. I. du Pont de Nemours & Co., Inc. has put on record[7] an interesting example of how a systematic examination of the factors underlying a substantial improvement in the rate of return over a period of three months might bring to light certain unsatisfactory trends calling for speedy correction. During the first three months of the year, the rate of return of a certain division improved from 12.6 per cent to 15.4 per cent. The causal factors may be set out as follows:

| | % Rate of return | = | Earnings as % of sales | × | Turnover |
|---|---|---|---|---|---|
| Jan. | 12.6 | = | 17.1 | × | 0.736 |
| Feb. | 13.4 | = | 20.2 | × | 0.664 |
| Mar. | 15.4 | = | 22.7 | × | 0.679 |

Earnings improved, turnover decreased. Why did it decrease? Because investment rose while sales fell somewhat, thus:

| | Turnover | = | Sales $'000 | ÷ | Investment $'000 |
|---|---|---|---|---|---|
| Jan. | 0.736 | = | 148 | ÷ | 200.5 |
| Feb. | 0.664 | = | 137 | ÷ | 206.0 |
| Mar. | 0.679 | = | 143 | ÷ | 210.2 |

[7] In *Executive Committee Control Charts*, E. I. du Pont de Nemours & Co., Inc 1959, pp. 30-31. The illustration has been summarized and Figure 6 has been reproduced by courtesy of the company.

FIGURE 6
Relationship of Factors Affecting Return on Investment

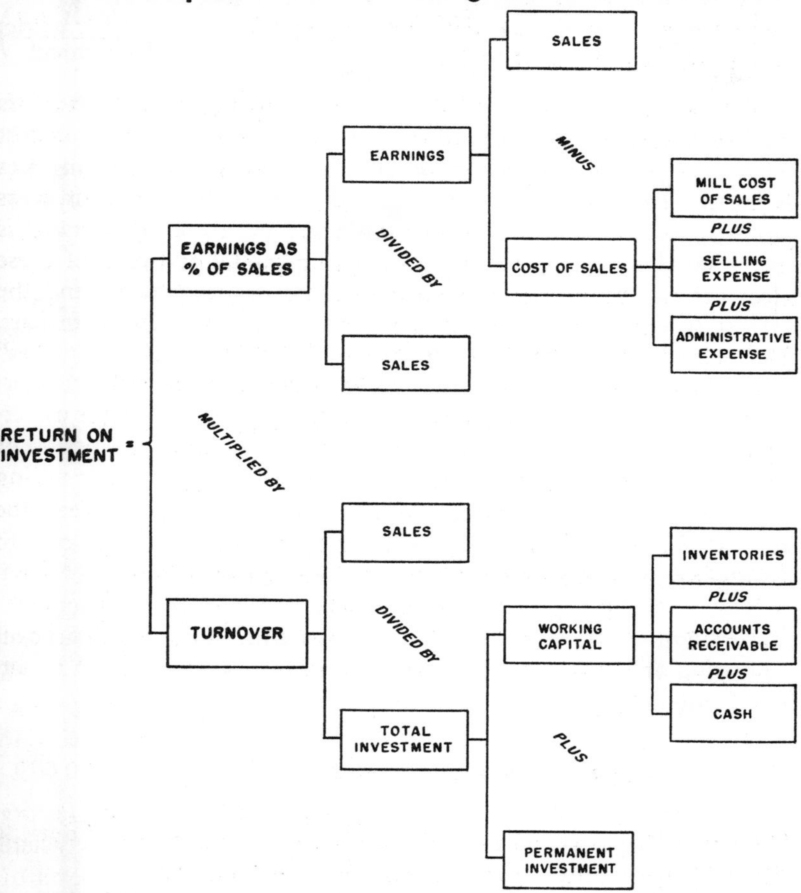


Further investigation of the rise in investment showed that it was inventory which caused the increase.

| | Total investment | = | Fixed investment | + | Working capital: Inventories | | Working capital: Other |
|---|---|---|---|---|---|---|---|
| | $'000 | | $'000 | | $'000 | | $'000 |
| Jan. | 200.5 | = | 143.7 | + | 26 | + | 30.8 |
| Feb. | 206.0 | = | 143.7 | + | 31 | + | 31.3 |
| Mar. | 210.2 | = | 143.7 | + | 36 | + | 30.5 |

Why did earnings improve from 17.1 per cent of sales in January to 22.7 per cent in March? An analysis of costs, which, of course, had fallen from 82.9 per cent of sales to 77.3 per cent as earnings had risen, showed that it was mill cost which had fallen sharply, while selling cost had fallen somewhat.

| Total costs as % of sales | | = | Mill cost as % of sales | + | Selling cost as % of sales | + | Admin. cost as % of sales |
|---|---|---|---|---|---|---|---|
| Jan. | 82.9 | = | 74.8 | + | 5.7 | + | 2.4 |
| Feb. | 79.8 | = | 71.9 | + | 5.3 | + | 2.6 |
| Mar. | 77.3 | = | 70.6 | + | 4.2 | + | 2.5 |

And why did mill cost decline? Because the rate of production had increased and fixed costs therefore were spread more thinly.

| | Production as % of capacity |
|---|---|
| Jan. | 86 |
| Feb. | 89 |
| Mar. | 92 |

Altogether, then, we have a picture of falling sales (perhaps because of falling selling expenses), rising production, and rising inventory. The analysis of the increase in the rate of return has brought to light a situation of imbalance which must be rectified if the division is not to get into deep water.

## Residual Income and the Cost of Capital

The rate of return, it has been argued, is only a satisfactory measure of the performance of a division in those instances where the divisional management has little or no control over the level of investment in the division. In such circumstances, the DGM is, in effect, given an investment of specified size and, to a great extent, of specified composition. He is instructed to maximize the return on it or, alternatively, to achieve a level of profit laid down for him as a target. This is a common enough situation, and in this situation it really does not matter much whether the DGM's target is expressed as a *rate* of return or as an absolute return in dollars. If the investment base is a given magnitude the determination of the rate automatically determines the return and *vice versa.*

But this is not the situation that a full-fledged division should be in. Full divisional autonomy implies, among other things, the right to exercise substantial influence on the scale of the division's operations. It also implies the right to determine the optimum scale of operations, and to be provided with the capital necessary to achieve that scale so long as the cost of the capital can be met. The corporate executives, on the other hand, have the right to say what the cost of capital to the divisions is to be: if capital is in strong demand by divisions, or is difficult to come by on terms which the directors are willing to accept, that cost may indeed be high. They also have the right and the duty to satisfy themselves, when a division undertakes to meet that cost as the price of additional capital for expansion, that there are solid reasons for confidence in the division's ability to carry out the undertaking. Once that confidence has been established, however, the division becomes a borrower from the corporation of which it is a part. It will never enjoy the degree of freedom from interference that an independent borrower in the capital market might expect to enjoy, but some approach to that kind of autonomy is implied by the very idea of decentralization by profit centers.

The great difference between a division's demand for capital and that of an independent borrower is that, unlike the latter, a division has no retained earnings, and does not even retain the funds set aside through its depreciation charges. This follows from the fact that, in the last resort, all the proceeds of divisional sales, less cash expenses, are centralized in the corporate treasury. All new investment in a division, therefore, whether it represents expansion or merely the replacement of used-up assets, has to be "externally" financed—externally, that is, from the point of view of the division. As a result, a division may be expected to be more sensitive than an independent concern to the price it has to pay for "borrowed" funds, for there is no way in which it can insulate itself from its one and only source of finance, the parent corporation.

Sometimes divisions discard assets as well as add to them. If a division finds that it has excess assets, it should be free to make out a case for their disposal. If it is charged for the capital it uses, it will have every incentive to liquidate, or to transfer to other divisions, assets which it can no longer profitably use. Against the savings in depreciation and interest will have to be set any losses on realization. Such losses (or gains), it has already been argued in a previous chapter, should be treated as divisional gains or losses unless the posal was the result of a decision taken over the division's

## The Cost of Capital

The cost of capital to be charged to a division to arrive at its residual income must obviously be determined as the product of two quantities—the amount of capital it employs, and the rate (or rates) of interest charged on that capital. The first of these two factors has already been discussed, but we have yet to choose the rate of interest to be used. Leaving aside for the moment the possibility of using more than one rate, it may be noted that the rate to be applied can fill a dual role. Not only can it be used in the determination of residual income, it can also be used in evaluating new investment projects brought forward by divisions for approval and authorization by head office. This budgetary aspect of the financial control of divisions will be touched on in a later chapter. It will, however, already be apparent that the determination of the cost of capital and the process of capital budgeting are not unrelated subjects.

"The cost of capital," in the present context, does not refer to the actual expenditure of interest on borrowed funds alone. If that were our meaning, equity capital and retained earnings would represent cost-free capital. Funds really free of cost in use must be freely obtainable (i.e., without any sacrifice), and clearly neither equity capital nor retained earnings are free in that sense. The cost of capital, in the sense that we are now using it, is its opportunity cost. By this is meant the sacrifice which has to be made when any scarce resource is applied to one use and therefore shut out from another. Resources which are really free can be applied to all the uses in which they will show any positive return at all without any valuable use being shut out. Capital is rarely free of cost in this sense, and certainly never for more than a short time.

The concept of the cost of capital has been much discussed in recent years,[8] particularly in connection with problems of capital budgeting, where a rate of interest has to be decided on for use in evaluating new investment projects. Our present purpose in trying to define the cost of capital is the evaluation of the results of past investment,

[8] For six contributions to this discussion, see Part III of *The Management of Corporate Capital,* Ezra Solomon (ed.), Glencoe, Illinois: The Free Press, 1959; also *The Theory of Financial Management,* Ezra Solomon, New York: Columbia University Press, 1963, *passim.*

rather than of prospective investment, by setting up the maximization of the excess of net earnings over the cost of capital employed as the goal for divisions to aim at.

Consider, first, a company financed wholly by equity capital. Any expansion in a division could be said to cover its cost of capital only if the equity stockholders were no worse off after the expansion than they were before. In order that a stockholder should not suffer, other things being equal, the value per share of his holding should not be reduced by the expansion. For this position to be secured, the additional investment in the division must earn or must promise to earn a rate of return at least equal to the *expected earnings yield (without the expansion) on the current market price of a share of stock* in the company.[9] This is the rate at which the market capitalizes the company's expected earnings, and it constitutes the company's cost of capital.

It must be noted that it is the ratio of expected earnings (without the expansion resulting from the contemplated additional investment) to the market price of stock which is used here, not the ratio of current earnings to market price. The use of current earnings, in the case of a so-called "growth" company, would give an unrealistically low capitalization rate, since the market values the stock of such companies at more than can be justified by current earnings.

It should be further noted that the firm's internal investment policy and its dividend policy cannot rationally be considered apart from each other. Much of the company investment, and more often than not all of it, will be financed out of retained earnings. How, then, ought its total after-tax earnings be divided between the portion to be retained, and the portion to be distributed to stockholders? The answer to this question is complicated by the fact that stockholders will have their dividends further reduced by the personal income tax on dividends. If the tax is ignored, it is clear that a company ought not to withhold earnings from distribution unless, when invested in the company, they can expect to earn a rate of return at least equal to the cost of capital, as defined above. If they earn less, the stockholders would have been better off to have had the earnings distributed for they then could have reinvested them in the company's stock to get

[9] This definition accords with that put forward by Ezra Solomon in his own paper, "Measuring a Company's Cost of Capital," reprinted in *The Management of Corporate Capital,* pp. 128-140. See also *The Theory of Financial Management,* Chapter IV.

the expected earnings yield on the sum so invested. As mentioned above, the personal tax on dividends complicates the issue, for the amount retained out of the dividends will be different for different stockholders, according to the tax bracket in which they fall. What has been said above will be true of those stockholders whose dividends are for any reason exempt from tax.[10]

So far we have considered only a company wholly financed by equity capital and retained earnings. If debt financing is used to provide some of the capital invested in divisions, then the cost of capital is not the cost of raising money from any one source. It is, rather, the weighted average of all of them. The rationale of this view is that debt financing, unaccompanied by any equity finance, is inconceivable. Any new issue of debt commits, so to speak, a slice of equity capital for its support. It follows that the weights to be used in computing the weighted average cost of capital should be derived from the projected financial structure which the company has set itself as a target, rather than the structure which it happens to have at the present time. As an illustration, suppose a company with equity capital having a market value of \$6 million and an expected earnings yield of eight per cent makes a \$1.5 million issue of five per cent bonds at par and considers that a 4:1 ratio of equity to debt is likely to be maintained in the foreseeable future. Then the weighted average cost of capital for this company is 7.4 per cent arrived at as follows:

| | | |
|---|---|---|
| Equity: | \$6,000,000 @ 8% — | \$480,000 |
| Bonds: | 1,500,000 @ 5% — | 75,000 |
| | \$7,500,000 | \$555,000 |

Weighted average: $\frac{555{,}000}{7{,}500{,}000} \times 100 = 7.4\%$

Should a single rate of interest be used to represent the cost of capital in all divisions? Should we not recognize that, if the divisions were separate businesses, by reason of the variations in the riskiness of their undertakings they would not all have to pay the same price for the capital raised? The answer to these questions is to be found in the fact that the divisions are not separate businesses and their

[10] For a fuller discussion of this point see Ezra Solomon, *The Management of Corporate Capital,* pp. 133-4.

effect on the riskiness of an investment in the parent corporation cannot be assessed by looking at them one at a time. Just as an insurance company reduces the uncertainty of its loss experience by increasing the spread of the risks it insures, just as an investor reduces the uncertainty of his investment income by increasing the size and variety of his portfolio, so diversification in a divisionalized business aims to reduce the risks borne by the corporation. It does this by offsetting the risks associated with the separate divisions. Thus the addition of a divisional activity which is in itself quite risky might actually *reduce* the riskiness of the whole corporate enterprise. For this reason, the riskiness of a division is not to be assessed by looking at it in isolation from the rest of the business. For this reason, also, a single corporate cost of capital can quite appropriately be used throughout the company, without regard to the supposed riskiness of any division considered as a separate entity.

It is worth noting that, of those few companies participating in this study which charge their divisions for the use of capital, none attempts to discriminate between divisions. While this in itself is sound enough, the fact is that the rate charged to divisions seemed in general to be determined rather crudely, and in some cases it had not been varied for a decade or more. A company's cost of capital is hardly likely to remain unchanged for so long a period. It goes without saying that the rate of interest used in determining residual income should be varied from time to time in response to changes in conditions in the capital market.

# INTERDIVISIONAL RELATIONSHIPS

CHAPTER VI

If a divisionalized company could arrange its affairs so that its divisions had no dealings of any kind with each other it would have removed one of the principal complexities of divisional profit measurement. It would also, however, have lost a valuable feature of decentralization, namely, the capacity to enjoy the fruits of division of labor and of specialization while simultaneously benefiting from integration to a greater or less degree. The fact that a divisionalized company is more than the sum of its parts is evidenced through the intricate pattern of interdivisional relationships which can establish itself within a large divisionalized company.

That the pattern may indeed be intricate is well exemplified by the relations existing between the divisions of a large company in the electrical and electronics industry. The company is organized into the following divisions:

Lighting products
Electronic tubes
Radio, TV, phonographs
Defense systems
Wire, metal and plastic parts
Chemical and metallurgical materials
Semiconductors.

A complete list of transfers of components and other intermediate products between divisions would be too lengthy to reproduce; but the list would include the following as typical examples:

Tungsten powder from Chemical and Metallurgical Materials Division to Tubes Division (for coating TV picture tubes)

Receiving and picture tubes from Tubes Division to Radio-TV-Phonograph Division

Lamp bulb parts from Parts Division to Lighting Division

Germanium and silicon from Chemical and Metallurgical Division to Semiconductors Division for manufacture of semiconductors

Semiconductors from Semiconductors Division to Defense Systems Division.

In this company, the minor portion of sales in each one of the supplier divisions goes to another division of the company and the major portion to outside sources many of which are competitors of the company. Prices to other divisions of this company are, therefore, essentially the same as prices to outside customers.

Whenever transactions between divisions make up more than a negligible proportion of the total transactions, it is obvious that the division's relative profitability can be very much affected by the formulae used for pricing interdivisional business. The more important these interdivisional transactions become, the more dependent is the whole system of profit measurement on the system of transfer pricing. Unfortunately, as the performance of one division becomes increasingly bound up with the affairs of other divisions, it also becomes more doubtful whether separate profit responsibility, the hallmark of a full-fledged division, continues to be feasible.

## Real or Fictitious Profit Responsibility?

In discussing the prerequisites for successful divisionalization in Chapter I it was pointed out that an essential condition, if a division's separate profit responsibility was to become a reality, was that the division must be substantially independent of other divisions, both in respect of its production facilities and of its marketing organization. The apparent advantages of decentralization through delegated profit responsibility has caused some companies to adopt a semblance of this system where it was not appropriate, and a set of more or less arbitrarily chosen transfer prices has been one of the instruments which has made the system appear to work. Here is part of a description of the methods used by a functionally organized company to set up separate profit responsibilities for the manufacturing and selling sides of the organization:

> The manufacturing division sells to the sales division at an agreed-upon price, which besides covering the cost of materials, labor and overhead, must also include in its overhead charge an amount to cover interest on investment.
>
> The sales division is broken down by product managers—one for each group of products requiring a similar type of effort. . . . Transfers from manufacturing become finished goods in the sales division and cost of sales on the sales profit-and-loss statement as they are sold. The sales division profit-and-loss statement picks up the usual deductions and allowances, selling expenses, advertising, commissions, and freight. In addition, it is charged for development engineering based on engineering development orders.
>
> The preparation of separate profit-and-loss statements for manufacturing and for sales has the effect of setting up each group as if it were in business for itself. Where excess manufacturing costs previously were buried in cost-of-sales figures in a composite statement, the sales group can now scrutinize the transfer prices readily. Frequently it sends its field engineers into the factory to determine whether certain tight specifications need be so tight. . . . In the past, the sales department might have been tempted to sell merely to increase volume, without regard to the profitability of the items or size of the resulting production run. Now it makes certain that the items which are sold will have sufficient margin to realize an adequate return. Likewise, the sales department realizes that the factory must be kept loaded with optimum production runs in order to keep transfer prices competitive.
>
> The manufacturing manager is also more conscious of performance because he realizes that his results will be clearly spelled out in a separate statement. It is true that standards and variances from standard accomplish the same type of control and constitute an important analysis function in the controller's department. But being responsible for results on a profit-and-loss statement which is scrutinized not only by the officers of the company but by the board of directors as well, creates an aura of responsibility not readily attainable through reporting by conventional methods.[1]

[1] Thomas S. Dudick, "How an Electronics Manufacturer Sharpened Cost Responsibilities," *The Controller* (now *Financial Executive*), February 1960, pp. 53 and 60. In view of the comments which follow it is perhaps significant that the company had previously been organized into product divisions and had changed over to a functional type of organization.

"The preparation of separate profit-and-loss statements for manufacturing and for sales" is said to have "the effect of setting up each group as if it were in business for itself." But does it? It does not seem to be contemplated here that either side of the business might choose not to trade with the other, an essential choice associated with being in business for oneself. The fact is that the fates of the two divisions here are inextricably intertwined, and the fiction of separate profit responsibility can serve no useful purpose. A manufacturing business lacking a sales organization would not last long if it were in business for itself. Nor would it consistently sell its products at cost (including interest on capital) as this manufacturing division apparently does. Again, the sales division of this business seems to expect to pay higher prices for the products it buys from the factory if the factory is not "provided with optimum production runs." This is not how independent businesses operate. As an independent concern, the factory would probably charge lower, not higher, prices if it were short of work. Shortage of work would certainly not entitle it to charge its customers more than the competitive price. It is difficult to attach much significance to the "profits" attributable to the departments in a situation such as this.

It is perhaps worth recalling here the conclusions of an earlier study on this point:

> . . . where the activities of two or more divisions of a company are in fact highly interdependent, it is very difficult to allocate total company profits among the divisions in a rational, precise manner. Under these circumstances, it becomes questionable as to how much weight can be placed upon these divisional "profits" in determining the effectiveness of the divisional executives. However convenient it would be for top management to have a single profit figure to summarize divisional performance to serve as a divisional incentive, it may turn out that such a simple but unrealistic criterion is less helpful than the more subjective but realistic bases which are commonly used for judging divisional management.
>
> The notion often expressed, that formal profit-and-loss statements are useful and necessary to stimulate "profit consciousness," appeared (from the study) to be largely unfounded. A high level of profit consciousness was observed among executives at all levels. There was no lack of understanding that profit is the final score for the company as a whole. But for his own score card, each operating executive generally wanted data that would indicate *the effect of his own operations* on profits. With a few exceptions, a profit-and-loss state-

ment was not regarded as the most effective report for this purpose. The exceptions were primarily managers of relatively self-contained divisions—men responsible for both manufacturing and sales functions.[2]

The fact is that nothing is to be achieved by a system of fictitious profit responsibility such as the one described above which cannot be achieved without it. As is pointed out in the quoted passage itself, standards and variances from standard can accomplish the same type of control. They can do it without any pretense that the two sides of the business are independent of each other. The company's real problem seems to be one of communication between the board of directors and the operating departments. The fiction of departmental profits has apparently been created because this is the only way to attract the board's attention to the activities of segments of the business, as distinct from the business as a whole. It is difficult to believe that there are not other and better ways of doing that.

The oil companies have grappled with this problem for years and have not all reached the same conclusions. An integrated oil company carries on several distinct activities: domestic crude production, domestic pipe lines, overseas production, overseas pipe lines, domestic products pipe lines, marine transportation, manufacturing (refineries) and marketing are the main ones. This excludes chemicals, which in most cases are treated as a separate division of the business and are often organized as a separate subsidiary company. Some of these activities can reasonably be regarded as substantially separate businesses. The pipe lines, for instance, are common carriers whose rates are regulated by law. These controlled rates obviously provide the transfer prices used for charging the other parts of the business for the services of the pipe lines. The production of crude oil can also, though not quite so satisfactorily, be treated as a separate profit-earning activity. Domestic crude produced can be credited to the production department at publicly available posted prices. However, while these are the prices independent producers obtain, they may not represent, with complete satisfaction, the prices a company refinery would have to pay the company's own producing department in an arm's length transaction after taking into account the large and steady outlet it provides for the producers. Crude pro-

---

[2] Herbert A. Simon, et al., *Centralization vs. Decentralization in Organizing the Controller's Department,* New York: Financial Executives Research Foundation (formerly Controllership Foundation, Inc.), 1954, pp. 41-42.

duced and sold overseas has its own clearly identifiable costs and revenues. Crude produced overseas and brought to refineries in the United States can be valued at its "domestic replacement cost," i.e., at the cost of the domestic crude which it replaces at the refinery, minus the import duty and shipping costs which imported crude has to bear. In all these cases, therefore, with the availability of transfer prices which are reasonably free from contention, it does no great violence to the facts to treat these departments of the company as separate profit centers, having the requisite degree of profit independence.

It is far from clear that the same can be said of manufacturing, marketing and marine transportation, even though these activities are the responsibility of separate departments. It is illuminating to compare the practices of two important companies in their handling of this problem.

Company J charges its marketing department and credits the refinery with refined products valued at Platts Oilgram prices, less a small deduction per gallon negotiated between the two departments. Thus the refinery gets a firm price for its products as they pass out of the refinery gate. The impact of local gasoline price wars and similar disturbances is borne by the marketing department. This arrangement, incidentally, has only fairly recently replaced another one, which gave the marketing department a firm margin for distribution (fixed by reference to what an independent distributor would get for this service) and leaving the refinery to bear the brunt of fluctuations in its "net-back." The marine department is not expected to make a profit on the services it provides for the company's other departments but charges for its tankers at cost, broadly speaking. However, in certain instances, the department can make a profit by hiring out its own tankers to charterers for coastal trade and replacing them by chartered tankers at a lower rate. Here, the question arises as to whether it is the cost of operating its own tankers or the cost of chartering outside tankers which should be charged to the refinery. Presumably, in an effort to get the best of both worlds, the company uses both methods, one for accounting purposes and the other in its statistical statements. Added to the above evidence that the company has less than complete confidence in its transfer pricing procedures so far as manufacturing, marketing, and transportation are concerned is the fact that these procedures are presently undergoing a renewed and thorough review.

Company K, until a few years ago, adopted somewhat similar methods, except that it went further and required its marine department to operate at a profit, as did its manufacturing and marketing departments. Eventually, however, the weaknesses in the system were considered to be too great to justify its continuance, and the three departments are now treated as a single profit center. It was the difficulty of agreeing on realistic transfer prices which caused the abandonment of the previous system. Charter rates had been used for pricing tanker services, but were these to be long-term or short-term charter rates, spot rates or forward rates? Platts Oilgram prices had been used for pricing transfers from the refineries to marketing, but would not marketing have obtained a discount from an independent refiner in view of the volume of products handled? What about special products for which no posted prices were available? There were other reasons, too, for being sceptical about the significance of departmental profits. Because inventories were carried at LIFO, end-of-period transfers of inventory between departments could produce substantial fluctuations in profits. This difficulty could have been remedied, but when added to the real problem (that the three departments were not really independent profit centers) it reinforced the scepticism about the significance of departmental profits. This eventually led to the merger of the three departments for profit-reporting purposes.

## The Danger of Suboptimization

Since transfer prices are an essential part of the profit measurement system, they must, as accurately as possible, help management to evaluate the performance of the profit centers viewed as separate entities. They must also motivate them to act in a manner which is conducive to the success of the company as a whole. There is, unfortunately, a real possibility of conflict here, for a set of transfer prices suitable for evaluating performance may lead divisions to act contrary to the corporate interest. Contrariwise, a set of transfer prices providing the right motivation may leave certain divisions, currently contributing materially to corporate success, with losses showing on their divisional income statements. This matter will be taken up more fully at a later stage of the discussion.

The motivating aspect of transfer prices is of primary importance. It is clear that a system which makes it possible for a division to add to its own profit while reducing that of the corporation as a whole is not to be tolerated. A badly chosen set of transfer prices may, however, do just that. For example, a division supplying another with an intermediate product may be in the position of a monopolist supplier. By taking advantage of its own position it could hold the division it supplies up to ransom. The parent corporation could perhaps afford to take a detached view of the situation if the amount which the transferor division could add to its own profit merely offset the diminution in the profit of the transferee division. But it is more than possible that the transferee division will lose more than the transferor division can gain. An illustration will make this point clear.

Division A of a company is the only source of supply for an intermediate product which is converted by Division B into a saleable final product. A substantial part of A's costs are fixed. For any output up to 1,000 units a day, its total costs are $500 a day. Total costs increase by $100 a day for every additional thousand units made. Division A judges that its own results will be optimized if it sets its price at $0.40 a unit, and it acts accordingly.

Division B incurs additional costs in converting the intermediate supplied by A into a finished product. These costs are $1,250 for any output up to 1,000 units, and $250 per thousand for outputs in excess of 1,000. On the revenue side, B can increase its revenue only by spending more on sales promotion and by reducing selling prices. Its sales forecast would look like Exhibit XIX.

## EXHIBIT XIX

| Sales (Units) | Revenue net of selling costs (per thousand units) $ |
|---|---|
| 1000 | 1750 |
| 2000 | 1325 |
| 3000 | 1100 |
| 4000 | 925 |
| 5000 | 800 |
| 6000 | 666 |

Looking at the situation from B's point of view, we can compare its costs and revenues at various levels of output while considering both its own processing costs and what it is charged by A for the intermediates which A will supply. The relevant information is set out in Exhibit XX.

The exhibit makes it clear that the most profitable policy for Division B, in the circumstances, is to set its output at either 2,000 or 3,000 units a day and to accept a profit of $350 a day. If its output is more than 3,000 or less than 2,000 it will make even less profit.

With Division B taking 3,000 units a day from it, Division A's revenue, at $0.40 a unit, is $1,200, and its total costs are $700. Therefore, A's separate profit is $500 a day. Adding this to B's profit of $350 a day, we get an aggregate profit for the corporation of $850 a day.

Assume now that the company abandons its divisionalized structure and instead of having two profit centers, A and B, it combines them into a single profit center with responsibility for both production of the intermediate and for processing it to completion. Let us further suppose that, apart from this change of structure, all the other conditions previously present continue to apply. Then the market conditions which formerly faced Division B now confront the single profit center. Its costs are equal to the combined costs of A and B eliminating, of course, the charge previously made by A to B for the supply of intermediates. The schedule of costs and revenues for the single profit center will then appear as shown in Exhibit XXI.

Exhibit XXI shows that the single profit center will operate more profitably than the two divisions together formerly did. By making and selling 4,000 units a day it can earn a profit of $900 or $50 a day in excess of the best result achieved by the combined activities of Divisions A and B.

The company is seen to have been paying a price for the luxury of divisionalization. By suboptimizing (i.e., by seeking maximum profits for themselves as separate entities), the divisions have caused the corporation to less than optimize its profits as a whole. The reason was, of course, that Division B reacted to the transfer price of $0.40 a unit by restricting both its demand for the intermediate and its own output of the finished product. By making for itself the best of a bad job, it created an unsatisfactory situation for the company. But who can blame it? Assuming that the instructions to its DGM were to maximize the division's separate profit, it did just that, given the conditions confronting it. The responsibility for the final result really lay with Division A. Yet it is not fair to blame that division either, for it too was only carrying out instructions in seek-

## EXHIBIT XX

| Division B's output (units) (1) | B's own processing costs (2) $ | A's charge to B for intermediates @ $0.40 a unit (3) $ | B's total costs (4) = (2) + (3) $ | B's revenue (net of selling costs) per 1000 units (5) $ | B's total revenue (6) = (1) × (5) $ | B's profit (loss) (7) = (6) — (4) $ |
|---|---|---|---|---|---|---|
| 1000 | 1250 | 400 | 1650 | 1750 | 1750 | 100 |
| 2000 | 1500 | 800 | 2300 | 1325 | 2650 | 350 |
| 3000 | 1750 | 1200 | 2950 | 1100 | 3300 | 350 |
| 4000 | 2000 | 1600 | 3600 | 925 | 3700 | 100 |
| 5000 | 2250 | 2000 | 4250 | 800 | 4000 | (250) |
| 6000 | 2500 | 2400 | 4900 | 666 | 4000 | (900) |

## EXHIBIT XXI

| Output (units) (1) | Cost of producing intermediates (2) $ | Cost of processing to completion (3) $ | Total cost (4) = (2) + (3) $ | Total revenue* (5) $ | Profit (6) = (5) — (4) $ |
|---|---|---|---|---|---|
| 1000 | 500 | 1250 | 1750 | 1750 | — |
| 2000 | 600 | 1500 | 2100 | 2650 | 550 |
| 3000 | 700 | 1750 | 2450 | 3300 | 850 |
| 4000 | 800 | 2000 | 2800 | 3700 | 900 |
| 5000 | 900 | 2250 | 3150 | 4000 | 850 |
| 6000 | 1000 | 2500 | 3500 | 4000 | 500 |

* Taken from column (6) of Exhibit XX.

ing to maximize its own profit; and a transfer price of $0.40, while it leads to a less than optimal result for the corporation, does maximize A's own profit.

One further feature of this illustration is worth noting. So far as its own profit was concerned, it was a matter of indifference to Division B whether it sold 2,000 or 3,000 units. We assumed that it decided to sell 3,000. If it had chosen to sell only 2,000, its own profit would have been unaffected, while A's profit would have been cut from $500 to $200, so that the corporate profit would have been diminished by $300. In a situation like this, negotiations about the price between A and B would probably have prevented this further damage to the corporation resulting from suboptimization. But it is unlikely that the divisions, left to themselves, would arrive at an optimal solution from the corporate point of view.

## Theoretical Basis of the "Market Price" Rule for Transfer Pricing[3]

The management of the single profit center whose results are set out in Exhibit XXI arrived at the conclusion that 4,000 units was its optimal output through comparison of incremental costs with incremental revenue for each prospective addition to output. Pushing output beyond 4,000 did not pay because an extra 1,000 units would have added $350 to costs while adding only $300 to revenues. The fact that incremental costs are made up of two parts (the cost of producing the intermediate product and the cost of processing it to completion) does not affect this result. Nor, from the point of view of the firm as a whole, should the result be affected if responsibility for the two operations happens to be split between two responsibility centers.

The second responsibility center (second, that is, in the chain of processes) can only do what is best for the company when deciding how much of the first division's production to take if it has knowledge of the other division's incremental costs. Leaving these decisions to divisions to work out for themselves implies that transferor divisions should offer their products to other responsibility centers at a figure not in excess of the incremental cost of producing them.

[3] Much of the theoretical analysis which follows stems from the work of Jack Hirshleifer. His two articles, "On the Economics of Transfer Pricing," *Journal of Business*, July 1956, pp. 172-184, and "Economics of the Divisionalized Firm," *Journal of Business*, April 1957, pp. 96-108, present the most rigorous treatment of the transfer pricing problem yet achieved.

This result appears to be a very far cry from the most common basis for fixing transfer prices, namely, the price of the transferred product on the outside market, provided the product, in fact, has an outside market. Actually, however, a close examination will show that *if the transferred product can be bought and sold in a competitive market,* the "incremental cost" rule and the "market price" rule for transfer pricing are not in conflict.

If there really is a competitive market for the transferred products, a transferee division can satisfy its needs for intermediate products by buying them outside at the going price. It will be in the company's interest that it should do so to prevent another division from incurring *incremental* costs of a greater amount in supplying the intermediate. To do otherwise would cause the company to incur a greater cost in production of the intermediate than in buying it. If the transfer price of the intermediate is set at its market price, the transferor division can supply as much as it wishes (which will be as much as it can produce without incurring incremental costs in excess of the price it will get), leaving the transferee division to acquire any additional supplies it may need by outside purchase. Alternatively, the transferor division may be able and willing to supply more of the intermediate at the market price than the consuming division can use. In that case, the correct course is for the supplying division to go on producing so long as its incremental cost is below the market price. It can sell on the market any output not taken by the other division.

The theoretical grounds for the conclusions arrived at in this chapter are much more easily and effectively demonstrated by the use of graphical methods than by lengthy verbal or arithmetic demonstrations. Readers wishing to pursue the theory of transfer pricing are referred to Appendix A of this chapter for a graphical treatment of the subject.

### *Extension of the analysis—More than one consuming division*

We must not confine our attention solely to situations in which a single supplier division faces a single consuming division. In practice, it is quite common to find one supplier division supplying intermediate products to two or more other divisions which incorporate the intermediate in final products for sale to outside customers. Thus, one company has a steel division which supplies steel in various forms to other divisions which, respectively, make steel strapping for packaging, hardware for the construction industries and power and hand tools. An oil company supplies feed-stock from its refineries to several chemical divisions grouped together into a separate chemicals subsidiary. This situation is so common as to need no further illustrations. So long as the common intermediate can be bought and sold on a free market (as in the above examples), the foregoing reasoning calls for only slight adaptation to make it fit a situation where a supplier division confronts a number of outlets. Each of the divisions using the intermediate can estimate the net incremental revenue to be obtained by adding to its consumption and processing of the intermediate for sale as a final product. These net incremental revenues can be aggregated for all the consuming divisions. Before the right course for the supplying division and the several consuming divisions can be determined, this aggregate net incremental revenue, the incremental cost of the supplying division, and the competitive price at which the intermediate can be bought and sold on the market must all be looked at together. The theoretically correct course is to set the transfer price equal to the competitive market price.

The divisions which consume the intermediate product will each require that quantity of it which equates its market price (this is also its transfer price) with the net incremental revenue derived from processing the marginal unit taken. The supplier division will wish to produce at that level which equates its incremental cost with the market price of the intermediate. If this level exceeds the aggregate demand of the consumer divisions, the supplier division must sell its surplus output on the outside market; if, on the other hand, the aggregate demand of the consumer divisions exceeds the amount which the supplier division wishes to produce at the market price, then the consumer divisions should make up their supply from external sources at that price.

So far we have dealt with two situations. In one a supplier division and a consuming division face each other; in the other a supplier division faces two or more consuming divisions. A third common situation is the one in which several supplying divisions are making components for a single consuming division which, in turn, assembles them into the finished product. Automobile manufacturers provide an obvious example. If the assumption holds that the components can be freely bought and sold outside the company at a competitive price (a doubtful assumption in the automobile case) no important variation in the conclusions so far reached is called for. Transfers should take place at the market price, and the supplying divisions should produce in such volume as will equate their marginal costs with the transfer (or market) price. The consuming division should decide what quantity of components it requires at the market prices thereof, and should acquire these quantities from the supplying divisions (if they are prepared to supply that much), or by purchase on the market in such quantities as are necessary to supplement the internal transfers. Supplying divisions which can profitably produce more, at the market price of their components, than the consuming division requires should dispose of their extra output to outside buyers.

### *A practical modification of the "market price" rule*

It will be apparent that in the highly theoretical conditions postulated in the foregoing discussion, the total profit of the company would be unaffected if the supplier division did no business with the other divisions, but sold the whole of its output on the market, leaving the consumer divisions to buy all their requirements outside. In real life, however, such behavior would not be likely to leave the company's profit unchanged. The supplier division would incur selling expenses in making outside sales which it does not incur on interdivisional transfers. It will also incur collection expenses and, sometimes, bad debts. It would probably cost the consuming divisions no more, on the other hand, to buy from another company than to buy from another division of their own company. If the supplier division really does charge the full market price, therefore, the other divisions will not be driven by self-interest to take their supplies from it; and if they do not, the corporation will be poorer to the extent of the selling expenses incurred by the supplier division in disposing of its output to outsiders.[4] In recognition of this fact, many companies modify the "market price" rule for pricing interdivisional transfers. They deduct from the market price a margin estimated to cover either the whole, or a part, of the selling and collection expenses and bad debts which the transferor division saves on internal transfers as compared with outside sales.

---

[4] On the theoretical issues involved, see J. R. Gould, "Internal Pricing in Firms When There Are Costs of Using an Outside Market," *Journal of Business,* Vol. 37, No. 1, January 1964, pp. 61-67.

The "market price" rule as used in practice provides not only for this but also for other modifications of pure market price as the basis of transfer pricing. It will be worth while to look at some of the modifications which are in use by companies participating in this study.

## *Company A*

1. When the product is sold regularly and in reasonable volume to outside customers, transfers are to be made at no more than the best price given any outside customer, less (a) division selling expense and (b) freight, allowances, cash discount, etc., allowed such customer.

2. When the product is not regularly sold outside in reasonable volume but is similar to one which is manufactured by other companies and can be purchased outside, transfer is to be made at no higher than the best competitive price the purchasing division can obtain with quantity, quality and delivery considered. Where the outside vendor allows cash discount, freight, etc., similar allowances are given.

3. The above formulae on pricing do not set minimum prices. The vendor division may set a lower price on any product transferred.

*Comment.* Where the transferred product is also sold outside, a deduction from the competitive price is made for selling expenses not incurred, to encourage divisions to buy inside. As cash discounts are not given on payment of interdivisional invoices, these discounts are allowed for in the transfer prices.

In arriving at the maximum transfer price where transferred products are not also sold outside, no deduction from the competitive price is made for selling expenses not incurred by the transferor division. If this maximum price were charged, therefore, there would be no incentive for the purchasing division to buy internally rather than externally. This may involve the company in loss, though there is an "escape clause" in that the transferor division may charge less than the maximum allowed. Use of the "escape clause" would substitute a negotiated price for the market price.

## *Company B*

Customer list price is used as the basis for pricing transfers of products for which such a list price exists. From this amount a discount is to be deducted as described below. However, if the calculated discount is less than that given to any class of customer, the higher customer discount is to be used.

The calculcated discount is to be determined annually for each product on the basis of the ensuing year's annual budget. It is to be expressed as a percentage of the list price and is to allow for the following factors:

Average cash discount
Average freight allowed to customers
Seasonal quantity discount (for certain products only)
Budgeted selling expense
Share of gross margin applicable to selling operations.[5]

*Comment.* This company applies the market price method only to products sold outside (since for others there can be no customers' list price). The inclusion in the discount of "share of gross margin applicable to selling operations" is somewhat unusual. The argument is, apparently, that if the transferor division is not to recover selling expenses from the transferee division, it should not recover the share of gross margin which these expenses (or at least the related capital) are deemed to generate. This approach reflects in part the great importance which Company B attaches to "return on capital."

## *Companies C, D and E*

These firms have wholesaler organizations (operating as separate divisions) which serve as outlets for the products of the manufacturing divisions. They also sell other companies' products. Transfers to the wholesale divisions are made at the normal wholesale prices.

## *Companies F, G, and H*

In pricing transfers between manufacturing divisions, these companies make a flat percentage deduction from the prices charged to outside customers, to allow for selling expenses. In two cases the deduction is five per cent, in another it is ten per cent, in another it is three per cent. Some of the lower percentages here represent only

[5] This is calculated by taking a proportion of the commodity gross margin (as a percentage of gross sales) after deducting the selling expenses (also as a percentage of gross sales). The proportion is determined by taking the proportion of capital employed in selling operations to total capital employed.

one half of the estimated selling expenses, the transferor division being allowed to benefit by the retention of the other half.

## The Difficulty of Determining Market Price

Enough has been said already to suggest that the concept of market price is not so simple as it might at first sight appear. In anything short of ideal conditions, there may be much discussion between divisions regarding the proper market price of transferred products.

> Granted the premise—that there is a free, open and virtually limitless market for the product, at an established, known price—the appropriateness of the measure (for transfer pricing) is virtually unchallengeable. . . . Unhappily, the applicability of the method is severely limited by the absence of dependable market price quotations on a majority of industrial products.[6]

Several factors conspire to create this situation. The transferred product may have special characteristics which differentiate it from other varieties of what may loosely be termed the "same" product. As a result, the market for it may, in fact, be quite restricted. This means that the ruling price will not be independent of the activities of the two divisions. In particular, it is likely to be sensitive to any quantities which the supplying division sells on the market, or which the consuming division buys on the market. In the limit, of course, where the transferred product is really unique in important respects, it can no longer be said to have a "market" at all. Well short of this point, however, a so-called market price may be so hedged with qualifications that it may have no immediate validity for transfer pricing purposes. There may be discounts for particular types of trader or for different conditions of sale. A given price may mean many different things according to the terms relating to delivery, payment, service and warranty which constitute part of the deal. Posted prices may not have the significance they appear to have if transactions are infrequent. The price for a given commodity may be widely different in a long-term contract from what it would be in an isolated transaction. The price obtainable by a seller may be very different from the price payable by a buyer, when selling expenses and the other costs of finding a customer are taken into account.

All these complications are symptoms of a single condition—the

[6] Howard C. Greer, "Divisional Profit Calculation—Notes on the Transfer Price Problem," *NAA Bulletin*, July 1962, p. 8.

market for the transferred product is not perfectly competitive. In a perfectly competitive market there would be one price for the product—and that price would not be sensitive to the quantities bought or sold by the divisions of a single company. There would be uniform conditions of sale, and selling expenses would be unimportant, if not completely absent. In real life, such markets are not often encountered. Modest degrees of imperfection have to be accepted, and in the markets for basic raw materials—steel, wood pulp, basic chemicals, lumber and the like—conditions approximate closely enough to those of perfect competition to make market price an appropriate basis for transfer pricing.

There is, however, a serious question whether, when we move into the field of manufactured products, the ease with which large quantities of a particular product can be bought and sold on the market and the absence of dependence of the product's market price on the quantity of the item handled by the firm's divisions are sufficiently assured to justify using market price for pricing transfers between divisions.

It is clear that the use of an unrealistic market price—one at which unlimited quantities cannot, in fact, be bought and sold—strikes at the very root of the market price basis of transfer pricing. The assumption which underlies such a basis is that when all divisions react to the market price in seeking to maximize their own profits, by so doing they maximize the corporation's. If the market price is a realistic one, any excess of interdivisional demand over supply (or of supply over demand) can be cleared on the outside market and *corporate* results can be optimized. But if the transfer price is not a realistic market price, the supplying division may be induced to supply less or the consuming divisions may be induced to take less than that quantity which is "ideal" from the corporation's point of view.

## Transfer Prices in an Imperfect Market—The Marginal Cost Rule

If a good competitive market for the intermediate product is lacking, or if for any other reason there is not a well-defined market for it independent of the quantity bought or sold by the divisions of the company themselves, then another basis of transfer pricing has to be found. In seeking that basis, we find that all the theoretical analysis (see Appendix A to this chapter) points in the same direction. The transfer price conducive to optimal decision-making, in that it will lead the divisions to maximize the corporation's profits, is the marginal or incremental cost of the transferor division for that output (we can call it the ideal output) at which this marginal cost equals the transferee division's net marginal revenue from using the transferred products. Even when there is an outside competitive price which can be used, the marginal cost rule still holds. The transferor division should produce up to the point where its marginal cost equals the competitive price, so that by setting the transfer price equal to the competitive price, we are also setting it equal to the transferor division's marginal cost for its marginal unit of output.

If two or more consumer divisions face the supplier division, a staff department will have to intervene to set the transfer price in accordance with the marginal cost rule, collecting the information it needs for the purpose from the divisions. Some illustrative figures may serve to explain the theory which lies behind this procedure. Suppose Division A is the supplier division and Divisions B and C are the consumer divisions. After deducting its own processing costs, the total net revenue and the marginal net revenue derived by Division B from various quantities of intermediate are:

Division B

| Quantity of intermediate processed lbs. | Total net revenue $ | Marginal net revenue $ |
|---|---|---|
| 1000 | 600 | 600 |
| 2000 | 900 | 300 |
| 3000 | 1100 | 200 |
| 4000 | 1200 | 100 |

Similarly, for Division C we have:

Division C

| Quantity of intermediate processed lbs. | Total net revenue $ | Marginal net revenue $ |
|---|---|---|
| 2000 | 1200 | — |
| 3000 | 1800 | 600 |
| 4000 | 2100 | 300 |
| 5000 | 2300 | 200 |
| 6000 | 2400 | 100 |

Division A, the producing division, faces the costs conditions set out as follows:

| | Division A | |
|---|---|---|
| Quantity of intermediate produced lbs. | Total cost $ | Marginal cost $ |
| 4000 | 2000 | — |
| 5000 | 2100 | 100 |
| 6000 | 2250 | 150 |
| 7000 | 2425 | 175 |
| 8000 | 2625 | 200 |
| 9000 | 2925 | 300 |
| 10000 | 3325 | 400 |

The staff department charged with the responsibility of setting transfer prices has to cross-add the quantities at each level of marginal net revenue in the schedules submitted by Divisions B and C and compare the aggregate quantities so arrived at with the quantity produced by Division A at a corresponding level of marginal cost. At some level of marginal net revenue and marginal cost, the aggregate quantity which will be taken by B and C and the quantity which can be supplied by A will be equal. This level of marginal cost gives us the desired transfer price. Exhibit XXII brings together information from the above figures and shows how the demands of Divisions B and C and the supply from A will be equated at 8000 pounds (marked with a star for emphasis) if the transfer price is set at $200 per 1000 pounds of intermediate.

Having set the transfer price in the manner described, not only are total demand and supply adjusted to each other in the way most profitable to the corporation, but the allocation of the supply between the two consuming divisions is also effected correctly. The transfer price will do the allocating, so long as the supplying division has enough capacity to meet the demands made on it at the price set. This is implicit in the assumptions we have been making. We shall examine the situation where there is a shortage of capacity later.

It will be noted that the absolute level of net revenue obtained by Divisions B and C per 1000 pounds of the intermediate is quite different in the two divisions. This does not matter. It is the *incremental* net revenue which is relevant in determining the volume of the intermediate to be produced, not the total net revenue (so long as this shows a profit over the fixed cost, for if it does not, production should cease altogether). Hence it is the incremental net revenue which, with incremental cost, sets the transfer price.

## EXHIBIT XXII

| Aggregate quantity taken by Divisions B and C which will yield marginal net revenue per 1000 lbs. shown in column 2 | Marginal net revenue per 1000 lbs. to Divisions B and C from quantities of intermediate product shown in column 1 | Marginal cost per 1000 lbs. incurred by Division A in supplying quantities of intermediate product shown in column 4 | Quantity which can be supplied by Division A at marginal cost shown in column 3 |
|---|---|---|---|
| (1)<br>lbs. | (2)<br>$ | (3)<br>$ | (4)<br>lbs. |
| 4000 + 6000 = 10,000 | 100 | 100 | 5000 |
| | | 150 | 6000 |
| | | 175 | 7000 |
| 3000 + 5000 = 8000* | 200 | 200 | 8000* |
| 2000 + 4000 = 6000 | 300 | 300 | 9000 |
| | | 400 | 10,000 |
| 1000 + 3000 = 4000 | 600 | | |

The existence of a noncompetitive outside market for the intermediate (i.e., one in which the price of the product is wholly or partly dependent on the action taken by Division A) is easily fitted into this analysis. The quantity saleable outside at each level of marginal revenue must be added to the quantities which will be taken by the consuming divisions, and an optimal output for Division A arrived at as before. The transfer price will be set equal to the marginal cost at the optimal output, and the consuming divisions will take what they want at that price. In the outside market it is the marginal revenue, not the selling price, which is equated with the transfer price. The selling price to outside customers must therefore be above, perhaps considerably above, the internal transfer price. For further clarification of this point, the reader is again referred to Appendix A to this chapter.

The rule we have now arrived at is that *transfer prices should be set equal to the marginal cost of supply, not at just any output, but at one particular equilibrium output.* What this rule means is that, assuming a company's object is to maximize profit, the production policy best for it if it were organized as a single profit center is also best if it is organized divisionally. If the firm were organized with a single manager in charge of both the production of the intermediate and of its conversion into the final product, the most profitable course would be to push production to the point where the marginal cost of output equalled the marginal revenue to be obtained from it. From the company's point of view, this policy does not cease to be right just because the responsibility for production is divided between two or more profit centers. What the procedure represented in Exhibit XXII does is to bring together (as if it were the responsibility of a single decision-maker) the relevant information about the revenue and cost functions relating to the intermediate. The profit-maximizing quantity of it to be made, and the transfer price which will secure its correct distribution among its competing uses, are then determined simultaneously.

Strong reinforcement for the marginal cost rule is to be found whenever a choice has to be made between buying an intermediate needed by a division or having it made by another division and transferred. Within a division, "make-or-buy" decisions, if made rationally, call for a comparison of the cost of buying outside with the *incremental* cost of producing the article inside. The nature of the decision, from the company's point of view, is not changed simply because the intermediate would have to cross divisional lines if made internally. The use of incremental cost as the basis of transfer pricing will enable the make-or-buy decision to be made just as it would be in a nondivisionalized firm. If there is a competitive market outside for the intermediate in which the divisions are really free to buy *and* sell, there is no problem. In the absence of such a market, however, it is clear that some common bases of transfer pricing—full standard cost, or full standard cost plus a return on investment—could cause a division to buy an intermediate outside because the price was below the transfer price, even though the *incremental* cost of production internally in another division would have been below the outside price. Obviously in such a situation, outside purchase would add more to the company's outlays than production within the company would have done. Such purchases would therefore reduce the company's profit (or keep it below what it would have been) even though the purchasing division, looked at by itself, might be better off as a result of the outside purchase.

All the discussion so far has been concerned with the activities of ngle-product divisions, or at least the transferor division discussed ıs made only a single product. This does not closely resemble real fe. Fortunately, however, while the problem of determining the *verage* total cost of each of a number of products made by a multi-oduct division is considerably more difficult than determining the erage total cost of the one product made by a single-product di-sion, the determination of the separate *marginal* costs of several roducts made by the same division is not much more difficult than nding the marginal cost of a single product, as long as extreme ac-uracy is not important. The reason for this is that fixed costs do ot enter into marginal costs. Each product's marginal cost is made o only of those cost items for which the product itself is responsible. ot that this is quite as simple as it sounds, for the marginal cost of xpanding the output of product M might show up in the form an increase in the cost of making N (through the necessity to ork overtime, perhaps, on N). Still, we are at least spared the ecessity of apportioning the divisional fixed costs over the several roducts made by the division since, so long as they really do stay xed, they are irrelevant to the ascertainment of marginal costs.

## Relative Neglect of the Marginal Cost Rule in Practice

Investigation of the transfer pricing policies actually used by the rms participating in this study showed, as already stated, that the ost common method of fixing transfer prices was to set them equal the outside market price of the transferred product, or to some ariant of this figure adjusted to pass on the saving in selling costs or a part of the saving) to the transferee division. In one case nly was there any overt reference[7] to marginal cost or anything ose to it. Even here, marginal cost played a subsidiary role. This mpany used market price for transferred products which had a ublished market price (steel was the main one in this case); and here there was no published market price, transferred products ere to pass at the lower of total (standard) cost plus 10 per cent r the outside competitive price. There was, however, a proviso that o products were to be transferred at less than the transferor divi-on's "out-of-pocket costs" defined as the "total of the additional

[7] The term "overt reference" is used here because a number of companies left ansfer prices to be negotiated between the divisions concerned. Negotiated prices ay in some cases have been "marginal cost" prices.

costs that will be incurred because of undertaking the additional pr
duction." If the outside price was below out-of-pocket costs, the pro
uct was to be purchased externally. However, an investigation as
the reason for this would usually be made. Since out-of-pocket cost
as defined, are the same as marginal or incremental costs, the ru
adopted by this company does recognize a role for incremental cost
Many firms not referring to out-of-pocket costs would perhaps ha
subscribed to this company's rule if they had thought that the poss
bility of outside prices being below their own out-of-pocket costs w
more than a remote one.

How is this neglect of the marginal cost rule by divisionalized firn
to be explained? Three reasons may be suggested:

1. Some firms are subject (or believe they are subject) to leg
or institutional restrictions on their freedom to choose the transf
price basis most suitable for them.

2. There are a number of situations, not yet discussed, in which
is difficult or impossible to use marginal cost pricing.

3. The use of marginal cost pricing by a division for a substanti
part of its output (where transfers to other divisions make up
large part of its activity) interferes more or less seriously with th
use of divisional profit as a measure of performance.

None of these objections to the use of marginal cost as a basis f
transfer pricing is trivial, and all call for further discussion.

### *Institutional objections to marginal cost pricing*

Are there any legal constraints on a company's right to choo
the basis for interdivisional pricing which it considers best suite
to its needs? For example, where a division sells a product both
other divisions and to outside customers, can the transfer price b
different from the outside price? Some managers seem to think no
They feel that any such difference would contravene the Robinsor
Patman Act of 1936, which makes it unlawful to discriminate i
price between different purchasers unless the price differential can b
justified by differences in cost. Such a view must surely be unfounde
Otherwise, transactions between divisions would be subject to r
strictions not applying to transactions between departments within
division, or between departments of a nondivisionalized firm. It
difficult to believe that this could have been the intention of Congre
when it passed the Act.

The position is less clear when a division is separately incorporated ; a subsidiary company. The Supreme Court has held a parent com-any and its subsidiaries to be capable of conspiring together in estraint of trade.[8] It may be, therefore, that a charge of illegal dis-:imination would be more likely to succeed where a division was subsidiary than where it was not incorporated. Until the courts pecifically decide this point, it must remain in doubt.

There seems to be less doubt about another kind of government iterference with transfer pricing, namely Canada's antidumping egislation. U.S. companies selling goods to divisions and affiliates 1 Canada are bound to transfer them at the market price (where iere is one), sales at any lower figure being penalized as dumping. Iowever, these transactions are on the line, if they are not over it, iat separates domestic and foreign transactions. In accordance with ur purpose of excluding the latter from this study, we shall not onsider them further.[9]

Even when divisional executives did not raise the Robinson-Pat-ian argument against setting transfer prices below the prices charged o outside customers, they did sometimes raise a related objection—hat customers would resent paying higher prices than other divisions f the company had to pay. This argument is probably no more than a ationalization of objections really based on other grounds. How vould customers know what transfer prices other divisions were harged? How could they resent what they did not know? While no oubt this argument against marginal cost pricing is sometimes ompelling, it seems doubtful whether it is generally valid.

Any argument about marginal cost pricing which concerns itself vith the relations between the firm and its outside customers (for he same product) implies, of course, that there *are* outside custom-rs, that there is, in fact, a market for the product. The wider the narket, the more likely it will be to approximate a freely competitive narket and the more likely it will be that market price is the ap-propriate basis for transfer pricing, in accordance with the analysis liscussed earlier in this chapter; and where market price can ap-propriately be used between divisions, the interests of outside cus-omers will automatically be safeguarded. However, the outside

---

[8] See, for example, Kiefer-Stewart Co. vs. Jos. E. Seagram & Sons, Inc. et al., J.S. 211-1951.

[9] For further discussions of these questions, see Williard E. Stone, "Legal Im-lications of Intracompany Pricing," *Accounting Review,* January 1964, pp. 38-42.

market may be a limited one or, for other reasons, may be too d pendent on what the firm itself does to qualify as a perfect mark Then market price, as it becomes more difficult to determine, al becomes less appropriate. It eventually becomes a matter both f the divisions which are parties to the transfers and for the corpor tion's top management to judge whether the case for marginal cc pricing, already explained, is strong enough to stand against the i stitutional pressures (and other pressures yet to be discussed) whi favor "market price."

### *Marginal cost does not always work*

Throughout the earlier theoretical discussion of transfer pricin it was assumed that:

1. The cost of the intermediate products transferred between d visions was a continuous function (in the mathematical sense) the volume of output of the transferor division; that is, all the co lines implicit in the discussion were drawn as in Figure 7 (a) rath than as in Figure 7 (b).

2. The transferor division always had the capacity to meet all d mands made on it up to the point where the incremental cost further output equalled the incremental value of the output to tl firm.

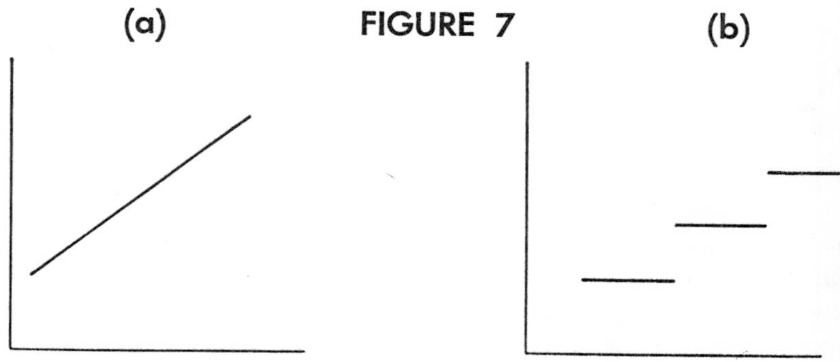

FIGURE 7

These assumptions will often be realistic enough for practical pu poses. But there will also often be situations where it is impossib to ignore the fact that the cost function is "stepped" rather tha smooth, that production facilities are inadequate, or that other nece sary resources constitute a bottleneck which restricts the output o the intermediate below what is needed to satisfy everybody. In these circumstances, marginal cost pricing will not, if the matter is to be settled between divisions without interference from above, result in a satisfactory allocation of the intermediate product.

The fact of discontinuous jumps in the *variable* cost of output is usually, in practice, not sufficiently important to invalidate the traditional type of marginal analysis we have been using since a smooth line can usually be substituted for the stepped line (e.g., in Figure 7 (b)) to provide an acceptable approximation to the facts. The refusal of what are usually called "fixed costs" to stay fixed in the face of expanding output is, however, another matter. The fact that further expansion in output will, from time to time, be held up by a need for heavy expenditure on additional space or equipment cannot be shrugged aside. These expenditures, or the need for them, are, of course, another name for short-run limitations on capacity. In the face of these additional costs, the marginal analysis we have been using hitherto breaks down.

## "Shadow Prices" as Transfer Prices

The existence of capacity constraints in the divisions making intermediates complicates the transfer pricing problem considerably. Until fairly recently, there was no effective way of handling them. Now, however, mathematical programming can be used to perform two rather remarkable things simultaneously. One is to provide a production program which will make the best (i.e., the most profitable) use of the limited capacity in the intermediate division. The other is to provide a set of values, or "shadow prices" as they are sometimes called, to be attached to the scarce resources limiting output. It is a fairly simple matter to go from the value of the resources to the value of their products, and these values could be used as transfer prices. However, for reasons which will be explained later, it is not recommended that they should be so used. Nevertheless, these shadow prices do have great significance of a somewhat different kind. A proposal will be made that they be given a role in connection with long-range planning, leaving the allocation of the limited capacity for producing intermediate products to be made by programming methods. This, as we shall see, will involve the sacrifice of a measure of decentralization or, more exactly, will require the conversion of decentralized units which may formerly have operated as profit centers into nonprofit-making service centers. But before we examine this proposal, we must see what is meant by allocation by programming methods.

Limiting the discussion to linear, as distinct from nonlinear, programming, we have to recognize that certain simplifications in the statement of operating conditions have to be accepted to give effect to the assumption of linearity on which linear programming is based. Thus, in Exhibit XXIII which follows, selling prices and unit variable costs will be taken as constant over the output range in question.[10] This means that the "contribution" made by each product is also taken as constant. It is the total contribution from all products which the optimal program will maximize, within the capacity constraints imposed by the situation.

Division B sells two products, $B_1$ and $B_2$, made out of materials produced by Division A, but used in different proportions. Product $B_1$ sells for $8.00 and $B_2$ for $14.00. The required quantities (per unit of $B_1$ and $B_2$) of the materials produced by Division A (which are known as S, T, and V) and A's maximum productive capacity per week are shown in Exhibit XXIII.

### EXHIBIT XXIII

| | S | T | V |
|---|---|---|---|
| Quantities used per unit of product: | | | |
| $B_1$ | 2 lbs. | ½ lb. | 1 lb. |
| $B_2$ | 2 lbs. | 2 lbs. | 3 lbs. |
| Maximum productive capacity per week in Division A | 4000 lbs. | 3000 lbs. | 4800 lbs. |

The variable costs of producing S, T, and V (per pound) are $1.00, $0.50 and $0.75 and Division B's costs of processing them and converting them into the two final products are $2.00 per unit of $B_1$ and $1.75 per unit of $B_2$.

There is no outside source of supply for S, T and V.

These facts are put together in Exhibit XXIV.

We can now formulate the company's problem. It is to decide

[10] Linear programming can be applied to situations with falling demand curves and increasing cost curves, the "curves" being replaced by a series of line segments. To attempt to introduce these conditions into our illustration would, unfortunately, make it unduly complicated for our present purposes.

how much of products $B_1$ and $B_2$ to manufacture in order to maximize the total contribution made by the products, while yet limiting the demands for the raw materials made by Division A to quantities within the capacity of that division.

## EXHIBIT XXIV

| | Products | |
|---|---|---|
| | $B_1$ $ | $B_2$ $ |
| Selling price per unit | 8.00 | 14.00 |
| Variable costs: | | |
| Division A—materials | | |
| S | 2.00 | 2.00 |
| T | 0.25 | 1.00 |
| V | 0.75 | 2.25 |
| | 3.00 | 5.25 |
| Division B—processing | 2.00 | 1.75 |
| Total variable costs | 5.00 | 7.00 |
| Contribution per unit of product | 3.00 | 7.00 |

This is a familiar product-mix type of problem with which linear programming is well adapted to deal, even when the number of products and constraints is many times greater than the two products and three constraints used in this case. It would not be appropriate here to devote space to a general description and discussion of linear programming.[11] What is of particular interest to us in the present

[11] For a simple introduction to the subject, see Alan S. Manne, *Economic Analysis for Business Decisions,* New York: McGraw-Hill, Inc., 1961, chapters 1 and 2, or Bierman, Fouraker and Jaedicke, *Quantitative Analysis for Business Decisions,* Homewood, Ill.: Richard D. Irwin, Inc., 1961, chapters 14-16. Nontechnical discussions are to be found in articles by Robert Dorfman, "Mathematical or 'Linear' Programming," *American Economic Review,* December 1953, and A. Henderson and R. Schlaifer, "Mathematical Programming," *Harvard Business Review,* May-June 1954. For a fuller treatment see Saul Gass, *Linear Programming: Methods and Applications,* New York: McGraw-Hill, Inc., 1958, or Naylor & Byrne, *Linear Programming,* Belmont, California: Wadsworth, 1963. An article by C. F. Day, "Shadow Prices for Evaluating Alternative Uses of Available Capacity," *NAA Bulletin,* May 1959, pp. 67-76, provides a simple introduction to the idea of shadow prices.

context is that in reaching an optimal solution to the product-mix problem (the primal solution, as it is called) we obtain, as a valuable by-product, a set of values or shadow prices for the materials S, T and V which represent their contribution to the final profit produced by $B_1$ and $B_2$. These values are given by what is known as the dual solution. The optimal program in this case turns out to be the production by Division B of 666 units of $B_1$ and 1,333 units of $B_2$ per week, which, at contributions of $3.00 and $7.00 a unit respectively, yields a total weekly contribution of $11,330.[12] This volume of $B_1$ and $B_2$ calls for weekly outputs of 4,000 pounds of S, 3,000 pounds of T, and 4,667 pounds of V.[13] Thus, the only spare capacity left is 133 pounds of V per week. The dual solution tells us that a pound of S is worth $0.83 over and above its variable cost; a pound of T is worth $2.67 more than its variable cost; and V is worth nothing more than its variable cost.

What do the figures provided by the dual solution mean? They mean that when the resources of the two divisions are being used in the most profitable way, the profit yielded by the products included in the optimal program can be imputed to the *scarce* resources used to produce them. *Scarce* here refers to those resources which effectively limit further expansion of the program (in this case S and T). The third material, V, is not scarce in this technical sense since a certain amount of V capacity is left idle by the optimal program and therefore, no part of the profit is attributed to it in the dual solution. The shadow prices of the two scarce ingredients show the amount by which total profits would be increased if the division making the materials could increase its productive capacity of each of them by one pound. It follows from the assumption of linearity that total profit would increase by the same amount for every additional pound of capacity, whether the capacity increase were one pound or a multiple of one pound.[14]

We can satisfy ourselves that the shadow prices of the materials exactly exhaust the profit contributions of the products. In this case

---

[12] The computation leading to this solution will be found in Appendix B to this chapter.

[13] Subject to small rounding differences.

[14] As a useful exercise, the reader may care to rework the computation in Appendix B to this chapter, substituting a capacity constraint for material of 300 pounds of T instead of 3000 pounds. When the new optimal program has been arrived at, total profit will be found to have increased by $2.67, the shadow price of one pound of T.

if we evaluate the quantities of ingredients which go into a unit of $B_1$ and $B_2$, using the prices arrived at in the dual solution, we get:

$B_1$ is worth (2 x \$0.83) + (½ x \$2.67) + (1 x 0) = \$3.00
$B_2$ is worth (2 x \$0.83) + ( 2 x \$2.67) + (3 x 0) = \$7.00

Material V is not valuable, in the present sense, because it is not scarce. It would not be worth the company's while to spend anything on expanding Division A's capacity for making V because it is unable to make profitable use of all its existing capacity.

The shadow prices which have been computed could not be used directly as transfer prices. To turn shadow prices into transfer prices, we would have to add on the variable costs of the materials—information which was contained in the original terms of the problem and used to arrive at the profit contribution made by each of the two final products. Adding shadow prices and variable costs for the materials, we get:

| | S | T | V |
|---|---|---|---|
| Variable cost per pound | \$1.00 | \$0.50 | \$0.75 |
| Shadow price per pound | 0.83 | 2.67 | — |
| Transfer price per pound | \$1.83 | \$3.17 | \$0.75 |

These transfer prices would be the counterparts, in a situation where productive capacities are restricted, to the incremental costs which, earlier in this chapter, we saw to be the theoretically "right" transfer prices where production of the transferred products could be expanded without restriction by simply paying the incremental cost. Indeed, since the only capacity constraints we are really concerned with are the effective constraints, and since the constraint on the supply of V, in the optimal program, is not an effective one (V is in effect unlimited in supply), it should not be surprising that the transfer price shown for V is the same as its variable cost per pound (which in this case was taken as being constant, and therefore equal to its incremental cost per pound).

## The Possibility of Conflict Between Ideal Transfer Prices and Divisional Profit Responsibility

Certain transfer prices have just been described as the "theoretically right" prices, and it may well be asked what this means. Briefly, at these transfer prices, the activities of the two divisions taken together would be the same as if they had been jointly organized as a single profit center, instead of as two separate profit centers. With any other prices, as has already been demonstrated, one division or the other might maximize its separate profits, but the profit of the second division would be diminished more than the profit of the first would be increased; or where capacity restrictions operate, the division so limited would not have the proper incentive to eliminate them. However, one very important question has, until now, been neglected. Where the transferred product does not have a market price freely determined in a competitive outside market, would the use of these corporate-profit-maximizing transfer prices be consistent with the philosophy of decentralization through divisionalization?

The first thing to note is that these ideal prices cannot always be set by the supplier division on its own because it may not have all the information to enable it to do so. This will be apparent in the unlimited capacity case delineated in Exhibit XXII. Here, the level of output for Division A which would equate the *company's* marginal revenue from the intermediate product and the *division's* marginal cost of making it could only be determined by someone in possession of both Division A's cost data and data relating to the markets for the products of Divisions B and C. If there had been an outside market for A's intermediate, this would also have to be taken into account before the correct transfer price could be set. The same principle operates where two or more divisions supplying components feed them into an assembly division. Only when the data for all divisions are put together to give a composite picture can the right levels of output and the right transfer price be determined.

There is, as a matter of fact, one important case in which the supplier division could arrive at the theoretically correct transfer price on its own. That is the case where its marginal cost is constant over the relevant range of outputs. This implies an absence of capacity constraints. If marginal cost is the same at all relevant output levels, then the transfer price has only to be set at this figure, and the consuming division's demand for the intermediate at this transfer price can be left to determine the supplying division's level of output. Even if marginal cost is not precisely constant, it will, in a great many cases, be near enough to constancy to make this, for all practical purposes, a realistic enough assumption.

But important as this exception is, it *is* an exception. In the limited capacity case, where resort to linear programming was necessary to reach an optimal solution for the company, it is again true that such a solution could have been reached only by someone having information both from the division which made the final product and the division which made the materials that went into it. The objective function was derived from Division B's market data and from information about the variable costs of both Divisions A and B. The information about capacity constraints, in this case, would have had to come from Division A. Thus neither division alone could have worked out an optimal program from the company's point of view.

It seems to follow that transfer prices, in these circumstances, could not be determined by applying any simple formula (e.g., standard cost) within the transferor division alone. Nor could they be left to emerge from a process of bargaining between the divisions, with each division concealing from the other as much information as possible about its own operations. The only sensible course would be to set up a headquarters staff department charged with the function of setting transfer prices wherever the absence of a free market for the transferred product ruled out the adoption of an outside market price as the transfer price. The staff department would have the power to call for cost and market data from the divisions concerned, and the transfer prices handed down would then be calculated to maximize the company's profits, whatever they might do to the profits of one or another of the divisions.

But why, in these circumstances, bother about transfer prices at all? If divisions are not to be left free to regulate their relations with each other by means of freely negotiated prices, then why not directly dictate the types and volumes of products to be transferred instead of dictating the prices at which transfers are to pass between them? Though such dictation would seriously impair divisional autonomy, it at least would go straight to the point.

One answer to the questions just raised would be to point out that many divisionalized companies already do lay down in company regulations the bases to be used in fixing transfer prices. Although "negotiated prices" are often the basis used, where some other basis is laid down (e.g., full cost, full cost plus a specified return on capital, etc.), this is not usually thought of as dictation. If a ruling as to the basis to be used is not resented as a serious infringement of divisional autonomy, there is no reason why a ruling on a specific price or a set of prices should be so regarded. The same cannot be said of dictated production policies. This is one answer.

If this is thought to be less than wholly convincing, there is a second line of argument in support of dictated transfer prices. Even if handing down transfer prices from a staff department is an infringement of divisional autonomy, it is likely to be much less objectionable to divisions than direct interference with production and marketing plans. A staff department may set the transfer prices, but at least the divisions are left free to react to these prices as they see fit. If the prices have been properly set, the divisional reactions may be expected to conform with the interests of the corporation. A procedure of this type would be likely to engender much less frustration on the part of divisional managements than would the more obvious kind of dictation represented by an order to produce specified quantities of specified products.

While these arguments have force, it must be admitted that serious doubts remain as to the compatibility of dictated transfer prices with the idea of autonomous divisions seeking to maximize their contributions to the corporation's profits by maximizing their own. It is not, it should be noted, the idea of decentralization on which doubt is cast, but only on decentralization through the devolution of profit responsibility. Further, it is only those divisions engaged in the production of intermediate products, and which cannot[15] sell their output freely in a competitive outside market, whose position is being questioned. Nevertheless, any doubts which may persist about the diminished effectiveness of the profit motive as a regulator of the activities of a division (when the power of deciding at what price it will sell to other parts of the corporation is taken from it) are strongly reinforced when we face the difficulties of combining divisional profit responsibility with marginal cost pricing or with the use of "program" prices where there are effective capacity constraints in the transferor division.

Marginal cost pricing means that all units of transferred products are charged to the consuming division at a price equal to the incremental cost of the marginal unit. Reference to Appendix A will show that as long as the marginal cost line slopes upward—as long, that is, as incremental cost increases (however slightly) as output

[15] *Cannot,* not *does not.* It is the availability of the outside market, not the actual resort to it, which is important here.

expands—pricing all output at the incremental cost of the marginal unit will give the supplying division some contribution, over and above variable costs, towards its fixed costs and profit. This may or may not result in a net profit for the division, according to whether its fixed costs are heavy or not. If marginal cost is constant, marginal cost pricing will allow the supplying division to recoup nothing towards fixed costs. If marginal costs are diminishing, it would actually fail even to cover its variable costs. As a first impression, these consequences of marginal cost pricing do not seem to accord well, to say the least, with the use of profit as the mainspring of divisional activity.

These results, however, are not nearly so strange as they may seem at first sight. In the first place, as has already been pointed out, even where an outside competitive market price is available for pricing transfers, if the supplying division behaves rationally (and if its marginal cost increases as output expands), it will produce at the scale which equates its marginal costs with the outside price. To require it to price its transfers at marginal cost in these circumstances is, therefore, to require it to do what rationality will lead it to do in any case. Where there is no competitive outside price, to price transfers at marginal cost will leave the supplying division at least no worse off (except in the unusual decreasing marginal cost case) than if it did not supply other divisions with its products, for its fixed costs will have to be borne whether it supplies them or not. If marginal cost is rising with increasing output, it will be better off by the amount of the contribution it can earn towards fixed costs, though perhaps not as much better off as it would wish to be.

The conflict between the interests of the corporation and the interests of the supplying division resulting from marginal cost prices can, perhaps, be seen most clearly if we take the "constant marginal cost" case, which is undoubtedly very common in practice. In this instance, marginal cost pricing of transfers by a division lacking outside business will leave the division with a loss equal to its fixed costs. The products transferred to other divisions will enable those divisions to make a maximum contribution to the corporation's profit. The supplying division's part in the operation is obviously not to be judged in terms of its own profit-and-loss statement since all or most of the profit derived from the intermediates will go to the divisions making the final products. Here we have the very essence of the conflict between, on the one hand, the need for a corporate policy which will maximize corporate profitability, and, on the other hand, the desire to maintain divisional autonomy by relying on divisional profit both as the incentive which promotes efficiency and the measuring rod by which performance is to be assessed.

So much for an intermediate-producing division which is not short of capacity. So long as it has surplus capacity, it cannot complain that having to supply other divisions at marginal cost prevents it from seeking more profitable outside markets, for it has the capacity to do both. If the situation changes and the division finds it does not have sufficient capacity to satisfy all the demands made on it (internal transfer prices being kept at marginal cost), the company again has the problem of making the best use of limited resources and it will need, as before, a programming solution to optimize results. The company does not have to use the dual prices derived from the programming solution as transfer prices, but if it does, the prices for the intermediates in limited supply will exceed their marginal cost. Indeed, the situation will now be the reverse of the previous case for, as we have already seen, the shadow prices which the dual solution gives us are such as to impute to the scarce intermediates the whole of the profit produced by the combined operations of the supplying and the consuming divisions. This time the consuming division will be dissatisfied with the transfer prices for though it could be argued that this division would not lose anything by paying them, it certainly would not gain anything either.

Recent advances in the techniques of linear programming have increased their relevance to the problems of divisionalized firms. For instance, using the so-called decomposition method, an optimal allocation not only of scarce divisional resources but also of scarce corporate resources (e.g., capital) can be arrived at, while preserving in the divisions a considerable measure of decentralized authority. Yet "in the final analysis the output decisions are made and enforced by the central planner. Partly this is done by means of the persuasive powers of profit and pricing system. But at one stage of the operation a central decision though based on divisional plans and proposals must, at least in the linear case, be made and imposed directly on the divisions. . . ."[16] In other words, the use of programmed transfer prices does not, at least in the present state of the art, make

[16] William J. Baumol and Tibor Fabian, "Decomposition, Pricing for Decentralization and External Economies," *Management Science,* Vol. II, No. 1, September 1964, p. 2.

it possible to preserve the autonomy of the divisions as profit centers while at the same time ensuring that, left to themselves, they will operate optimally from a corporate viewpoint. The same thing seems to be true when, in the absence of effective capacity constraints in the divisions, transfer prices based on marginal cost would best serve the interests of the corporation but not, unfortunately, the interests of the supplying division.

In these circumstances, it seems best to recognize that there is no possibility of a truly arm's length relationship between the supplying and consuming divisions since one of the essential conditions of successful divisionalization—profit independence—cannot be satisfied. Accordingly, the supplying division should either be merged with another division (if it does all, or most, of its business with that one division) to form a single profit center; or if that solution is inappropriate because it does business with several other divisions, the supplying division should be given a separate status as a service center, rather than as a profit center. As such, it would have the responsibility of serving other divisions, but not of having to make a profit. This change of status is not to be confused with loss of status, though in some circumstances it does involve taking away from the service center, and entrusting to a staff department, responsibility for setting transfer prices.

The difficulty of combining marginal cost pricing or "programmed" pricing of transfers with full divisional status for divisions serving other divisions has led some authorities concerned with this problem to resist the conclusion just reached, and to advocate other bases of transfer pricing. These usually involve negotiated prices or some approximation to market price, even where no really free market exists. It has usually been argued that loss of the profit incentive would so diminish efficiency that the corporation would lose more from this cause than it would gain from the elimination of suboptimization. Typical of the advocates of marginal cost pricing who have felt bound to draw attention to this possibility is Paul W. Cook, Jr. who writes:

> A company might well find that the effects of incentives and profit evaluations, in terms of innovation, creativity, and hard work, far outweigh the disadvantages inherent in a somewhat illogical transfer price system and somewhat misleading financial reports.[17]

---

[17] Paul W. Cooke, Jr., "Decentralization and the Transfer Price Problem," *Journal of Business,* Vol. 28, No. 2, April 1955, p. 94.

Joel Dean, an advocate of negotiated prices, is less tentative in his language:

> Commercial abilities that are so desirable in a well-rounded division manager are stunted under marginal-cost transfer pricing. He is isolated from the pitfalls and opportunities of the market and is confined to the role of a service division manager.[18]

Certainly there is a danger here which must be recognized, a danger that more may be lost than gained by substituting a logical transfer-pricing system without profit responsibilities for an illogical system with it. Before attempting to implement the proposals which follow, the probabilities of gain and loss must be weighed. However, the profit spur is not the only way to maintain efficiency. Nondivisionalized businesses are not, invariably, markedly less efficient than those which are divisionally organized and so long as every effort is made to find and use other means of keeping the efficiency of service centers high, resorting to the profit motive for segments of a business where it is not appropriate is likely to do more harm than good. We may remind ourselves here that decentralization is not synonymous with divisionalization. In some circumstances, decentralization may work better without divisionalization.

## A Recommended Procedure

What we are seeking is more than merely a method of fixing transfer prices. We need a procedure for ensuring that transactions between divisions are of a kind and volume which will maximize corporate profits. The transfer prices used are not the only element in this procedure, but they are probably the most important element.

The procedure to be chosen in any particular situation must depend on the circumstances, and, in particular, on the answers to the following questions:

1. Is there a competitive outside market for the transferred products to which divisions may freely resort?
2. If not, do transfers take place in material amounts, or in potentially material amounts?
3. If there is no competitive outside market and transfers are material in amount, does the supplying division have surplus capacity or is it unable to meet all the demands made on it?

[18] "Decentralization and Intracompany Pricing," *Harvard Business Review,* July-August 1955, p. 70.

The significance of these questions will already be sufficiently cle We now have to formulate prescriptions based on the answers them.

* * *

*There is an outside competitive market for the transferred products, and divisions may freely resort to it.* It has already been made clear that everything points to the use of the outside price in this case. By maximizing their own profits, all parties to the transfers maximize the corporation's profits. Whether or not there are constraints on capacity, the outside price determines the value of the transferred product to the company, to the consuming division, and to the supplying division. In these circumstances, full profit responsibility of divisions supplying transferred products can be maintained.

*There is no outside competitive market for the transferred products, and transfers take place only in amounts which are not important and not potentially important.* In these circumstances neither the corporation nor the divisions can come to much harm, whatever basis for transfer pricing is used. The simplest solution is, probably, to leave the price open to negotiation between divisions. Experience indicates that negotiated prices tend to settle down at a figure based on the standard cost of the transferred product, plus a "fair" return on the capital deemed to have been used in its production. Since standard cost generally includes fixed overhead, from the theoretical viewpoint negotiated prices so determined are open to the objection already levelled against any transfer pricing method which turns one division's fixed costs into another division's variable costs by including them in a product price. Presumably, in the circumstances posed here, not much harm can be done. The proposal is to leave transfer prices to be negotiated between divisions only where the volume of transfers is not large, and is not potentially large. A *presently* small volume of transfers is a necessary, but not a sufficient, condition for it may be precisely an ill-chosen basis of transfer pricing which keeps the volume of transfers small when it should be substantial. The further condition, that the volume shall not be potentially large, has to be added.

One case of rather wide applicability which may fall into this category occurs when one division markets a final product made by another division because the producing division has the know-how and equipment which the product demands, while the marketing division has the kind of sales force required or knowledge of the market in which the product is sold. So long as the products in question are not large-volume items but are, rather, subsidiary items needed to complete a line, the best way to deal with this interdivisional transaction is for the producing division to take the actual sale proceeds and to pay the marketing division a selling commission for its services. This method of handling the situation generally works well and, once the rate of commission has been agreed to, it leads to few disputes. Transfers for sale which are substantial in amount are dealt with later as a separate case.

In all these cases, divisional profit responsibility should be maintained, even though resort to an outside market is not possible. More would be lost than could be gained here, usually, by following any other course.

*Transfers in significant or potentially significant amounts of a product for which there is no outside competitive market are made for sale by another division: the transfers are not a predominant part of the supplying division's business.* A common arrangement in such cases is to provide for "equal profit sharing," i.e., either equalizing the return on capital earned both by the producing and the marketing divisions (if the return on capital attributable to a single product or product group can be determined) or, more simply, equalizing the gross profit margin as a percentage of sales. To illustrate this latter arrangement, if Division A produced an article at a cost of $50 and Division B sold it at $100, "equal profit margins" would result in the transfer price being fixed at about $71,[19] since this would give a profit to A of $21 or about 30 per cent of the transfer price and B would make a profit of $29, close to 30 per cent on its selling price of $100.

Any such arrangement as this is clearly open to the objection already levelled against average cost as a basis for transfer pricing, i.e., that this procedure makes the cost to the buying division of increasing its volume of business greater than the cost to the company, with the consequential danger of loss to the corporation from suboptimization.

The procedure recommended is for the supplying division to charge for the "transfers for sale" in two parts:

---

[19] The transfer price, in this case, has to be the geometric mean of the cost and selling prices, i.e., $\sqrt{50 \times 100}$, or about $71.

1. A charge per unit of product, determined (as already described) by equating the marginal cost of the producing division with the marginal revenue of the selling division. This charge, therefore, covers the variable costs of the product and, perhaps, a part of the fixed costs as well.

2. An annual lump-sum payment for the franchise to handle the product. This should cover the contribution required from the product towards fixed costs and profit. The essential point is that the lump-sum payment, fixed by negotiation once a year on the basis of the *expected* volume of transfers, will not be affected by the actual volume of transfers. It will, therefore, not enter into the selling division's calculation of the amount of the product it ought to take. That division will, accordingly, not be deterred from acting to maximize the *company's* net revenue from the product.

Strictly, transfers of branded products from manufacturing divisions to a wholesale division would come within this category. Such a division usually handles other manufacturers' products as well, and the manufacturing divisions do not distribute their products exclusively through the wholesale division. The rule almost invariably followed in practice is for a wholesale division to be treated like an outside customer so far as prices are concerned. It seems probable that, in a desire not to discriminate between customers (even though one of them is an affiliate), this practice will continue. However, the procedure prescribed in the previous paragraph on economic grounds has much to commend it.

*There is no outside competitive market for the transferred products, transfers constitute a predominant part of the supplying division's business, and it can meet all probable requirements.* In these circumstances, the supplying division should operate as a service center, and transfers to consuming divisions should take place at standard variable cost. If the unit variable cost of transferred products does not vary or does not vary significantly with the amount produced (a very common case), the supplying service center (as we shall now call it) can periodically notify consuming divisions of the price at which it is prepared to supply intermediates. On the basis of this information the divisions can then formulate their requirements. If the supplying service center's unit variable costs are not independent of the volume of transfers, then it becomes necessary for a staff department to intervene. Information supplied by the service center about costs at different levels of output on the one hand, and information from the consuming divisions about their requirements at different levels of transfer price, must be collated by the staff department on the lines discussed earlier. The transfer price will be determined in the light of the staff department's judgment as to the price which will equate demand and supply. But once the transfer price has been set, divisions can be left to place their own demands on the service center, which has the responsibility to supply them.

The stipulation that standard, not actual, variable cost should determine the transfer price is intended to restrict the costs which the service center is allowed to recover to those causally related to variations in the demands made on it, and also to require it to bear variances from standard cost which are the result of its own inefficiencies. In order to give full effect to this principle, it will be necessary to revise the standards fairly frequently. There is, moreover, no reason why all uncontrollable price variances should not be charged to the consuming divisions. Attention has been drawn to the need to ensure that divisions calling for nonstandard products, or for variations from standard products, should bear the full (standard) incremental cost of meeting their requirements, to remove any temptation on their part to make excessive demands on the service center.[20]

What of the service center's fixed costs? They will not be recovered in the transfer price of its products if the recommendation just made is followed, but they have to be borne by someone. They could be charged to corporate headquarters. However, if that course of action were followed, and consuming divisions were to bear only the variable cost of the transferred products they used, their profits would be inflated by reason of their being able to turn these products to profitable uses while escaping a part of the costs of making them. It is not only the service center's fixed costs, in the ordinary sense, which they would escape, but also the burden of providing a return on the service center's capital. From the corporation's point of view, and to ensure that corporate profit is maximized, it is quite right that this should be so. The result, however, would be to falsify the picture of divisional profitability presented by the income statements of the transferee divisions.

---

[20] Paul W. Cook, Jr., "Decentralization and the Transfer Price Problem," *Journal of Business*, Vol. 28, No. 2, April 1955, p. 90.

The way to resolve this difficulty is to charge the service center's fixed costs (including its cost of capital) as *period* costs, and not as *product* costs, to those divisions using its products. The essential requirement is that the decisions of the consuming divisions concerning the volume of transfers to take should not be distorted by the conversion of the service center's fixed costs into the consuming divisions' variable costs by incorporating these fixed costs in the price of every unit of intermediate product which they consume. The divisions can be charged for the service center's fixed costs, while avoiding the distortion just referred to, by seeing that they each receive a monthly charge for a proportion of the fixed costs. This charge must not be directly related to the volume of intermediates which a division takes during the month, but should be based on a budgetary calculation of the proportion of the service center's capacity earmarked, so to speak, to serve the division. If the service center serves only one division, that division would assume, in the monthly charges it accepts, the whole burden of the service center's budgeted fixed costs. If the service center serves several divisions, each division should assume responsibility for a proportion of the service center's budgeted fixed costs, its proportion being determined by the proportion of the service center's capacity which it budgeted (before the start of the year) to use during the year. It is assumed here that the service center does not have a substantial amount of surplus capacity.

The use of the service center's *budgeted* fixed costs and the division's *budgeted* demands on capacity as the bases of the charges made to divisions for the fixed costs of the intermediates used has three advantages over the use of "actual" data. First, the service center is left to carry any spending variances over budget, and is not able to pass them on to its customer divisions. Second, the system eliminates any danger that fixed costs will enter into the divisions' decisions about the volume of intermediates to take during the year. Third, the closing of divisional books will not be delayed each month by the necessity to wait for service center charges based on actual costs for the month. If, on the other side, it is thought that the system here recommended provides a temptation for divisions to underbudget their demands for intermediates, thus attracting to themselves a smaller charge for service center fixed costs for the ensuing year, it need only be pointed out that in most cases underbudgeting in this respect could not be effected without underbudgeting other phases of its activities. No division is likely to undertake this step lightly for the sake of a small short-run advantage.

It was explicitly assumed above that the service center's capacity was fairly well matched to its needs and that it did not have a substantial amount of idle capacity. But suppose that the service center supplies several divisions and the demand by one or more of them for its products declines, leaving it with considerable unused capacity. Should the allocation of its fixed costs to the other divisions, as period costs, be increased accordingly to assure full absorption? The answer must surely be no. Rather, by leaving the unabsorbed fixed costs as an adverse volume variance in the operating statement of the service center, both its management and top management will be alerted to the need either to find new outlets for its products, or to reduce its fixed costs.

*There is no outside competitive market for the transferred products, transfers do take place in significant amounts, and the supplying division or service center does not have the capacity necessary to meet all requirements.* The difference between this situation and the preceding one lies not in the transfer-pricing policy recommended for use. It lies, rather, in the role of the central staff department which has responsibility for interdivisional relations. In the situation posed here, there is not sufficient capacity to make all the intermediates demanded by consuming divisions and the best allocation of the scarce resources cannot be made either by them alone or by the producing division alone. Only a department which can take a corporate view of cost and revenue potentials can achieve this. The best allocation will be arrived at by programming methods, as has already been explained. Once the optimal solution has been reached, there seems to be no reason why the division producing the intermediates should not be instructed to implement it, to use its resources in the prescribed manner and to supply specified quantities of products to specified consuming divisions.

Once a decision has been made to dictate to the producing division in this way, thus depriving it of true divisional status (so that we shall again refer to it from now on as a service center), transfer prices lose at least part of their planning significance. They cease to be important in arriving at short-run decisions about the volume and allocation of transfers. There is, however, still the long-run question as to how worth while it is to add to the inadequate capacity. As we have already seen, the shadow prices found in the dual solution to the programming problem throw valuable light on that question. The shadow prices are, therefore, well worth calculating, even if they are not used for routine transfer-pricing purposes. There is also the question of the effect of whatever transfer prices are to be used on the profits of the divisions taking the transferred products. For that purpose, there is no reason to depart from the methods recommended in the immediately preceding situation where capacity constraints were not operative. We can use variable costs at the programmed outputs as transfer prices, with budgeted fixed costs being allocated as period costs to the divisions taking the transferred products.

## Intracompany Services

It has just been suggested that, in the absence of a competitive outside market for transferred products, a division whose primary purpose is to make intermediate products for other divisions should operate as a nonprofit-making service center, rather than as a division, and that it should charge for products supplied to divisions on a two-part tariff. The absence of an outside market lies behind this proposal and, if it is appropriate for products produced internally, it is, presumably, also appropriate for services provided internally. Rarely can it be said of a service center, such as a maintenance department or a quality control department, that it is free to sell its services outside the firm, even if divisions are free to purchase some services outside.

There may be some exceptions to this rule, however. A trucking department might just as easily sell transportation (subject to the law) when it has idle capacity as buy it when it has too little and, in such a case, it is appropriate that the division should operate as a profit center and charge the market rate for its services. Most service departments are not, however, almost by definition, market-oriented. There is, then, much to be said for a two-part tariff as a means of charging divisions for their services. The divisions should then tend to demand services up to the point where the incremental value of the services equals the incremental cost of providing them. Each division will bear its proportion of the service center's fixed costs, but not in such a way as to affect its judgment as to how much of its services to take. Ideally, this should ensure that an optimal amount of services will be provided and used within the firm.

## Inventory Valuation and the Transfer Problem

If the recommendations made earlier in this chapter are followed, transfers of products between divisions will be made on either of these bases: (a) market price, where a realistic outside market exists for the transferred product, or (b) variable cost, as determined by a central staff department on the basis of information provided by the division or service center, its fixed cost being allocated to customer-divisions on the basis of the use of its capacity which they budget to make.

It follows that a division which is holding, on an accounting date, an inventory of materials or products supplied by another division or service center must value this inventory accordingly. Where the transfer was made at market price, the division will have no difficulty in attaching a value to the inventory and the only problem will be that of the corporate accounting staff in eliminating the inter-divisional profit from the consolidated figures. Where the variable cost basis of pricing was used, the matter will be easy to handle in a division which uses direct costing, and less easy if it uses absorption costing. If the division holding the inventory uses direct costing, the transfer price at which it was acquired will already express its direct cost. The charge to the division for the supplying division's fixed costs, made on a periodic basis, will fall quite naturally into a group with the division's own period costs, and will be written off in the period to which the charges relate. If the division uses absorption costing, some of the charges for fixed costs will have to be allocated to inventory. The allocation cannot be done precisely for the division holding the inventory knows nothing about the supplying division's fixed costs except the total charge made to it in respect to each period. It can, however, be done with sufficient precision by allocating the fixed charge each quarter, say, between transferred products sold and those still held in inventory in proportion to their variable costs. This is, in effect, applying to the valuation of the inventory of transferred products the same type of adjustment as was prescribed in Chapter IV for the more general purposes of bringing inventories valued at direct cost onto an absorption cost basis. The similarity of treatment is to be expected, since we are really dealing with the same problem. The difference is only that here we are exclusively concerned with inventories resulting from transfers between divisions, not with inventories in general.

## Interdivisional Market Relationships

The impact of divisions on each other is not confined to the transfer of products between them. They may compete for markets, as do the products of the Ford Division and the Lincoln-Mercury Division of the Ford Motor Company. They may compete with each other for labor or other resources. Their products may complement each other and so help to expand each other's markets as when different divisions of a company make floor tiles and floor polish, cameras and roll films, or phonographs and records. One division's purchases may encourage its supplier to become a customer of another division, and so add to that division's profit.

These interdivisional relationships have an important bearing on the significance of the results which appear in a division's income statement. When the Lincoln-Mercury Division sells a Mercury Monterey to a customer who would otherwise have bought a Ford Galaxie, it has not added to the profits of the Ford Motor Company as much as it has added to its own divisional profits. If, on the other hand, the customer would have bought a Chevrolet Impala if he had not bought a Monterey, what was added to divisional profits has also been added to corporate profits. The opposite effect is seen where the products of different divisions complement each other. When the sale of a camera increases the sales of roll film, the Camera Division's contribution to corporate profits is understated by the profit on cameras which appears in its divisional accounts, for the profit on film appears somewhere else.

This has significance for the evaluation of divisional performance and for policy-making. A division thought to be performing badly profit-wise may be able to claim that, though its own operations are unprofitable, it is making an important contribution to corporate profits through the results of other divisions. For policy-making purposes, in deciding how much it is worth spending to promote the sales of cameras, or the best price to charge for cameras, it is not only the resulting revenue from cameras but also the revenue from the increased sale of film which should be taken into account.

These relationships are by no means peculiar to divisionalized firms. They exist to a greater or lesser degree between the items manufactured by any multiproduct firm. The problems to which they give rise are, however, particularly acute where competitive or complementary products are handled by different divisions, for then different people will receive the praise for success or the blame for failure. This suggests that one simple way of dealing with these interactions is to prevent or at least to minimize their occurrence, by drawing divisional boundaries in such a way that the demand for every one of Division A's products is independent of the demand for every one of Division B's. A moment's thought will show that if this advice were followed completely, many companies now divisionalized would have to abandon the divisional type of organization altogether. Nevertheless, there is a core of good sense in the idea, for it will often be possible to arrange divisional boundaries so as to bring within one division products which compete directly, or which are obviously complementary. The reason for doing so is, of course, not the elimination of an awkward accounting problem but, instead, the chance to economize in marketing resources and to minimize the danger of loss from suboptimization.

However, there are clearly many cases where nothing less than abandoning the whole divisional organization would eliminate interdependence of demand between divisions. A container company with divisions making, respectively, cans, bottles, cardboard and plastic containers, all of which are substitutes for each other for certain purposes, is a case in point. Indeed, there are many companies which promote direct competition between divisions which could, without much difficulty, be combined. The major American automobile companies provide obvious examples. Such companies must have satisfied themselves that the gain in efficiency and keenness which such competition develops more than outweighs any waste of corporate resources resulting from interdivisional competition. The question we should like to answer is: Can we reflect in the financial statements of a division (1) any part of its net income which has been earned at the expense of another division, and (2) any contribution to the net income of other divisions not reflected in its own financial statement? If we could measure these amounts, their reflection in the financial statements of divisions would be tantamount to the system of taxes and subsidies proposed by Hirshleifer[21] to penalize or compensate divisions whose operations diminish or contribute to the profits of other divisions.

Our own judgment is that a scheme of this kind is still no more than an interesting theoretical idea, which would be difficult enough to implement if the relationship between divisions remained stable for any length of time. However, it is quite incapable of being imple-

[21] "Economics of the Divisional Firm," *op. cit.*, p. 100.

mented with our present apparatus in the face of constantly changing market relationships between the divisions. This does not mean that it is a waste of time to give thought to the matter, however, for even if precise values cannot be attached to the parameters of the problem, a qualitative judgment about the accuracy with which accounting results reflect the true contribution of a division to corporate prosperity will usually be better than no judgment at all. Our present incapacity to do more may, moreover, one day yield to more powerful tools than those now in our possession.[22]

## Interdivisional Transfers and Government Contracts

We have discussed the problem of transfer pricing under the assumption that the firm is always free to adopt whatever internal policies are most likely to maximize the corporate profit. A somewhat special situation, however, faces companies doing a substantial amount of work on defense contracts for the Government. Such companies are not free, at least so far as these contracts are concerned, to adopt arrangements between divisions which result in contract costs unacceptable to the defense agencies.

Defense contracts generally fall into one (or more than one) of four categories:

1. *Fixed price contracts.* The company gets the contract as the result of a firm competitive bid, or the product is one with an established market price.
2. *Cost-plus-fixed-fee contracts.* The Government reimburses the company for the actual cost of completing the contract, and in addition pays a fixed sum as the company's profit on the contract. This sum is usually determined by reference to the *planned* cost of the contract.
3. *Redetermination contracts.* Here the contract price is fixed after a specified percentage of the contract has been completed and some experience has been gained of the difficulties involved.
4. *Incentive contracts.* A target price is set before the contract begins. When, at the end, the cost of the contract has been determined, the Government pays the target price plus a percentage (e.g., 75 per cent) of any excess cost or minus a per-

[22] In their article "Decomposition, Pricing for Decentralization and External Economies," William J. Baumol and Tibor Fabian claim that the decomposition technique has a contribution to make here also, *Management Science,* Vol. 11, No. 1, September 1964, pp. 1-32.

centage of any saving. Thus the company bears part of the excess costs, or alternatively, receives part of any economies it can make.

It is idle to pretend that our analysis of the transfer pricing problem which confronts a company operating in an ordinary competitive market has direct relevance throughout that large sector of the economy now engaged in working for the Government under any but the first of the four types of contract. Yet, even here, it is not without some relevance since market price is now widely permitted as the basis for transfer pricing, within a company engaged on defense contracts, for components and subassemblies which are also competitively bought and sold in a free market. However, where components not so traded are the subject of transfers, anything but "full cost" is inappropriate as a basis for charging transfers between divisions.

Suppose two divisions of a company are engaged on a single defense contract, one making components which are assembled by the other. If the contract is one for which a firm price has been quoted by the assembly division, the components division's transfer price will become the assembly division's cost (or part of it, at least). Though a relatively high transfer price will increase the first division's profit and reduce the second's, the price paid by the Government and the profit made by the company will be unaffected. Not so, however, if the contract price is set at cost-plus-fixed-fee. In that case, if the assembly division is regarded as the "principal contractor" and *its* cost is the basis of the price charged to the Government, then any profit included by the components division in its transfer price becomes part of the assembly division's cost. If the "fixed fee" is negotiated by reference to this cost, it is clear that there may be an element of double-counting in the company's profit margin on the contract.

The Government's procurement regulations now distinguish between components made by a division of the contracting company for which there is an alternative market source of supply and those for which there is no alternative source. In the first case, the division making the components is allowed to charge the market price (if the Government specifically agrees to the arrangement in advance) and to keep any profit it can make. The principal contracting division then includes this price in its costs. In the second case, where there is no market for the components, only their cost can be included in the cost charged to the Government and the allocation between divisions of any profit made by the principal contracting division on the contract is a matter to be settled internally. One common method is to divide the profit between divisions in proportion to the planned cost of the work done by them.

Government contracts on which several divisions work are apt to give rise to some unexpected difficulties, and cooperation among divisions in such circumstances has often been less than spontaneous. In one company, one division, in tendering for a cost-plus-fixed-fee contract, takes the lead and acts as the principal contractor. If it uses components purchased outside the firm, it has no difficulty in justifying the inclusion of their cost in the contract costs, and is able to retain the whole of the fixed fee for itself. If it uses components made by other divisions of the company, on the other hand, the total cost of the contract may possibly be a little less, the fee may be the same or even less than it would otherwise be, and the lead division now has to share the fee with the other divisions. If there is no alternative outside source of supply for the components and the components division overruns its estimated cost, the principal contracting division has to justify the extra cost to the Government. If the extra cost, or part of it, can be held to be due to that division's failure to state its requirements precisely, it may even have to relinquish still more of its fixed fee to the components division. This difficulty would not arise if components were being purchased from outside at a firm price. The result is to make intracompany supplies even less attractive to the principal contracting division, and to encourage it to find alternative means, outside the company, of complementing its own activities.

There is no easy way of eliminating these difficulties. They can be minimized by making divisions engaged on government work as self-contained as possible. To go beyond a certain point in this direction involves, however, sacrifice of too many of the benefits of divisionalization. For the rest, the closest possible liaison between the various parts of the firm engaged on the government work, by means of a committee structure or otherwise, must be secured. Essentially the problem arises because part of the company is operating in a market economy and part is operating as an adjunct of government, and no single set of rules will operate effectively in two such different sectors. Perhaps the remarkable thing is not that the problem exists, but that divisionalized firms cope with it as well as they do.

# Appendix A to Chapter VI

## A GRAPHICAL TREATMENT OF THE THEORY OF TRANSFER PRICING

It is impossible to discuss the economic theory of pricing in purely verbal terms without some loss of rigor. The reader who wishes to study the theory of transfer pricing further is therefore invited to pursue the matter with the aid of this appendix.

### The Intermediate Product Has a Competitive Market

Figure 8(a) depicts the position where a division using an intermediate product (Division B) is supplied both by transfers from another division (Division A) and by purchases in a competitive market from outside suppliers. Figure 8(b) shows Division A being willing to supply more of the intermediate than Division B wants and disposing of some of its production on the outside market. In both charts, units of product produced or sold are measured horizontally, and dollars per unit of revenue or cost are measured vertically.[23]

Taking Figure 8(a) first, the horizontal line $P_B$ represents the demand curve for the final product of Division B. The market for this product, it will be supposed for the purposes of this illustration, is perfectly competitive, so that the price per unit obtainable by Division B is independent of the quantity sold since the division's sales do not represent more than a small part of the total industry sales of the product. From the unit revenue $P_B$, Division B has to recoup its own costs of processing the

[23] Putting both the intermediate and the final product into a single diagram creates a problem of scale. What kind of units are measured along the horizontal axis? The answer must be that two scales are needed, though they are related to each other. The two scales use different units, which are respectively (1) units of final product and (2) the quantity of intermediate product required for each unit of final product. It follows that each diagram assumes a particular state of technology.

intermediate. These processing costs will consist of certain fixed costs of operating the process, together with the variable costs per unit of processing carried out. The fixed costs will be relevant in deciding whether a process shall be instituted or not, or whether it shall be continued or not. They are not relevant to short-term questions about the level of operations once the equipment and other fixed costs have been determined. In pursuing these short-term policy questions, therefore, we can ignore the fixed costs and concentrate on the variable or incremental costs of operations. How these incremental costs will react to changes in the level of operations will vary from situation to situation.

FIGURE 8(a)

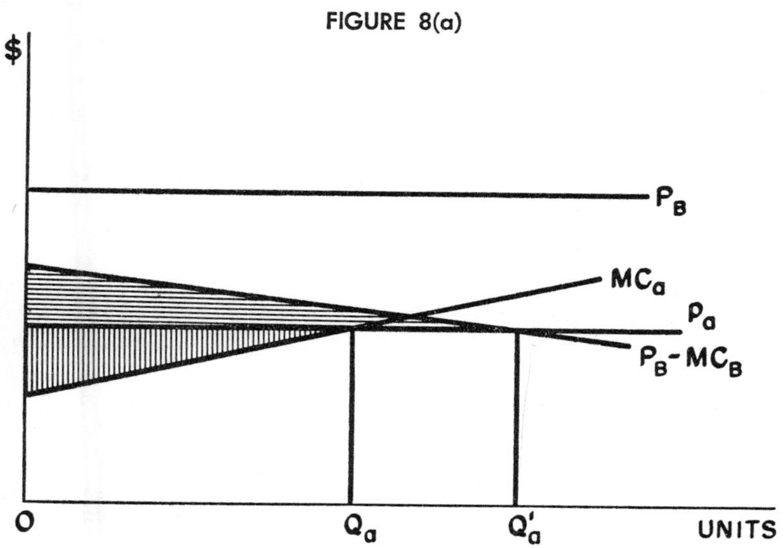


In the present situation, we will assume that they increase somewhat as the scale of the operation expands (because less efficient labor and equipment has to be drawn in to feed the expansion). The incremental cost of processing is not shown explicitly in Figure 8 but what is left of the sales revenue (per unit) after meeting these costs is shown by the line $P_B - MC_B$ (standing for the price of product B minus the marginal cost of processing the intermediate which goes into it). This line falls from left to right, because an increasing marginal cost of processing is being deducted from a constant selling price per unit of the final product. The line represents the net revenue earned by Division B for each additional unit of the final product which it sells, subject to the recovery of its fixed costs and to the further deduction of the cost of the intermediate which it uses, whether this is bought outside or obtained by transfer from Division A.[24]

Division A's costs also can be segregated into those which are fixed over the relevant ranges of output[25] and those which vary more or less directly with the level of output. As with Division B, so with Division A: The fixed costs have an important bearing on whether the process shall be brought into existence, and whether it will be kept in existence, but not on the scale at which it will be operated while it is in existence. Since this is the question in issue here, we can confine our attention to the variable or incremental or marginal costs of the division which are represented by the line $MC_a$. It is shown as rising from left to right as production expands, for reasons similar to those already put forward in explanation of the rising marginal cost of processing the intermediate in Division B. Division A is not the only source of the intermediate, which can be bought competitively on the outside market at a price of $p_a$ per unit. The unlimited availability of the intermediate at this price is represented by the horizontal line $p_a$.

The correct courses for the two divisions are now clear. Division B should buy the intermediate and process it so long as it adds more to its revenue by so doing than it adds to its costs. It can profitably use a total of $OQ'_a$ units so long as it pays no more than the market price $p_a$ whether its supplies come from Division A or the outside market.[26] Any consumption of intermediate in excess of this quantity will add more to its costs than it adds to its revenue. Any consumption less than this will leave it with unsatisfied opportunities for profit.

Division A will be prepared to supply only $OQ_a$ units at a price $p_a$; for supplying more than this will add more to *its* costs (as shown by the line $MC_a$) than it will add to its revenue. Thus Division B will get $OQ_a$ of its supply of the intermediate from Division A, and $Q_aQ'_a$ by purchase on the market. No better result than this can be found for the firm as a whole.

If Division B were to obtain more that $OQ_a$ of its supply of intermediate from Division A, the additional cost to the *firm* of supplies in excess of this amount would be greater than if they were bought outside

---

[24] Straight lines are used here and elsewhere in this chapter to represent various functional relationships. Where the facts demand it, curves can, of course, replace the straight lines.

[25] In the diagrams which follow, for ease of exposition the output ranges over which fixed costs are deemed to remain fixed are greatly exaggerated. This exaggeration must be kept in mind in interpreting the diagrams, which really relate to the range of operations which can be carried out *within existing capacity constraints*. Something will be said about these constraints later.

[26] More strictly, a consumption of $OQ'_a$ units will be more profitable or less unprofitable than any other level of consumption. Whether in fact the division makes a profit will depend on whether it is more or less than covering its fixed costs.

at the price $p_a$. If Division B were to obtain less than $OQ_a$ from Division A and bought more of its supply outside, the firm would again be incurring a greater cost for the intermediate than it need incur. Setting the transfer price equal[27] to the outside market price is the best way to make the two divisions act in the best interest of the corporation while seeking the most favorable result for themselves.

FIGURE 8(b)

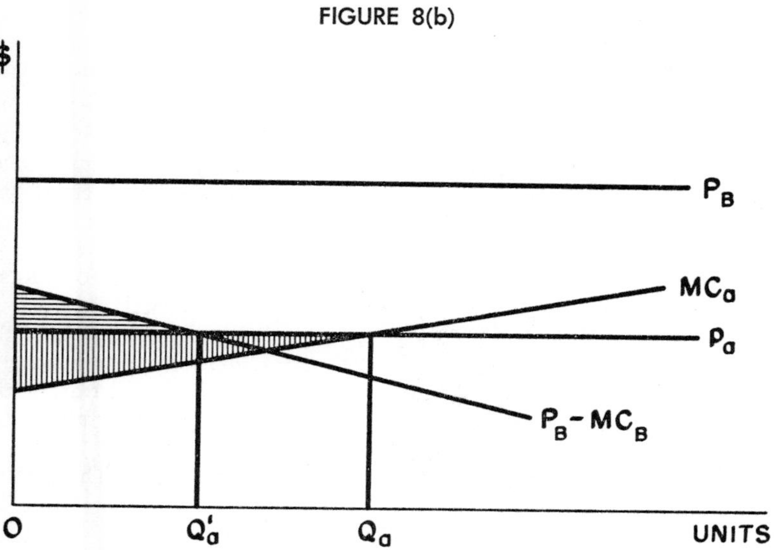


Figure 8(b) is simiiliar to Figure 8(a) and uses the same notation, but Division B's costs of processing the intermediate are now higher than they were in the previous situation and, therefore, though the line $P_B$ is in the same position as before, the line $P_B - MC_B$ is lower, showing Division B as having less net revenue left from the sale of successive units of its final product than it had in Figure 8(a). This causes the line $P_B - MC_B$ to cut the line $p_a$ to the left of the point where the line $MC_a$ cuts it (whereas in Figure 8(a) these positions were reversed). This means that at the price $p_a$ which the intermediate commands on the outside market, Division A is willing to supply a quantity $OQ_a$ (as before), because producing up to that point adds more to its revenue than it adds to its costs, since up to that point the line $MC_a$ is below the line $p_a$. Division B, on the other hand, is prepared to accept only the quantity $OQ'_a$, for to take more than this would add a greater amount to its costs than it would add to its (net) revenues, the line $P_B - MC_B$ being below the

[27] Or nearly equal to it. Some minor adjustments were discussed on pp. 174-177.

line $p_a$ at all points to the right of $Q'_a$. Since Division A can profitably pro duce $OQ_a$ but Division B can only profitably take $OQ'_a$ at the rulin price $p_a$, the correct course for Division A is to sell $Q'_aQ_a$ of its outpu on the outside market. These outside sales add to the corporation's prof as well as to the division's.

In both charts, Division A's profit (subject to fixed costs) is repre sented by the vertically hatched area, while Division B's profit (subjec to its fixed costs) is represented by the area of horizontal hatching.

### Imperfectly Competitive Market for the Final Product

In the situations covered by Figures 8(a) and 8(b), the market for th final product marketed by Division B was perfectly competitive, so th the price obtainable per unit sold was independent of the quantity sol This implies that Division B does not command more than a small pa of the total market for its product. But if this does not hold and the d vision has to take account, in deciding how much of its product to mak and sell, of the impact of volume on price, then the market conditior for the final product cannot be represented by a horizontal line such a the lines $P_B$ in Figures 8(a) and 8(b). Instead, we have to show th price line as falling from left to right, since the division can only achiev an increase in volume by accepting a lower price or by increasing th selling costs per unit, so that in either case the result is a fall in th net proceeds per unit sold.

This situation is represented in Figures 9(a) and 9(b). The slopin

FIGURE 9(a)

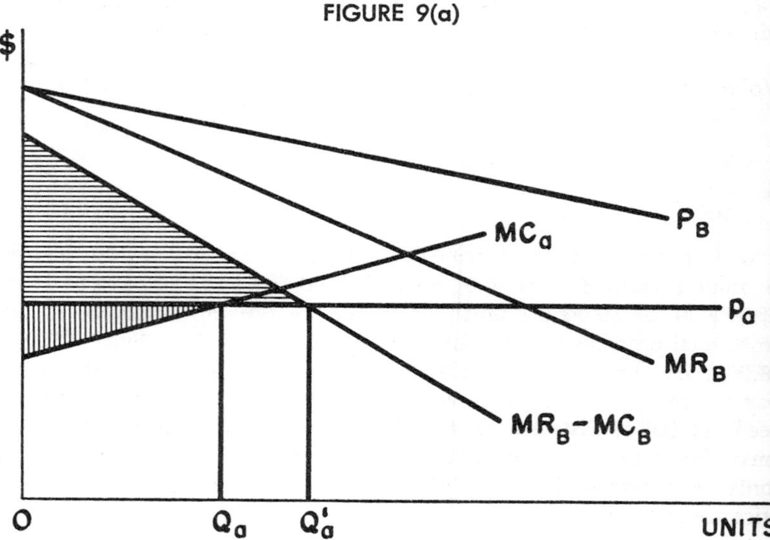

FIGURE 9(b)

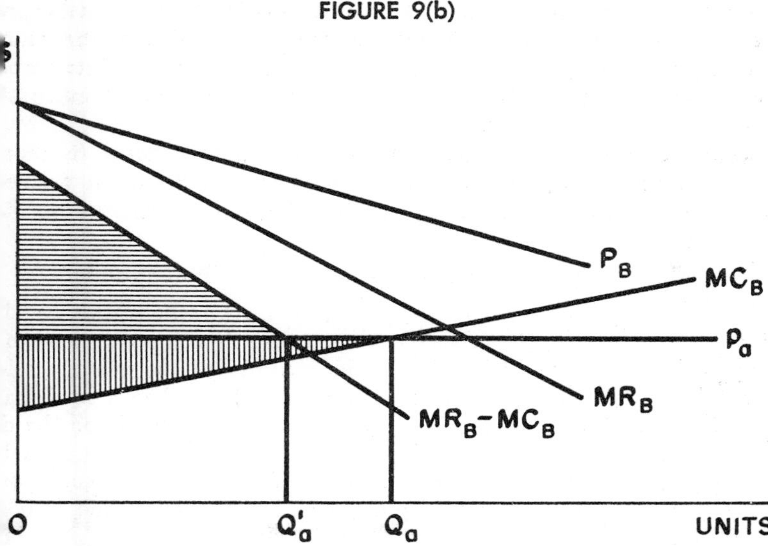


ne $P_B$ shows the relation between selling price and volume or, more real-tically, net sales proceeds per unit and volume, as already explained. rom this line we can derive the marginal revenue line ($MR_B$) for ivision B. This shows the incremental sales proceeds from each addi-onal unit sold, and it will always be below the $P_B$ line. The under-ing data represented by the two lines, over a small part of their length, ight look as follows:

| olume sold | Price per unit | Marginal revenue per unit |
|---|---|---|
| 300 | $10.00 | $ —— |
| 400 | 9.00 | 6.00 |
| 500 | 8.00 | 4.00 |
| 600 | 7.00 | 2.00 |

will be seen that the incremental revenue resulting from the increase volume from 300 to 400 units is $600, i.e. 400 @ $9.00 – 300 $10.00, or $6.00 per unit. When volume goes up from 400 to 500 nits, total proceeds go up from $3600 (400 @ $9.00) to $4000 (500 @ 8.00), i.e., by $400 for the 100 extra units, or $4.00 a unit. In this ay the marginal revenue curve can be derived from the price curve. It eed not fall consistently, as it is shown as doing in Figure 9, though it ust always lie below the price curve (except where the curve is hori-ontal, as it was in Figures 8(a) and 8(b), when marginal revenue and rice are identical).

From Division B's $MR_B$ curve we now have to derive the *net* margin revenue curve, showing the amount available for purchase of the inte mediate by Division B. This is obtained by deducting the division's ma ginal cost of processing the intermediate from the marginal revenue o tained from marketing the final product. The result is the $MR_B - M($ curve, which corresponds to the $P_B - MC_B$ curve in Figure 8, exce that in that situation the selling price per unit was constant (and ther fore equal to marginal revenue per unit, which was also constant) where now we have to start from a falling $P_B$ curve.

From here on, the correspondence between the two sets of curves complete. In Figure 9(a), as in Figure 8(a), Division B is willing acquire a quantity $OQ'_a$ of the intermediate at the ruling market price p for at any quantity less than this the division has an incentive to increa its purchases, since by doing so it can add more to its net revenues than adds to its costs. Division A, on the other hand, will be willing to supp only the quantity $OQ_a$ at the competitive price $p_a$, for outputs in exce of $OQ_a$ add more to its costs than to its revenues. Division B, therefor acquires quantity $OQ_a$ of the intermediate from Division A and an add tional quantity $Q_aQ'_a$ by purchase from outside. In the situation repr sented in Figure 9(b) Division A would like to supply the quantity OQ whereas Division B is prepared to take only $OQ'_a$. Division A, therefor sells $Q'_aQ_a$ on the outside market, and transfers $OQ'_a$ to Division both at price $p_a$. In both diagrams, Division B's profit, subject to its fixe costs, is shown as the horizontally hatched area, while Division A's prof subject to its fixed costs, is represented by the area of vertical hatching.

## Competing Demands for the Intermediate Product

Figure 10 depicts a situation in which two divisions, B and C, both u the intermediate produced by Division A but apply different process to it and produce different end products. Both Divisions B and C fa imperfect markets for their products, whereas the market for the inte mediate is perfectly competitive.[28] The left-hand section of the diagra

[28] It is appropriate at this point again to draw attention to the problem of sca Indeed, in Figure 10 the problem is even more acute than it was in the earlier agrams, for we are now trying to represent together not just a final product and intermediate but two (or more) final products and an intermediate. The soluti adopted earlier was to use two related scales, one measured in units of final produ the other in units determined by reference to the quantity of intermediate requir per unit of final product. Now with two or more final products, a different sol tion is called for. All three sections of Figure 10 must use a scale based on un of the intermediate. The right-hand section will use simple units of intermedia the other two sections will, respectively, use as their units the quantities of pro ucts B and C obtainable from one unit of intermediate. This procedure is necessa because the supply or use of the intermediate is the only thing that the three visions have in common.

FIGURE 10

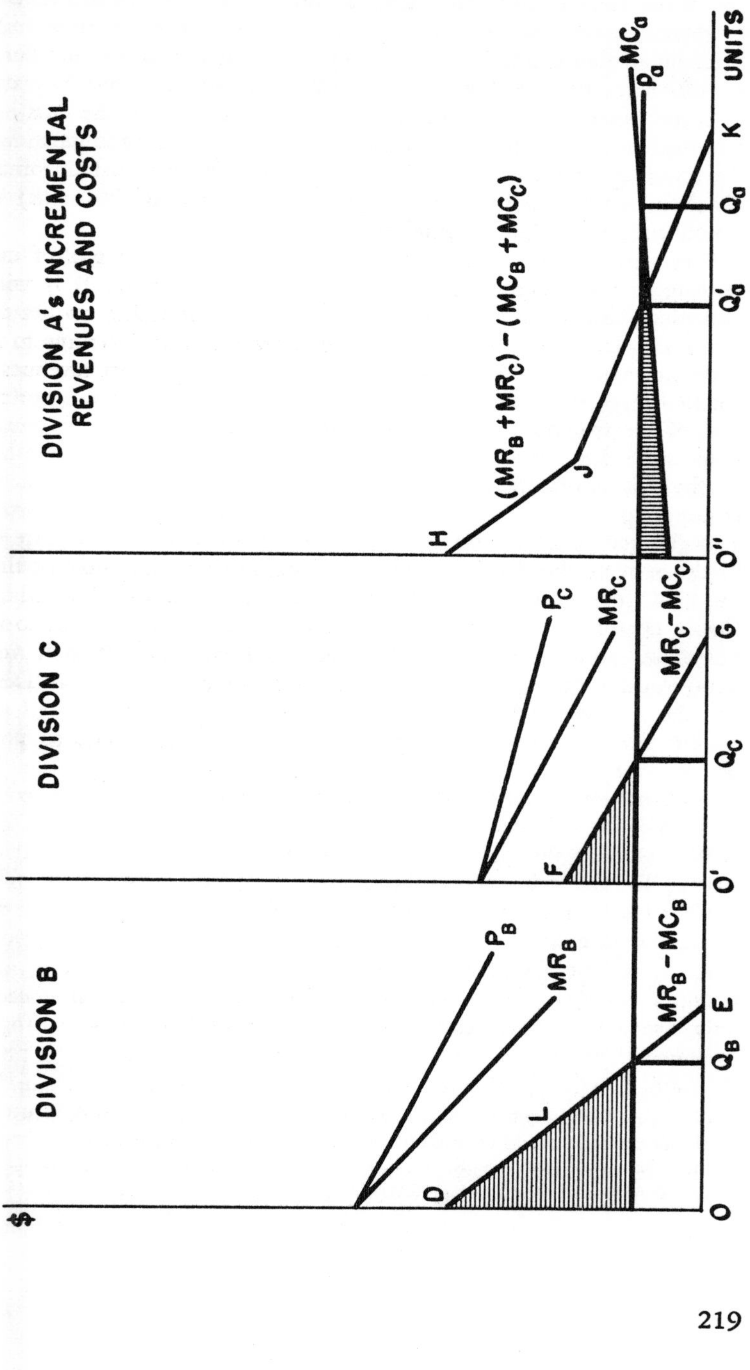

$
DIVISION B
DIVISION C
DIVISION A's INCREMENTAL REVENUES AND COSTS
D
L
$P_B$
$MR_B$
$MR_B - MC_B$
F
$P_C$
$MR_C$
$MR_C - MC_C$
H
J
$(MR_B + MR_C) - (MC_B + MC_C)$
$MC_a$
$P_a$
O
$Q_B$
E
O'
$Q_C$
G
O''
$Q'_a$
$Q_a$
K
UNITS

shows the market conditions facing Division B in the market for its final product, the line $P_B$ showing the relationship between volume and the price obtainable per unit. The marginal or incremental revenue per unit as volume increases is shown by the $MR_B$ line, and from this the marginal or incremental costs of producing product B (excluding the cost of the intermediate) are deducted to leave the incremental net revenue shown by the line DE. The central section of the diagram gives similar information about the market for Division C's product, with the line FG as the incremental net revenue line for product C.

The right-hand section of the diagram shows the aggregate situation relating to the revenue and cost conditions which confront Division A and which should determine its policy and that of the other two divisions concerning the supply of the intermediate. We first have to aggregate the "net incremental revenue" lines of Divisions B and C (the two lines labelled respectively DE and FG). This is done by taking the horizontal sum of the two lines. What this means is that we start by marking the point H on the vertical axis on the right-hand curve at the same height on the axis as the *highest* point on either of the other two curves, which is clearly point D. This gives us one end of the line of the horizontal sum. To get the other end, K, we measure out from O″ a distance equal to the sum of the distances OE and O′G. To get every other point on the HJK line we plot, at each successive vertical height above the base line, a horizontal distance from the vertical axis equal to the *sum* of the horizontal distances which the DE and FG lines are from their vertical axes. Point J on the HJK line corresponds to point L on the DE line and the line segment HJ corresponds to the segment DL, for all points on DE from L upwards are higher than *any* point on FG, so nothing has to be added to their values in obtaining the horizontal sum. From J to K, however, every point has an abscissa or horizontal value equal to the sum of the abscissae of the corresponding points on DE and FG.

We complete the right-hand diagram by drawing the horizontal price-line $p_a$ for the price which the intermediate commands on the market, and the marginal or incremental cost line $MC_a$ showing the amount which production of each additional unit of the intermediate adds to Division A's costs. It is now apparent that Division A will wish to produce a total quantity of $O''Q_a$ at a price $p_a$. Divisions B and C between them will only want to take the quantity $O''Q'_a$, and if we extend the line $p_a$ back through the other two sections of the diagram we can see that at price $p_a$ Division B will take a quantity $OQ_B$ and Division C will take $O'Q_C$. These quantities together equal $O''Q'_a$. As Division A's ideal output exceeds what the other two divisions between them are prepared to take at the intermediate's market price of $p_a$, Division A is left to sell the amount $Q'_aQ_a$ on the outside market.

As before, if Division A's marginal cost line $MC_a$ (in the right-hand section) had cut the $p_a$ line to the left of the HJK line's intersection with it instead of to the right of this intersection, this would have meant that Division A would be unwilling to supply as much of the intermediate as the other two divisions between them were prepared to take, and either one or both divisions would have had to have resort to the outside market to supplement the supply from Division A. Since we are assuming that the intermediate changes hands at a uniform price, $p_a$, everywhere in the market, it is a matter of indifference to the company whether Division B or C or both of them buy part of their supplemental supply outside the corporation; and as the same price rules inside and outside, it is a matter of indifference to the divisions also.

The profits of the three divisions are represented in Figure 10 exactly as they were in the other diagrams. The profits of the two divisions which consume the intermediate (B and C), subject to their respective fixed costs, are shown by the horizontally hatched areas, while the profit of the division which produces it (A), subject to its fixed costs, is shown by the vertical hatching.

## The Dangers of an Unrealistic Market Price

We can see the theoretical result of using an unrealistic market price as the transfer price for an intermediate product made by one division for use by another by using an adaptation of Figure 9. Retaining the notation used earlier, suppose that Division A manufactures the inter-

FIGURE 11(a)

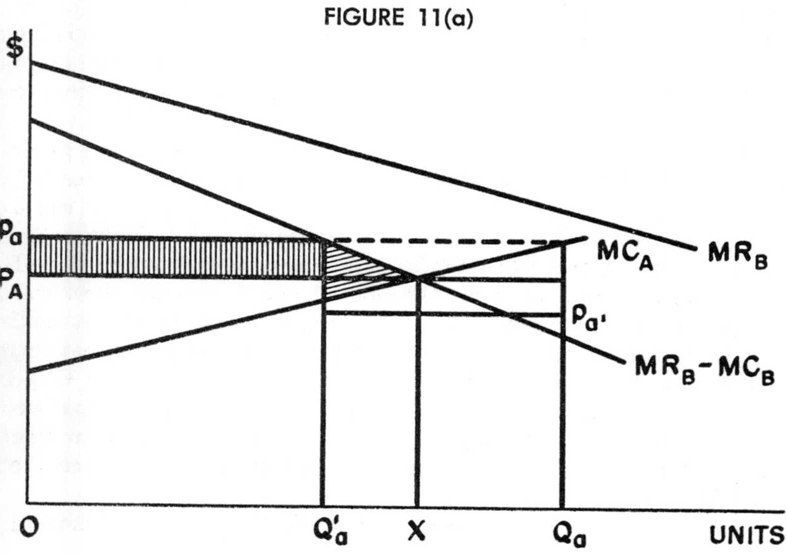

mediate and Division B converts it into a finished product. In Figure 11(a), the line marked $MR_B - MC_B$ corresponds to the similar line in Figure 9. It shows the marginal or incremental net revenue derived by Division B from the sale of successive units of the final product, after deducting the incremental conversion cost as output expands. The line, therefore, shows the additional value which Division B will attach to additional supplies of the intermediate. The line $MC_a$, as before, shows the marginal or incremental cost to Division A, as we move along the line from left to right, of expanding the output of the intermediate. The horizontal line $p_a$ shows the transfer price which has been fixed for the intermediate, just as it did in Figure 9. At this price, as before, Division B will only be prepared to take the quantity $OQ'_a$, while Division A would be happy to dispose of an additional quantity $Q'_aQ_a$ on the open market at the price $p_a$. However, suppose this time there is not a genuine outlet for Division A's surplus production except at a considerably lower price, say, at a price $p_a'$. Then at the ruling transfer price of $p_a$, Division A will limit its output to $OQ'_a$. Yet it is clear that if the transfer price had been set at $P_A$ instead of $p_a$, Division A would have been content to produce an extra volume $Q'_aX$ of the intermediate since its incremental cost of doing so would have been covered. Division B would have taken this extra supply, for its value to B would have been greater than Division A's extra charge for it. The corporation would have been better off as a result of the extra output of the intermediate to the extent of the extra profits represented by the shaded triangle, for this is the amount by which the aggregate profits of the two divisions together would have increased.

It is worth noting that a change in the transfer price from $p_a$ to $P_A$, while it would have resulted in an improvement in the company's profit by an amount represented by the area of the shaded triangle, would not have improved the profits of both divisions. At the new and lower transfer price, the area of the shaded triangle will be divided between the two divisions so that the part below line $P_A$ will go to Division A (its new total profit, subject to fixed costs, is shown by the triangle bounded by the vertical axis, line $P_A$ and line $MC_A$), while the part above line $P_A$ will go to Division B (whose total profit, subject to fixed costs, is now shown by the triangle bounded by the vertical axis, line $P_A$ and line $MR_B - MC_B$). However, while Division A gains its share of the shaded triangle when the transfer price is reduced, it loses the whole of the vertically hatched rectangle—its gain from increased volume is more than offset by the reduced transfer price it gets for the whole of its output. Division B, on the other hand, gains both from the increase in its volume and from the reduction in the transfer price it has to pay for the intermediate. B's gain is greater than A's loss, so the corporation is better off as a result of the change in price.

The effect of the change in the transfer price on the relative profitability of the two divisions need not always turn out to be as it was here. It is the shape of the cost and revenue functions in each particular case which will determine the effect of a given change in price on the relative positions of the divisions. It is, however, precisely because of the possibility of a conflict between the interests of the corporation and the interest of one or more of its divisions that the whole question of transfer prices is fraught with such difficulty.

FIGURE 11(b)

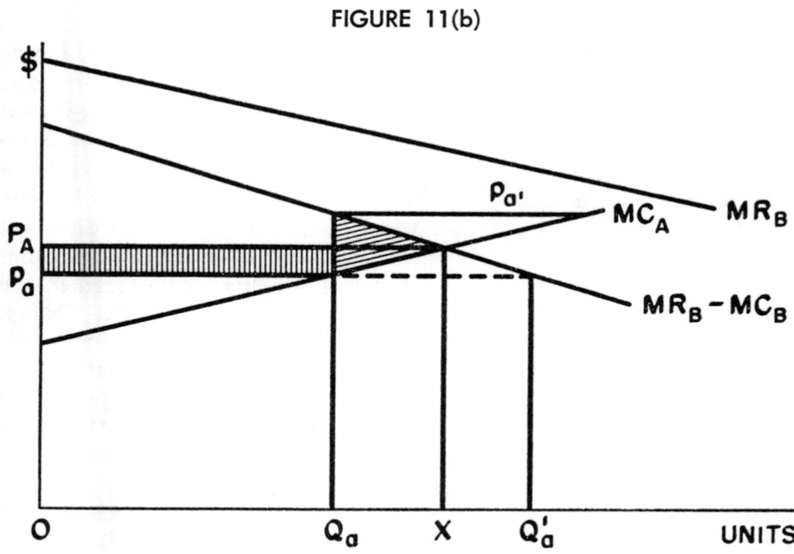


Using the same notation as before, Figure 11(b) shows a situation in which the transfer price, $p_a$, is set below $P_A$, the price which would equate the demand of Division B with the quantity which Division A would be willing to supply. At the price $p_a$, Division A will want to supply only the quantity $OQ_a$, while B will want to buy $OQ'_a$. The difference between $p_a$ and $P_A$ would not matter if $p_a$ were a truly competitive price, in the sense that Division B could buy a quantity $Q_aQ'_a$ at that price on the outside market, as was the case in Figure 9(a). But in the present situation suppose that it is found that, because of the effect of Division B's buying power in the market, it would have to pay a price $p_a'$ to secure outside supplies (though Division A could not command such a price as a seller, because of the imperfections of the market). Then Division B will have to be content with a supply of $OQ_a$. Setting the transfer price too low will cause the corporation's profit to be less than it might have been by an amount represented by the area of the shaded triangle. At the transfer price $P_A$, the company would have sold a quantity OX instead of only $OQ_a$, and its profit (the aggregate profit of the two divisions), subject as always to fixed costs, would have been represented by the large triangle bounded by the vertical axis, line $MR_B - MC_B$ and line $MC_A$. At the lower price $p_a$ for the intermediate and with the imperfect market for it outside, the firm's profit will be less than this by the area of the shaded triangle.

### Transfer Prices in an Imperfect Market—the Marginal Cost Rule

We have not yet reached the general rule for setting transfer prices where there is not a realistic outside competitive price for the transferred product, though we have come fairly near it in Figure 11. Two more steps will take us as close to it as we can come without an excessive amount of theorizing. Figure 12 presents the generalized situation where Division A makes an intermediate product which is used by two other divisions, B and C, and there is also an outside market for the intermediate, but because Division A represents a substantial supplier in this market, the price it can command is not independent of the volume sold. Though Figure 12 covers only two consuming divisions, more divisions can easily be added without affecting the principle which the diagram illustrates.

The diminishing increments of revenue from increasing sales of the intermediate in the outside market are shown by the falling $MR_o$ (marginal revenue from outside) line in section 3 of the chart. Sections 1 and 2 show ($MR_B$ and $MR_C$) the diminishing marginal revenue from expanded sales of the final products of Divisions B and C, and the two lower lines ($MR_B - MC_B$ and $MR_C - MC_C$) show their diminishing *net* marginal revenues from the conversion of the intermediate, this being the residue of their gross marginal revenues after deducting their marginal costs of conversion. By taking a horizontal sum of the three lines $MR_B - MC_B$, $MR_C - MC_C$ and $MR_o$ (proceeding in exactly the same way as was explained in connection with Figure 10), we can construct the line $ANMR_a$ (aggregate net marginal revenue for Division A) as shown in section 4 of the chart. We now draw in the line $MC_a$, showing Division A's marginal cost of expanding output. The distance from the vertical axis at which these two lines intersect is $O'''Q_a$. Division A will choose to produce a total quantity $O'''Q_a$ of the intermediate and the distribution of this quantity between the three uses to which it can be put is determined by drawing a horizontal line through the intersection and back to intersect the three lines which are aggregated to give $ANMR_a$. In section 3 of the chart, the intersection occurs vertically above $Q_o$ and $O''Q_o$ is therefore the quantity of the intermediate to be sold on the outside market. Proceeding similarly back through sections 2 and 1, we

FIGURE 12

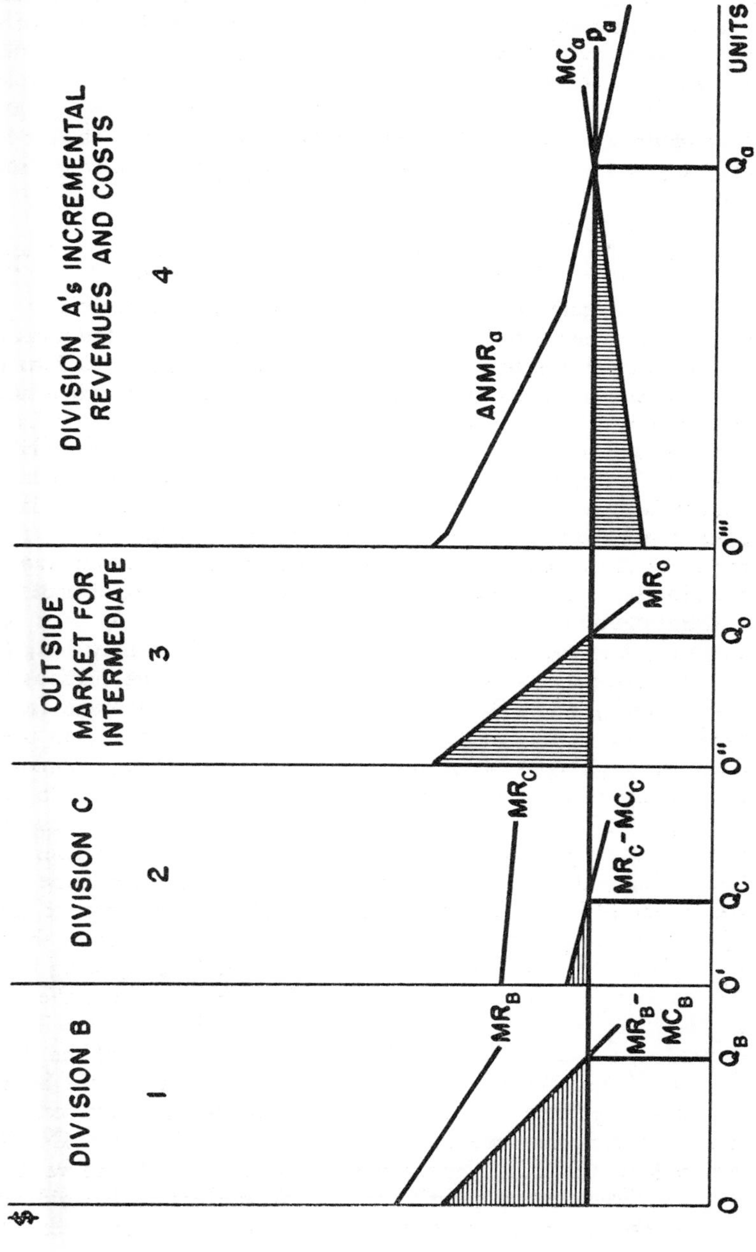

$
DIVISION B
1
DIVISION C
2
OUTSIDE MARKET FOR INTERMEDIATE
3
DIVISION A's INCREMENTAL REVENUES AND COSTS
4
$MR_B$
$MR_B - MC_B$
$MR_C$
$MR_C - MC_C$
$MR_o$
$ANMR_a$
$MC_a$
$p_a$
O
$Q_B$
O'
$Q_C$
O''
$Q_o$
O'''
$Q_a$
UNITS

arrive at $O'Q_C$ and $OQ_B$ as the quantities to be distributed to Divisions C and B. All that needs to be done to effect this distribution is for Division A to fix its transfer price at $p_a$, which is determined by the level of marginal cost at which the intersection takes place in section 4 of the chart. Faced with this transfer price, Divisions B and C will want to take just the quantities indicated, leaving $O''Q_o$ for sale on the market. The sum of $OQ_B$, $O'Q_C$ and $O''Q_o$ must, of course, equal $O'''Q_a$, for the line $ANMR_a$ was constructed by horizontally adding the abscissae of the points on the other three lines.

In Figure 12, as in the earlier charts, the profit of the division making the intermediate, subject as before to the division's fixed costs, is represented by the areas of vertical hatching, while the profits (subject to their fixed costs) of Divisions B and C, which use the intermediate, are shown by the areas of horizontal hatching. Division A's surplus over its fixed costs comes from three sources in this case, from Divisions B and C and also from sales on the outside market.

One important case remains to be dealt with, where several divisions supply different intermediates to an "assembly" division which alone markets a final product. This case is not to be confused with the one covered in Figure 12. In that situation, a division making an intermediate is faced with several alternative outlets. The present case is one wherein a single "final product division" draws supplies from a number of "intermediate" divisions.

It is obvious that the previous analysis cannot be applied here directly. Suppose we take as our example a division of an automobile company which markets an automobile incorporating an engine and a body supplied by two other divisions of the same firm. Our previous analysis would require the final product division to say what its net revenue function was after charging all incremental costs except the cost of the engines, and *also* to say what it would be after charging all incremental costs except the cost of bodies. Clearly, it cannot answer either of these questions until it knows the answer to the other. The only feasible course is to follow a somewhat different approach which will answer both questions at once.

A situation in which an engine division and a body division transfer their products to a third division which assembles them and markets them as automobiles is represented in Figure 13. Sections 1 and 2 show the marginal cost conditions in the components divisions, incremental cost per engine ($MC_E$) rising somewhat with expanding output, and incremental cost per body ($MC_B$) being almost constant. There is no empirical justification for these assumptions: they are made purely for the purpose of illustration and other assumptions might have been made just as well. In the right-hand section of the chart which relates to the assembled automobile, the line $MC_E$ is copied from section 1 and the line $MC_B$ (from

FIGURE 13

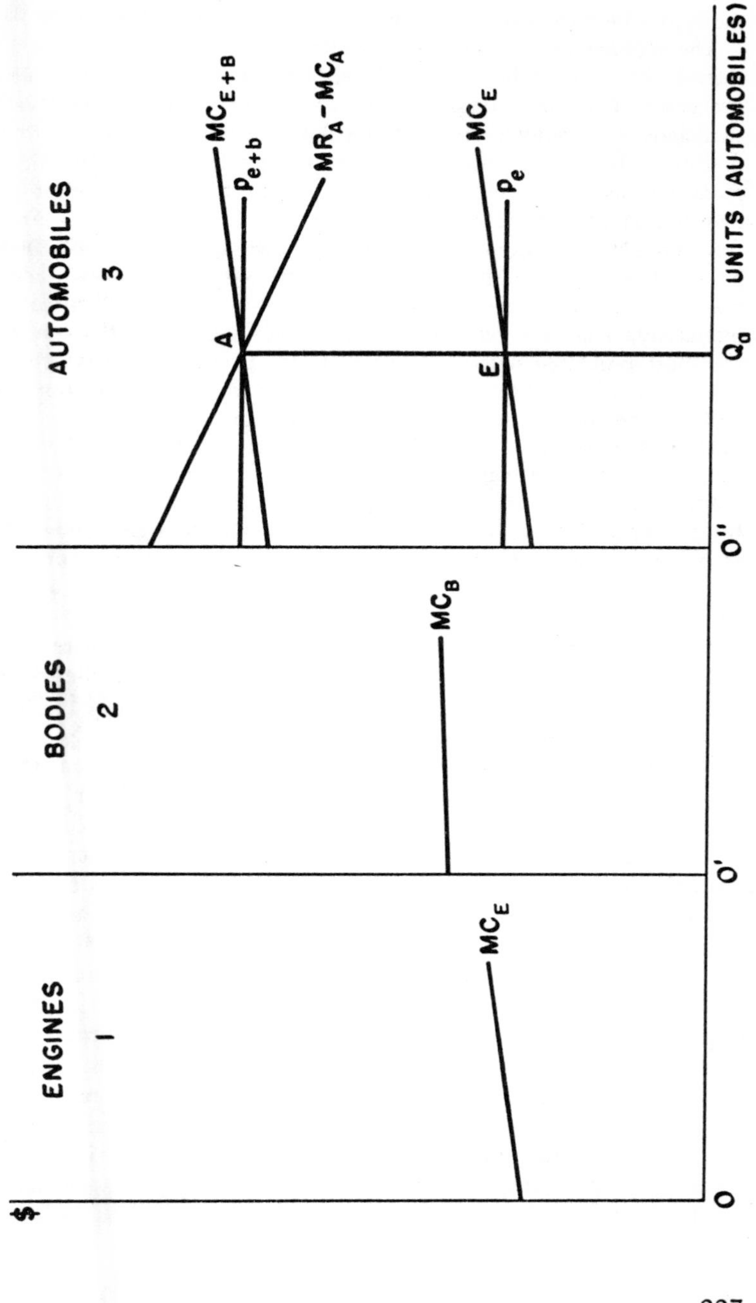

$
ENGINES
1
BODIES
2
AUTOMOBILES
3
MC_E
MC_B
A
MC_{E+B}
p_{e+b}
MR_A - MC_A
E
MC_E
p_e
O
O'
O''
Q_a
UNITS (AUTOMOBILES)

section 2) is added to it vertically, to give the line $MC_{E+B}$, representing the aggregate marginal cost of producing one engine and one body.[29]

The number of components so dealt with could (and should, in the interests of realism) be multiplied, but for the sake of simplicity we shall proceed as if no other components went into a car. For the same reason, we shall ignore the automobile division's own assembly costs. The automobile division now has to estimate its net marginal revenue, i.e., the marginal revenue from selling more cars minus the marginal cost of the two components to give the final product. The net marginal revenue function of the automobile division is shown in section 3 of the chart by the line $MR_A - MC_A$. This line intersects the aggregate marginal cost line for components ($MC_{E+B}$) at point A, and the distance of this intersection from the vertical axis (a distance equal to $O''Q_a$) determines the most profitable output of automobiles. This in turn determines the most profitable output of components—most profitable for the corporation, that is. The component divisions can be led to produce just the required quantities of components if the transfer prices are set at the level $p_e$ ($= EQ_a$) for engines and $p_b$ (which cannot directly be shown on the diagram but is equal to $p_{e+b} - p_e$, or AE) for bodies. Again, then, the correct transfer price is equal to the marginal cost of the transfer product when it is being produced at a level of output which equates its (or its final product's) marginal cost and marginal revenue.

---

[29] The problem of scale, which has already been noted, obtrudes itself here again. In the present illustration the assumption that each automobile will call for one engine and one body simplifies matters, and makes it possible to scale each section of Figure 13 in units. If we were to extend the illustration to cover a further components division making, say, wheels, the scale for that division would have to be in five-wheel units, since each vehicle would require five wheels (including a spare). The scale for each division, in other words, as before, has to be in terms of "per unit of final product," for in no other terms can the components be added together.

# Appendix B to Chapter VI

## COMPUTATION OF THE OPTIMAL PROGRAM FOR THE PRODUCT-MIX PROBLEM AND OF THE IMPLICIT PRICES OF THE TRANSFERRED MATERIALS

The terms of the problem can be expressed in the usual linear programming form as:

Maximize profit, P, when

(1) $P = 3\,B_1 + 7\,B_2$[30]

subject to

the S capacity constraint: $2\,B_1 + 2\,B_2 \leqq 4000$
the T capacity constraint: $\frac{1}{2}\,B_1 + 2\,B_2 \leqq 3000$
the V capacity constraint: $B_1 + 3\,B_2 \leqq 4800$

We add the condition that negative product quantities are ruled out, i.e.,

$$B_1 \geqq 0$$
$$B_2 \geqq 0$$

The constraint inequalities are first converted into equations by introducing "slack variables" representing unused capacity, if any, in Division A's operations. We shall call these $K_S$, $K_T$ and $K_V$ to represent idle capacity (in terms of pounds of output) in the production of S, T and V, respectively. The equations derived from the inequalities are, then:

$$2\,B_1 + 2\,B_2 + K_S = 4000$$
$$\tfrac{1}{2}\,B_1 + 2\,B_2 + K_T = 3000$$
$$B_1 + 3\,B_2 + K_V = 4800$$

---

[30] The symbols $B_1$ and $B_2$ here stand for the number of units of each product, not just their names.

or rewriting these to get expressions for the slack variables, we have:

| | |
|---|---|
| (2a) | $K_S = 4000 - 2 B_1 - 2 B_2$ |
| (2b) | $K_T = 3000 - \frac{1}{2} B_1 - 2 B_2$ |
| (2c) | $K_V = 4800 - B_1 - 3 B_2$ |

If we start out with zero outputs of $B_1$ and $B_2$ and all capacity in Division A idle, our *initial program* will be:

$$B_1 = 0$$
$$B_2 = 0$$
$$K_S = 4000$$
$$K_T = 3000$$
$$K_V = 4800$$

With this program, equation 1 (the objective function, as it is called) of course yields $P = 0$.

We can improve on this by introducing either $B_1$ or $B_2$ into the program. As a unit of $B_2$ yields the bigger contribution, we will start with that, introducing as much of it as possible. How much is possible can be found by turning to equations (2), setting $B_1$ and the K variables equal to zero (we want no $B_1$ and no idle capacity at this stage). We then get, for each kind of capacity

| | | | |
|---|---|---|---|
| (S) | $2 B_2 = 4000$ | or | $B_2 = 2000$ |
| (T) | $2 B_2 = 3000$ | or | $B_2 = 1500$* |
| (V) | $3 B_2 = 4800$ | or | $B_2 = 1600$ |

We now see that the restriction on the output of T stops us from making more than 1500 units of $B_2$, and the S and V constraints are at this stage, therefore, inoperative. We mark the T constraint with a star to show that it is the operative constraint, and introduce 1500 units of $B_2$ into the program.

Product $B_2$ has replaced $K_T$ in the program, and we can find out what the rest of the program now looks like if we rewrite equation 2 (b) to get $B_2$ on the left, and substitute the resulting expression for $B_2$ into the objective function and the other equations, thus:

Rewriting equation (2b): $2 B_2 = 3000 - \frac{1}{2} B_1 - K_T$

So $B_2 = 1500 - \frac{1}{4} B_1 - \frac{1}{2} K_T$

Substituting this expression in the objective function (equation (1)) and the other constraint equations (equations (2)), we have:

$$P = 3 B_1 + 7 (1500 - \tfrac{1}{4} B_1 - \tfrac{1}{2} K_T)$$
$$K_S = 4000 - 2 B_1 - 2 (1500 - \tfrac{1}{4} B_1 - \tfrac{1}{2} K_T)$$
$$K_T = 0$$
$$K_V = 4800 - B_1 - 3 (1500 - \tfrac{1}{4} B_1 - \tfrac{1}{2} K_T)$$

Simplifying and collecting terms, these equations become:

(3) $P = 10{,}500 + \frac{5}{4} B_1 - \frac{7}{2} K_T$
(4a) $K_S = 1{,}000 - \frac{3}{2} B_1 + K_T$
(4b) $K_T = 0$
(4c) $K_V = 300 - \frac{1}{4} B_1 + \frac{3}{2} K_T$

As $B_1$ and $K_T$ are both zero in the *second program,* this program thus stands as follows:

$$\begin{aligned} P &= 10{,}500 \\ K_S &= 1{,}000 \\ K_T &= 0 \\ K_V &= 300 \\ B_1 &= 0 \\ B_2 &= 1{,}500 \end{aligned}$$

Looking at the new objective function, equation (3), we can quickly see that we have not arrived at an optimal solution, for it still has a positive term in it, $B_1$. If we increase $B_1$, therefore—it now stands at zero—we can increase P, the profit. We therefore go to the last set of constraint equations (equations (4)) to see by how much $B_1$ could be increased. Remembering that $K_T$ is zero, if we reduce $K_S$ and $K_V$ to zero (if we use up all idle capacity in those processes) we have:

for S, from (4a) $\frac{3}{2} B_1 = 1000$ so $B_1 = 666$*
for V, from (4c) $\frac{1}{4} B_1 = 300$ so $B_1 = 1200$

We star the S constraint to show this is now operative, for to have enough V capacity for 1200 units of $B_1$ is no good if the S capacity will only permit us to make enough of S to give 666 units of $B_1$: and we introduce 666 units of $B_1$ into the program.

Product $B_1$ having replaced $K_S$, we rewrite equation (4a) with $B_1$ on the left hand side, thus:

$$\frac{3}{2} B_1 = 1000 - K_S + K_T \quad \text{or} \quad B_1 = 666 - \frac{2}{3} K_S + \frac{2}{3} K_T$$

We substitute this expression for $B_1$ in the objective function and the constraint equations (equations (3) and (4)) just as we did before when $B_2$ was introduced into the program. This gives us

$$\begin{aligned} P &= 10{,}500 + \tfrac{5}{4} (666 - \tfrac{2}{3} K_S + \tfrac{2}{3} K_T) - \tfrac{7}{2} K_T \\ B_1 &= 666 \\ B_2 &= 1500 - \tfrac{1}{4} (666 - \tfrac{2}{3} K_S + \tfrac{2}{3} K_T) - \tfrac{1}{2} K_T \\ K_S &= 0 \\ K_T &= 0 \\ K_V &= 300 - \tfrac{1}{4} (666 - \tfrac{2}{3} K_S + \tfrac{2}{3} K_T) + \tfrac{3}{2} K_T \end{aligned}$$

Again simplifying and collecting terms we have

$$
\begin{array}{ll}
(5) & P = 11{,}330 - \tfrac{5}{6} K_S - \tfrac{16}{6} K_T \\
(6a) & B_1 = 666 \\
(6b) & B_2 = 1333 + \tfrac{1}{6} K_S - \tfrac{4}{6} K_T \\
(6c) & K_S = 0 \\
(6d) & K_T = 0 \\
(6e) & K_V = 133 + \tfrac{1}{6} K_S + \tfrac{8}{6} K_T
\end{array}
$$

Inspection of equation (5) shows that we have reached an optimal solution, for apart from the profit of $11,330 it contains nothing but negative terms, so that giving $K_S$ and $K_T$ values in excess of zero would only reduce the profit. The *final* and *optimal* solution at which we have arrived is therefore:

$$
\begin{array}{l}
P = \$11{,}330 \\
B_1 = 666 \text{ units} \\
B_2 = 1333 \text{ units} \\
K_S = 0 \\
K_T = 0 \\
K_V = 133 \text{ lbs}
\end{array}
$$

This is the primal solution, the solution to the product-mix problem in terms of which our original equations were set up. The dual solution can be read straight off the objective function (equation (5)) simply by taking the coefficients of $K_S$ and $K_T$. These tell us that a pound of S is "worth" five-sixths of a dollar or $0.83 and a pound of T is "worth" sixteen-sixths of a dollar or $2.67. The significance of this information is discussed in the body of the chapter.

The method used above to reach the primal solution is a "slow-motion" version of the simplex method as it would be used in practice, and which is explained in any of the numerous books on linear programming. In a practical problem involving more than a few products and constraints, the use of a computer to reach an optimal solution becomes virtually a necessity.

# BUDGETARY CONTROL OF DIVISIONAL OPERATIONS

## CHAPTER VII

By its system of budgets, more than by any other means, top management of a divisionalized company maintains control of its divisions while allowing them a large measure of freedom in the day-to-day and month-to-month conduct of their operations. It is important to understand that such freedom can be allowed at all only because certain limits within which that freedom is to be exercised have been accepted by both sides in advance. The presentation of budgets by a division, and the need to obtain corporate management's approval of them, is the modest price which a division pays for the extensive powers of decentralized decision-making which it enjoys. It may also be noted that the cost of budgeting is part of the price which the company pays for the benefits of a divisional form of organization. As one writer puts it, "a decentralized profit center system . . . requires a more sophisticated and expensive budgeting and planning system to overcome the problems of communication, coordination, and evaluation that profit decentralization creates."[1]

Budgets serve several different purposes, all of them related to each other. They incorporate an organization's plans. They provide motivation by means of the targets built into them. They contain a means of self-evaluation for those responsible for the budget center, since

[1] John Dearden in "Mirage of Profit Decentralization," *Harvard Business Review,* November-December 1962, p. 147.

the budget provides them with a bench mark. Also, budgets offer a means of control of the budget center by the higher echelons to which it is answerable—control of the power to spend (through capital expenditure budgets, for example) and control in the different sense of evaluation of performance. It is not our purpose here to discuss budgeting in general, and in any case it already has a substantial literature of its own.[2] It is the special role which budgets play in divisionalized companies which will occupy almost all our attention. There are many other problems of budgeting which such companies share with nondivisionalized businesses, but these will not concern us except quite incidentally.

Ultimately, the success of a division and of its management must be measured in terms of profitability. Even though in the short run there may be many other indices of success, sooner or later these must express themselves in terms of profit or, what is really the same thing, in terms of an increase in the net worth of the enterprise. But measures of profitability or increase in net worth, like other measures, take on much greater significance when they are related to something else than when they are looked at in isolation. One obvious bench mark is the performance of other divisions; another is the past performance of the division itself. But both of these, while useful, are imperfect. Comparison with other divisions can only be effective after adjustment has been made for differences in size, differences in market situation, and a host of other factors, some of them incapable of being reduced to figures. Comparison with the division's own past performance may also be vitiated by changes of circumstance which may make it difficult, if not impossible, to judge, for example, whether an apparent improvement in results really represents a better managerial performance or not. More fundamentally, however, comparison of present performance with past performance is comparison with an undefined and undetermined standard. It is, of course, something to be able to say that a division has done "better" this year than it did last year; but this does not tell us very much if we do not know

[2] A good treatment of budgetary control is to be found in *Cost and Budget Analysis* by John Dearden, Englewood Cliffs, N. J.: Prentice-Hall, Inc., 1962. *Business Budgeting* by Burnard H. Sord and Glenn A. Welsch, New York: Financial Executives Research Foundation (*formerly* Controllers Institute Research Foundation and Controllership Foundation), 1958, is an extensive survey of management planning and control practices. *The Impact of Budgets on People* by Chris Argyris, New York: Controllership Foundation, 1952, is a short but penetrating study of some of the human problems created by budgets.

whether last year's performance was satisfactory or not. The point about a comparison of actual performance with budget is that the assumptions on which the budget was based, and the level of performance which was built into it, will have been (or at least should have been) carefully specified when the budget was drawn up. It should therefore be possible to say not merely whether results are better or worse than they previously were, but how good or how bad they are on some predetermined scale. It is the difference, in fact, between having a thermometer to measure today's temperature as against merely being able to say that today is colder than it was yesterday.

It is exceedingly difficult, if not impossible, to separate the control uses of budgets from their role as an embodiment of the firm's plans. This double role is not without its difficulty, for what constitutes a "good" budget from one point of view may not be so "good" from the other. For planning to be effective, it must be realistic. That is, it must be based on accurate forecasts of what will be achieved. For control purposes, on the other hand, it may be quite legitimate to encourage a division to set its sights a little higher than it can confidently be expected to achieve. There is a conflict of evidence as to whether, left to themselves, divisions will in fact tend to err on the side of optimism or of pessimism in drawing up their budgets. Some corporate controllers with whom the question was discussed thought that divisions generally kept something in hand and budgeted below their true capabilities so as to reduce the risk of failing to achieve their budget. Others thought that a divisional manager would rather be rebuked once, for failure to achieve his budget, than be rebuked twice, once for not aiming high enough and a second time for failure to do well enough. Whichever of these views is right, the point is that both of them seem to expect characteristics of budgets, when they are used for control purposes, which are not altogether consistent with what is required from a realistic plan. This suggests that control budgets should, perhaps, not necessarily be identical with planning budgets. However, the ideal to be aimed at is clearly that the same set of figures should serve both purposes.

## Divisional Responsibility for Budgets and Its Limitation

There is widespread acceptance of the idea that those held answerable for failure to achieve a specified level of performance should have participated in setting that level. At least, they should have accepted it as a reasonable one, one by which they are prepared to be judged. However, while all financial men pay lip service to these ideas, they may mean very different things by "participation" and "acceptance." As Argyris points out,[3] this may sometimes be only "pseudo-participation" with the forms of participation in setting budget levels and accepting them, but without the substance thereof. This danger, however, is likely to be more serious at lower levels of management (among the plant supervisors whom Argyris questioned, for example) than among divisional managers, who are both financially more literate themselves and have financial staffs to assist them. Even at this level, pseudo-participation is not unknown. But usually divisions do exercise a genuine responsibility for preparing their own budgets.

This responsibility, however, is exercised within limits. If it were not so, corporate management would presumably be bound to accept the judgment of the division management about the results to be expected of it. This is not a position which corporate management is likely to accept. It is, it is true, reasonable for those in charge of a division to claim that they understand its problems better than anyone else. On the other hand, top management can fairly claim to enjoy a broader view, and to know better how the plans of other divisions may impinge on any one of them. More important, perhaps, it knows which of the DGM's can be expected to err on the side of overoptimism, which on the side of excessive caution. Fortunately, the budgetary procedure can provide some built-in checks designed to prevent divisional and head office thinking about the future from moving too far apart.

The principal means of coordination are usually embodied in a planning or budget manual. In virtually all divisionalized companies, the corporate financial management provides divisional managements with a manual of instructions setting out in detail how they are to exercise their budgetary responsibilities. The major purposes of one such manual are quoted at length here because they provide a good description of the more important ways in which central direction is imposed on divisional budgeting without reducing divisional participation in the process to pseudo-participation:

---

[3] Chris Argyris, *The Impact of Budgets on People,* New York: Controllership Foundation, Inc., 1952, p. 28.

The major purposes of this planning manual are to

1. Set forth in one place applicable policy statements (or references thereto) and interpretations which describe the approach desired by company management in the development and conduct of the annual planning program by the divisions.
2. Provide company-wide assumptions and other planning data which are not readily available to divisions and which require consistent representation by all participants in the planning program.
3. Recommend guidelines which may assist divisions in analyzing and evaluating their performance budget proposals.
4. Delineate the specific information required from divisions which summarize, in financial terms, the *results* of their annual planning process, and which also serves to:

    a. Provide the organized financial planning data for evaluation of the course(s) of action proposed for the conduct of the company's businesses.
    b. Establish a specific performance commitment for [the budget year] by each division to the president of the company.
    c. Provide the basis for development of the company budgets for [the budget year].
    d. Establish standards against which actual performance for [the budget year] will be measured. To assure that such standards are useful as control tools to division management and to the company, the profit budget and the asset budget will be constructed within the responsibility accounting policies and procedures set forth in the finance policy and procedure manual.
    e. Provide for a review of critical planning parameters extending through [the next four years] so that the company may properly consider earnings and investment requirements relative to its over-all objectives.

5. Suggest methods and techniques for developing and expressing basic planning data so that corollary use may be made of this information for short-term planning and analysis, and in the evaluation of alternatives to aid in day-to-day decision-making.

The manual secures, by several different means, the coordination of divisional policies with corporate policies. There is, first, a statement by corporate management of its basic economic assumptions about conditions within which the company and its divisions will operate during the planning cycle (defined by this company as the next four years). Divisions are required to modify these assumptions in the light of certain specific considerations which they are to examine before proceeding to prepare their own budgets. Then there is a statement of over-all financial objectives which have been established by the company based upon analysis of the current and immediate future business activities which constitute the company and the general performance rates which could logically be expected from such types and mix of businesses. The objectives are stated in terms of a specified percentage return on sales, a rate of asset turnover, and a resulting return on assets employed but, of course, alternative ways of stating these objectives might have been chosen. The statement of general company objectives does not render unnecessary the formulation of separate divisional long-term objectives. Indeed, divisions are specifically required to develop such objectives for their particular businesses with the help of the corporate financial staff and with the concurrence, when the objectives have been formulated, of the corporate management.

Some companies, not content simply with long-term objectives for the divisions, give divisions a target to aim at more directly in their budgets for the ensuing year. This target may be one of over-all profitability. It may be in terms of a specific task, e.g., to achieve a specified percentage improvement in sales or a specified reduction in costs. Formulating this objective *before* the division presents its budget, it is claimed, makes it much easier for the division to accept it. Once the budget has been drawn up, it is likely to become a matter of divisional pride to stand by it, to find reasons why it should not be altered. To set up the target first, to get the division to build that target into its budget, is to associate the division with it much more closely. The result is a correspondingly greater chance of winning the division's commitment to achieving the agreed-on goal.

Long-range forecasts, are, nevertheless, useful in providing guidelines within which short-term budgets are to be drawn up. Most companies look more than one year ahead, and some look as many as 15 years into the future. Five years is common for the long-term view, with less and less detail being filled in for the remoter part of the quinquennium. Long-term budgeting, quite apart from its value in helping to cordinate corporate and divisional planning, has a salutary effect on divisional management in that it diminishes the risk of overemphasizing short-run success at the expense of the long view.

If divisions have to think about long-run results every year, when the long-term forecast is revised, the effect of their immediate plans on the less immediate success of the business can hardly be overlooked.

The budgeting timetable itself provides further means of achieving coordination. The company whose budget manual has already been referred to divides its planning program into two distinct phases. First are the preliminary discussions between divisions and head office which take place during the first half of September. Before they are held, however, divisions must submit estimates of net sales by product lines, product costs and other division costs (totals only for each), division margin, profit after tax, new capital requirements (total only), total assets employed and manpower (in a few broad categories). These estimates are for the ensuing year and for three years thereafter. The budget and the forecast actual figures for the current year are also shown on the form. The causes of divergence between the current year's forecast actual results and next year's estimates have to be explained at this stage.

When agreement in these preliminary discussions of the division's broad plans has been reached, the volumes and prices of interdivisional transfers are negotiated between divisions. Buying divisions make their requirements known by the end of September, and the acceptance of these "orders" by supplying divisions is settled early in October. Divisions complete their budgets by the end of October; submit them to head office at the beginning of November; and the review by head office is completed by the end of the third week of November. While the divisions break down their budgets by months during a further two and one-half weeks, the company proceeds with consolidation of the divisional budgets and its own staff department budgets. There is a final review of the budget prior to its approval just before Christmas.

But suppose that, in spite of all that can be done to keep divisional and head office plans in step, top management is dissatisfied with a division's budget when it finally comes to head office for approval. It can, of course, be sent back for revision, with reasons why the revision is requested. These reasons may or may not commend themselves to the division. If they do not, then the best procedure seems to be to leave the division with its own budget, but to make an appropriate adjustment in the head office consolidation of the divisional budgets to bring the division's contribution to the corporate results into line with what top management thinks it will be. Such an adjustment, up or down, would be made without notifying the division, in order to make the corporation's plans more realistic. This procedure exemplifies the distinction between control budgets and planning budgets, for though the head office figures will have been adjusted in the interests of realistic planning, it seems appropriate that the division should still be judged by reference to its own forecasts.

## Budget Revisions

The distinction between the planning and control uses of budgets again comes to the fore when the question arises of revising a division's budget during the budget year because of changed circumstances or new information. For planning purposes, it is generally agreed that it is futile to cling to a plan once it has become evident that events have passed it by. Many companies require divisions to revise their budgets quarterly; sometimes, however, a moving forecast of the next three months is presented on a monthly basis. However the revision is made, no one argues that the original budget should be adhered to for planning purposes, once it has ceased to embody current expectations.

There is not the same unanimity, on the other hand, as to whether actual performance should be compared with the original budget or with later revisions. The case for using the original budget is that it alone represents the formal target agreed on between the division and corporate management, and to abandon it as the basis for judging the division as soon as conditions look adverse may be tantamount to accepting an excuse as a reason. The case for using the revised budget as the bench mark is that to do otherwise is to require the division to report and explain the same variances month after month, once the impossibility of attaining the original budget has become obvious. This is a persuasive argument. The revision of the budget will be known to those by whom the division's performance is being judged and they may, therefore, be presumed to understand the significance of the variances being currently reported.

In an attempt to get the best of both worlds, however, some companies compare current actual figures both with the original budget and a revised "forecast" (this word is sometimes used to distinguish the revised figures from the original "budget"). Then the deviation, if any, between actual performance and both the original targets and the targets as revised in the light of more recent knowledge can be examined.

## Cost Control and Flexible Budgets

The significance of variations from budget, so far as costs are concerned, depends on the nature of the costs in question. A distinction is commonly made between variable costs, period costs, and programmed costs, and this distinction is a very useful one. *Variable costs* (which differ with the level of activity) will ordinarily be limited to direct costs of manufacturing and to some direct costs of selling and distribution. *Period costs* (such as administrative salaries, fixed and semifixed manufacturing overhead, other occupancy expenses and similar items) are more a function of time than of activity, although many important items in this category, such as clerical salaries or storekeeping expenses, will show some variability with the volume of production or sales. *Programmed costs* (such as advertising, sales promotion and research and development) are not directly related to current activity but are determined by managerial decision. It is clear that different methods are appropriate for controlling each of these three cost categories.

Variable costs are best controlled by the use of standards. Differences between the actual and standard costs of products manufactured in a division's plants will then be analyzed and explained by means of the variances thrown up by the system of standard costs. So will variances between actual and budgeted plant period costs which are included in the division's product costs. Detailed consideration of plant cost variances will be the responsibility of plant managers and, if serious enough, of division management. Normally they would not demand the attention of the corporate management. For divisional budgeting and reporting, it is enough to show the cost of goods sold, perhaps broken down by products or product groups, but without showing its detailed make-up. The summary of manufacturing cost variances maintained by the division will enable it to explain variances between budgeted cost of goods sold and the actual cost.

Manufacturing overhead, though a period cost, will be included in the product standard costs of a manufacturing division unless the division is using direct costing. Differences between actual overhead and the overhead absorbed at standard rates will also appear as variances and will be analyzed accordingly. To calculate the volume variance, if any, a flexible budget will be used to give the expense allowances appropriate to the achieved level of activity for comparison with the actual expenses. If direct costing is used, manufacturing overhead will not be taken up in the product standard costs, but the use of a flexible budget to enable a distinction to be drawn between a spending variance and a volume variance need not thereby be affected.

When we turn to administrative expenses and indirect selling and distribution expenses, flexible budgets seem to be a less popular means than might have been expected of accounting for variances between budget and actual expense. The reasons given for not using flexible budgets are not always very convincing. Thus the argument in favor of a fixed budget that it puts pressure on for economy in expenses when activity increases is all very well, but it ignores the opposite effect when activity falls. The argument that "flexible budgets are fine in theory but don't work in practice" is not borne out by those companies that have found that they can work in practice so long as enough effort is put into them.

A flexible or variable budget requires a very careful study of cost variability, using engineering cost studies, statistical investigations and any other methods that can be brought to bear on the problem. In budgeting the types of expense now under discussion, personnel is the governing factor in determining the level of expense, while equipment is at most an ancillary factor. Hence, the first step in the construction of a flexible budget will be to set up manning tables showing the numbers and categories of personnel needed at varying levels of activity. From this table a "stepped" budget of wages and salaries, fringe benefits and other attendant expenses can be derived.

Flexible budgeting applied to divisions provides for budget revisions in advance of events. There seems *a priori* much to be said in favor of requiring a division to give thought, at the time its budget is being prepared, to the effect that any change in the level of activity may be expected to have on expenditures. If the relationships between activity and expense can be agreed on between the division and corporate management as a routine part of budget preparation, some of the rancor which later budget revisions may generate can probably be eliminated. Investigation of the causes of variation in activity are not rendered unnecessary, of course, by flexible budgeting. Given the variation in activity, and with the expense variation likely to accompany it having already been determined, it becomes necessary only to investigate variances from this predetermined level of expense.

## Reporting Against Budget

Even if no comparison of actual performance with budget were ever carried out, the preparation of a budget would be a very worthwhile exercise, for it would formalize the planning process and raise it to a higher level of effectiveness. However, its use as a bench mark against which to measure actual performance obviously gives the budget great added value. The commonest reporting interval is the calendar month or the 4-4-5 (weeks) arrangement, but there is a growing tendency to report only the broad outlines of the operating picture every month, with fuller reports being rendered quarterly. To speed up the interim reports, all relatively fixed expenses may be prorated monthly on the basis of the budget figures, with departures from budget being picked up in the "actual" figures only at the end of the year or in the final quarter.

Since profit reporting has been discussed at length in previous chapters, it will not be taken up again here, nor will methods of analyzing variances between budget and actual results be discussed. Many companies are content merely to report actual results side by side with the original budget, but it is impossible to know what significance to attach to the deviations from budget when this is done. As a minimum, it seems desirable to reconcile budget and actual results by showing how much of the total variance between them is attributable to the following causes:

Sales price
Sales mix
Sales volume
Production efficiency
Production volume
Raw material prices
Wage rates
Expense variances
Variances from budgeted programmed costs.

It is dangerous, however, to generalize about what information concerning its divisions is important to a particular company. If, for example, all the products of a particular division show much the same rate of gross margin, sales mix will not be important. In a division with little or no manufacturing activities production variances can be ignored and, in a regulated industry, sales prices are unlikely to be an important cause of variation from budget. Ultimately, each company, and each division of each company, has to decide what information is needed to illuminate the truly significant aspects of its operating performance.

## Capital Expenditure Budgets[4]

However much autonomy divisions may enjoy in other matters, however much the management of a division may be encouraged to behave as if it were running an independent business, one ultimate form of control over divisions by corporate management will invariably be maintained: that is the control of capital spending. Such control is really very far-reaching for it is virtually impossible for a division to introduce new products or otherwise to change the nature of its business without spending money on new facilities. When it does so, the corporate control of investment steps in and makes itself felt.

Most companies submit capital expenditure proposals to a double scrutiny. The first one takes place when the division's budget comes up for approval. The amount of information to be submitted about a capital project will depend to some extent on the nature of the project—whether it is concerned (to use one company's classification) with voluntary improvements not resulting in a measurable return, or with cost-saving, or with the retention or expansion of sales. In any case, enough financial information will have to be given to enable the company's budget committee (or whoever carries out the function of a budget committee) to approve its claim for funds in competition with the claims of other projects from other divisions. The second scrutiny of capital expenditure proposals comes when the actual expenditure or commitment of funds has to be authorized. DGMs always have a limited authority to spend on investment projects. In some companies this limit is as low as $2,000, in others it goes as high as $150,000; most companies seem to place the limit at $25,000 or $50,000 for projects specifically included in the capital budget, with a substantially lower limit for unlisted projects. Higher and higher limits for authorized expenditures will usually be placed on the power vested in an executive vice president, the president, the executive committee of the board of directors, and the full board itself. In effect, then, the second scrutiny of smaller projects is carried out within the division itself. Indeed, since quite small projects, say up to $2,500, will usually be included in a "blanket" item in the division's capital budget, the first scrutiny of such projects is carried out there.

---

[4] A much fuller study of this area than is possible here will be found in *Managing Capital Expenditures* by Norman E. Pflomm, Business Policy Study No. 107, New York: National Industrial Conference Board, 1963.

On the other hand, one of the companies participating in this study dispenses with a capital budget and goes straight to the "spending authorization" stage. Every project has to be justified before the money is appropriated for it. Needless to say, the cash position of this company is a fairly easy one, and its procedure is quite unusual.

The advantages of taking a long view of normal operations have already been emphasized, and for progressive companies, which usually have more openings for investment than they have capital to invest, a long view of their capital investment plans is essential if a rational choice between alternative opportunities is to be made and funds are not to be wasted by being used in a hand-to-mouth manner. Hence, a five-year investment plan is commonly called for from divisions. Often an estimate is required, though with few, if any, details of what capital will be required at a still more remote time.

Nothing has a more direct impact on a company's future than the means used to select those investment projects which are to be approved and those which are to be rejected or at least to be held up. This problem of "capital rationing" has become, in recent years, the subject of a vast literature,[5] and we shall not examine here the relative merits of payback, rate of return, discounted cash flow, present value and other selection methods, all of which have their adherents. The best of these methods cannot be better than the predictions that go into them, and this is often used as a defense of the less sophisticated methods such as payback. It is quite right to remind ourselves that a sophisticated manipulation of erroneous data may be worse than a waste of time. However, assuming that a company and its divisions have done the best they can to read the future, it seems foolish to waste this effort by not making the best use of the data, even at a cost of some extra man-hours of financial analysis. It is very unlikely that this cost, with all the means of rapid computation now available, will approach the possible loss resulting from an ill-directed investment.

The selection of projects for inclusion in a division's capital budget, the approval of the budget, the authorization of the expenditure, the audit of the expenditure, and the bringing of the project into operation, is not quite the end of the story so far as financial control is concerned. Just as operating results are compared with budget, both

[5] See Chapter 4 of *Managing Capital Expenditures,* already referred to. A short bibliography appears on p. 59 thereof, and further references will be found in the bibliography at the end of this study.

to evaluate the results and to ensure conscientious budgeting, so the results of investment projects must be compared with expectations. Irresponsibility will creep into capital budgeting if it becomes known that claims made by divisions for projects sponsored by them will never be brought home to their door. The postaudit of all sizeable capital projects is essential, both to ensure conscientious budgeting and to gain whatever insight can be gained from past successes and failures. A common arrangement is to look at the results of a project 12 months after it goes into operation, but additional earlier and later audits are not unusual, especially for large projects or for projects not going according to plan. There is, of course, not the same need to carry out a postaudit of projects included in the budget on nonpecuniary grounds rather than on the basis of an expected measurable return. However, this points up the need for caution in accepting nonpecuniary justifications for investment proposals. Only rarely is it that nothing at all can be said about the effect of an investment on costs and revenues and divisions should be pressed to seek out such information even for projects which are not purely profit-seeking.

# A CASE STUDY IN BUDGETARY CONTROL OF DIVISIONS

# Appendix C to Chapter VII

In this appendix, an effective budget system is described—effective, th is, for the company for which it has been designed. It goes without sayin that not everything in it will be appropriate to other companies an smaller companies, particularly, will usually not need anything so elaborat

The company whose system is to be described has a national and inte national reputation and is a leader in its field. A good deal of its busine is done with the building trade, and it sells direct to contractors and wholesalers and, through its own wholesale division, to retailers. For mo budgetary purposes, the company looks five years ahead. The "budg year" and the next succeeding year constitute what is called the "planne period," and the last three years of the five-year period are the "projecte period." More detail is required for the planned period than for the lat period. A corporate budget review committee, made up of corporate e ecutives, is appointed each year by the president to review the division budgets and those of the central staff departments.

Exhibit XXV summarizes the company's annual profit plan, which cal for considerably less detail for the projected period (the last three years the five-year period) than for the planned period (the first two years Supporting schedules in respect of the planned period are shown in su sequent exhibits. The information about interdivisional sales and depreci tion at the foot of Exhibit XXV draws particular attention to items whic have already been included in the revenues and expenses shown earlier the statement. There is a separate supporting schedule of interdivisional sal and purchases, and the selling division is required to cross-check these wi the purchasing division. The budget for the projected period is obtained b projecting the expected results of the planned period, specifically takin into account the expected effects of such profit determinants as planne additions to or abandonment of facilities, cyclical movements in industri served by the divisions, planned results of cost reduction programs (r ferred to below), the planned introduction of new products, and know changes of material and labor costs resulting from long-term contracts

# EXHIBIT XXV

## STATEMENT OF INCOME

| Current Year 19— | | | | | Planned Period | | | | Projected Period | | | | | |
|---|---|---|---|---|---|---|---|---|---|---|---|---|---|---|
| Budget | % | Est. Actual | % | | 19— Budget | % | 19— Yr. 2 | % | 19— Yr. 3 | % | 19— Yr. 4 | % | 19— Yr. 5 | % |
| | | | | Gross sales | | | | | xxx | | xxx | | xxx | |
| | | | | Returns, allow., disc. | | | | | xxx | | xxx | | xxx | |
| | 100 | | 100 | NET SALES | | 100 | | 100 | | 100 | | 1.00 | | 100 |
| | | | | Cost of goods sold | | | | | | | | | | |
| | | | | Gross profit | | | | | | | | | | |
| | | | | Operating expense | | | | | | | | | | |
| | | | | Adm. and gen. expense | | | | | xxx | | xxx | | xxx | |
| | | | | Selling expense | | | | | xxx | | xxx | | xxx | |
| | | | | Adv. and sales promotion | | | | | xxx | | xxx | | xxx | |
| | | | | Research and development | | | | | xxx | | xxx | | xxx | |
| | | | | Admin. service charge | | | | | xxx | | xxx | | xxx | |
| | | | | Total operating expense | | | | | | | | | | |
| | | | | Operating income | | | | | | | | | | |
| | | | | Other charges (net) | | | | | | | | | | |
| | | | | PRE-TAX INCOME | | | | | | | | | | |
| | | | | Interdiv. net sales | | | | | | | | | | |
| | | | | U. S. | | | | | xxx | | xxx | | xxx | |
| | | | | Foreign | | | | | xxx | | xxx | | xxx | |
| | | | | Deprec. and amortization | | | | | | | | | | |

statutory requirements. The *general* effects of expected price-level changes are recognized in the statement only for the budget year, but not for later years of the period.

A breakdown of the planned results for the first two years between a division's main product groups[6] is called for, as shown in Exhibit XXVI. Return on investment (defined by this company as return on average gross assets for the year, including cash calculated as a percentage of annual net sales) is also computed by product groups on this form. Only nonoperating income or losses and excess or idle assets are allowed to escape allocation. Other supporting schedules follow. Exhibit XXVII shows net sales and gross profits by product lines for the budget year and second year; Exhibit XXVIII shows details of budgeted export operations for the same two years; Exhibit XXIX gives the breakdown by months of the statement of income for the budget year only, and Exhibit XXX sets out the division's expectations of the cash it will generate during the five-year period.

A separate statement (not reproduced) covers cash generation by foreign subsidiaries. Other statements (also not reproduced) showing supporting detail for the annual profit statement cover the financial figures for the budget year and second year, and the financial figures for the budget year itself are in turn supported by manning tables covering manufacturing, selling, sales promotion and advertising, research and development and administrative activities. The manning tables relating to salaried personnel also provide a reconciliation of salaries for the budget year with those for the current year, showing how any difference between the two years arises through personnel accessions and terminations, merit increases and other changes.

A particularly interesting feature of this company's budget system is the profit improvement plan which forms part of the annual budget. Each division is required to identify areas within its operations that fail to show

---

[6] The way in which a division classifies its products in product groups is a matter left to the division itself. A product group is defined by the company as "a group of closely related product lines homogeneous with respect to market, or more particularly with respect to function of the product within the market in which it competes." It is recognized that what constitutes a "product group" within a division may be determined or at least influenced by industry-wide reporting practices. The criteria by which product groups may be recognized include (a) the products' ultimate users, (b) marketing methods or channels of distribution, (c) design technicalities or operating characteristics. Where these criteria result in very large product groups, it may be desirable to split them into several smaller groups. A "product line" within a product group is defined as having the characteristics of (a) similarity of function, material and process of manufacture and (b) a common denominator in which to express sales and production quantitatively.

# EXHIBIT XXVI

## STATEMENT OF INCOME AND RETURN ON INVESTMENT BY PRODUCT GROUPS

| | Total Division | | | | | | (Product Group) | | | | | | (Product Group) | | | | | | Items Not Allocated | | | |
|---|---|---|---|---|---|---|---|---|---|---|---|---|---|---|---|---|---|---|---|---|---|---|
| | 19— Curr. | % | 19— Budg. | % | 19— Yr. 2 | % | 19— Curr. | % | 19— Budg. | % | 19— Yr. 2 | % | 19— Curr. | % | 19— Budg. | % | 19— Yr. 2 | % | 19— Curr. | 19— Budg. | 19— Yr. 2 | % |
| NET SALES | | 100 | | 100 | | 100 | | 100 | | 100 | | 100 | | 100 | | 100 | | 100 | xxx | xxx | xxx | 100 |
| Cost of goods sold | | | | | | | | | | | | | | | | | | | xxx | xxx | xxx | |
| Gross profit | | | | | | | | | | | | | | | | | | | xxx | xxx | xxx | |
| Operating expense | | | | | | | | | | | | | | | | | | | | | | |
| Adm. & gen. exp. | | | | | | | | | | | | | | | | | | | xxx | xxx | xxx | |
| Selling expense | | | | | | | | | | | | | | | | | | | xxx | xxx | xxx | |
| Adv. & sales prom. | | | | | | | | | | | | | | | | | | | xxx | xxx | xxx | |
| Res. & development | | | | | | | | | | | | | | | | | | | xxx | xxx | xxx | |
| Adm. serv. charge | | | | | | | | | | | | | | | | | | | xxx | xxx | xxx | |
| Total operating exp. | | | | | | | | | | | | | | | | | | | xxx | xxx | xxx | |
| Operating income | | | | | | | | | | | | | | | | | | | | | | |
| Other charges (net) | | | | | | | | | | | | | | | | | | | | | | |
| PRE-TAX INCOME | | | | | | | | | | | | | | | | | | | | | | |
| Gross assets | | | | | | | | | | | | | | | | | | | | | | |
| Asset turnover | | | | | | | | | | | | | | | | | | | xxx | xxx | xxx | |
| ROI | | | | | | | | | | | | | | | | | | | xxx | xxx | xxx | |

## EXHIBIT XXVII

### NET SALES AND GROSS PROFIT BY PRODUCT LINES

| | 19— Est. Actual — Current Year | | | | 19— Budget Year | | | | 19— Yr. 2 | | | |
|---|---|---|---|---|---|---|---|---|---|---|---|---|
| | Net Sales | | Gross Profit | % | Net Sales | | Gross Profit | % | Net Sales | | Gross Profit | % |
| | Units | $ | | | Units | $ | | | Units | $ | | |
| (Product Group) | | | | | | | | | | | | |
| (Product Lines—List) | | | | | | | | | | | | |
| Total (Product Group) | xxxx | | | | xxxx | | | | xxxx | | | |
| (Product Group) | | | | | | | | | | | | |
| (Product Lines—List) | | | | | | | | | | | | |
| Total (Product Group) | xxxx | | | | xxxx | | | | xxxx | | | |

— etc. —

EXCEPTION: Wholesale division will·furnish net sales and gross profit by branches in lieu of this schedule.

EXHIBIT XXVIII

EXPORT OPERATIONS
STATEMENT OF INCOME
MEMO ONLY

| | 19— Current Year | % | Planned Period 19— Budget | % | 19— Yr. 2 | % |
|---|---|---|---|---|---|---|
| Export sales | | | | | | |
| Sales for export | —— | —— | —— | —— | —— | —— |
| TOTAL NET SALES | | 100 | | 100 | | 100 |
| Cost of goods sold | —— | | —— | | —— | |
| Gross profit | —— | | —— | | —— | |
| Operating expense—direct | | | | | | |
| Export admin. charge | | | | | | |
| Agents' commissions | | | | | | |
| Advertising | | | | | | |
| Research and development | —— | | —— | | —— | |
| | —— | | —— | | —— | |
| Operating expense—allocated | | | | | | |
| Admin. and general expense | | | | | | |
| Selling expense | | | | | | |
| Adv. and sales promotion | | | | | | |
| New York admin. charge | —— | | —— | | —— | |
| | —— | | —— | | —— | |
| Total operating expense | —— | | —— | | —— | |
| Operating income | | | | | | |
| Other charges (net) | —— | | —— | | —— | |
| PRE-TAX INCOME | ==== | | ==== | | ==== | |

an acceptable return on investment. An "area" means, for a manufacturing division, a product group or (better still) a product line, and for the wholesale division it means a branch. Return on investment is recognized as a function of the rate of profit on sales and the rate of turnover of investment, and profit improvement programs are therefore to be directed at either increasing sales proceeds (through increases in volume and/or price), reducing costs or reducing the ratio of assets to sales.

For each product group which fails to show the minimum acceptable return on investment, a profit improvement summary (Exhibit XXXI) has to be prepared, and the figures for this statement are derived from the listings of detailed programs on Exhibits XXXI (a), (b), and (c). The letters on Exhibit XXXI are keyed to the corresponding letters on

## EXHIBIT XXIX

### STATEMENT OF INCOME
### BUDGET YEAR 19—

| | J | F | M | A | … | O | N | D | Total |
|---|---|---|---|---|---|---|---|---|---|
| Gross sales | | | | | | | | | |
| Returns, allow. & disc. | | | | | | | | | |
| NET SALES | | | | | | | | | |
| Cost of goods sold | | | | | | | | | |
| Gross profit | | | | | | | | | |
| Operating expense | | | | | | | | | |
| Adm. and general expense | | | | | | | | | |
| Selling expense | | | | | | | | | |
| Adv. and sales promotion | | | | | | | | | |
| Research and development | | | | | | | | | |
| Adm. service charge | | | | | | | | | |
| Total operating expense | | | | | | | | | |
| Operating income | | | | | | | | | |
| Other charges (net) | | | | | | | | | |
| PRE-TAX INCOME | | | | | | | | | |
| Interdivision net sales —U. S. | | | | | | | | | |
| Interdivision net sales —Foreign | | | | | | | | | |

EXHIBIT XXX

CASH GENERATION

| | Planned Period | | Projected Period | | |
|---|---|---|---|---|---|
| | 19— Budget | 19— Yr. 2 | 19— Yr. 3 | 19— Yr. 4 | 19— Yr. 5 |
| PRE-TAX INCOME | | | | | |
| Add: | | | | | |
| Depreciation & Amortization | | | | | |
| Gross Cash Generation | | | | | |
| Less: | | | | | |
| Capital Expenditures | | | | | |
| Increase (or decrease) in working capital, other than cash | | | | | |
| Increase (or decrease) in other balance sheet accounts (net) | | | | | |
| NET CASH GENERATION | | | | | |

the three related exhibits, which show how the figures in the profit improvement summary are obtained. It is, of course, the detailed programs for profit improvement which are the important part of this system. First, the gap between the standard of performance aimed at for the product group and the standard presently obtained has to be quantitatively defined. Then the programs to increase sales volume, to reduce costs or to reduce investment are listed, with their expected effect on income and investment.

As examples of sales increasing programs, the company lists programs to increase sales revenue per unit sold (e.g., by improving quality), pricing programs, programs to improve distribution, delivery or service, programs of sales training, advertising and sales promotion, and programs to expand capacity. This list is merely illustrative, not exhaustive. A similar list could be given of cost decreasing and investment minimizing programs. When the division has made its plans to raise the profitability of a particular product group, the final result on the profit improvement summary, in the columns headed "goals," will be to show that the minimum acceptable return on investment for the product group either can or cannot be achieved. If it can be achieved, the division is expected to proceed with the implementation of its programs once its budget has been approved. If it cannot be achieved, the division is expected to present plans for the discontinuance of the product group, or for one or more of its product lines.

## EXHIBIT XXXI

### PROFIT IMPROVEMENT SUMMARY
### (PRODUCT GROUP)

| | | Sales Increasing Programs | | Cost Decreasing Programs | | Asset Minimizing Programs | | Goals | |
|---|---|---|---|---|---|---|---|---|---|
| | 19— Current Year | 19— Budget | 19— Yr. 2 | 19— Budget | 19— Yr. 2 | 19— Budget | 19— Yr. 2 | 19— Budget | 19— Yr. 2 |
| Net sales | | A | D | | | | | | |
| Cost of sales | | B | E | G | I | | | | |
| Gross profit % of net sales | | | | | | | | | |
| Operating expense | | C | F | H | J | | | | |
| Pre-tax income Margin (% N.S.) | | | | | | | | | |
| Inventory | | | | | | K | N | | |
| Other working capital | | | | | | L | O | | |
| Fixed assets | | | | | | M | P | | |
| Total | | | | | | | | | |
| Asset turnover (Net Sales ÷ Gross Assets) | | | | | | | | | |
| ROI (Margin × Turnover) | | | | | | | | | |

NOTE: Amounts shown for budget and second year under sales increasing, cost decreasing and asset minimizing programs represent only incremental profit and asset improvement for each year. Goals for budget year represent add-through of current year and three budget columns. Goals for second year represent add-through of all columns. Alphabetic references are to Exhibits XXXI (a), (b), and (c).

## EXHIBIT XXXI (a)

### SALES INCREASING PROGRAMS
### (PRODUCT GROUP)

| | Increased Sales Volume or Realization | Cost of Increased Volume | Increase (Decrease) Expense |
|---|---|---|---|
| **Budget Year 19—** | | | |
| List specific programs for the budget year and carry totals forward to Exhibit XXXI as indicated ...................... | (A) | (B) | (C) |
| Totals | | | |
| **Second Year 19—** | | | |
| List specific programs for the second year and carry totals forward to Exhibit XXXI as indicated ...................... | (D) | (E) | (F) |
| Totals | | | |

NOTE: The additional inventories, receivables and fixed assets required to support increased sales volume should be footnoted on this schedule and the amounts carried forward to Exhibit XXXI opposite the appropriate caption in the sales increasing column.

EXHIBIT XXXI (b)

COST DECREASING PROGRAMS
(PRODUCT GROUP)

| | Manufacturing Cost Reductions | Operating Expense Reductions |
|---|---|---|
| **Budget Year 19—** | | |
| List specific programs for the budget year and carry totals forward to Exhibit XXXI as indicated . . . . . . . . . . . . . . . . . . . . . | (G) | (H) |
| Totals | | |
| **Second Year 19—** | | |
| List specific programs for the second year and carry totals forward to Exhibit XXXI as indicated . . . . . . . . . . . . . . . . . . . . . | (I) | (J) |
| Totals | | |

This final step, the discontinuance of a product group or product line, needs to be approached with circumspection, for the failure to achieve or to show prospects of accomplishing a desired rate of return on investment (investment being defined as the amount historically invested in assets) does not automatically point to the wisdom of abandoning the products. An abandonment decision has to be taken in the light of the amount of the investment which can be *taken out* of a project, not the amount

EXHIBIT XXXI (c)

ASSET MINIMIZING PROGRAMS
(PRODUCT GROUP)

| | Reductions In | | |
|---|---|---|---|
| | Inventory | Other Working Capital | Fixed Assets |
| **Budget Year 19—** | | | |
| List *specific* programs for the budget year and carry totals forward to Exhibit XXXI as indicated . . . . . . . . . . . . . . . . . . . . . | (K) | (L) | (M) |
| Totals | | | |
| **Second Year 19—** | | | |
| List *specific* programs for the second year and carry totals forward to Exhibit XXXI as indicated . . . . . . . . . . . . . . . . . . . . . | (N) | (O) | (P) |
| Totals | | | |

originally put into it. As pointed out earlier, abandonment decisions need to be examined with the help of *ad hoc* computations rather than by reference to data collected for other purposes. In this one respect, therefore, the profit improvement plan just described raises a doubt about its desirability; but in all others it should repay careful study by other companies. Incidentally, it is easily adaptable to the use of residual income instead of return on investment as a criterion of performance (in ac-

EXHIBIT XXXII

RESEARCH AND DEVELOPMENT EXPENSE

| Responsibility | 19— Current Year | Planned Period 19— Budget | Planned Period 19— Yr. 2 |
|---|---|---|---|
| Research | | | |
| (location) | | | |
| Product development | | | |
| (location) | | | |
| Product engineering | | | |
| (location) | | | |
| Totals | | | |

cordance with the recommendations made in earlier chapters), for increases in sales, reductions in cost, and reductions in investment are the factors which must be looked to for an increase in residual income, as well as for an increase in the rate of return.

The company classifies its research and development activities into three categories and requires divisions to budget accordingly:

*Research:* Scientific investigation directed ultimately to the creation of a new product, process, or other specific end result.

*Product development:* The use of research findings and other scientific data to improve an existing product or to develop a prototype or model of a proposed new product in commercial form.

*Product engineering:* Work beyond the development stage to bring a prototype or model of a new or improved product to a form suitable for normal production and marketing.

These classifications appear in Exhibit XXXII, which summarizes research and development expenses, by the location at which the work is to be done, for the current year and the next two years.

All research and development projects having a total cost of $10,000 or more, or which represent more than ten per cent of the total cost of the division's research effort (whichever is less) must be listed on Exhibit XXXIII. Smaller projects are grouped together and are shown in total as

## EXHIBIT XXXIII

### RESEARCH AND DEVELOPMENT BY PRODUCTS

Related to Volume and Profit Objectives

| Project No. | Description | Cumulative Expense to End of Current Yr. | Budget Year: Hours | Budget Year: Total Expense | Expense in Subsequent Years | Total Amount | Completion Date | Objectives: Net Sales | Objectives: Added Annual Profit | Objectives: Year |
|---|---|---|---|---|---|---|---|---|---|---|
| | Improved Products | | | | | | | | | |
| | (List projects carried forward) | | | | | | | | | |
| | (List new projects) | xx | | | | | | | | |
| | Minor projects (combined) | | | | | | xxx | xx | xx | xx |
| | | | | | | | xxx | xx | xx | xx |
| | New Products | | | | | | | | | |
| | (List projects carried forward) | | | | | | | | | |
| | (List new pioiects) | xx | | | | | | | | |
| | Minor projects (combined) | | | | | | xxx | xx | xx | xx |
| | | | | | | | xxx | xx | xx | xx |
| | Totals(*) | | | | | | xxx | xx | xx | xx |

(*) Amounts in budget year should agree with totals on Exhibit XXXII.

EXHIBIT XXXIV

RESEARCH AND DEVELOPMENT BY PRODUCTS

Related to Added Facilities Requirements and Marketing Expense

| Project No. | Description | Total Amount of R&D Expense Per Exhibit XXXIII | Additional Facilities Requirements | | Additional Marketing Expense | |
|---|---|---|---|---|---|---|
| | | | Amount | Year | Amount | Year |
| Improved Products | | | | | | |
| (List projects carried forward) | | | | | | |
| (List new projects) | | | | | | |
| Minor projects (combined) | | ——— | ——— | xx | ——— | xx |
| | | ——— | ——— | xx | ——— | xx |
| New Products | | | | | | |
| (List projects carried forward) | | | | | | |
| (List new projects) | | | | | | |
| Minor projects (combined) | | ——— | ——— | xx | ——— | xx |
| | | ——— | ——— | xx | ——— | xx |
| Totals | | ═══ | ═══ | | ═══ | |

minor projects. Major projects are classified as relating either to improved products or new products, and projects to be initiated during the budget year are separated from those already started and continuing in the budget year. If a project is not expected to reach completion in the budget year, its total anticipated cost to completion has to be shown. The net sales and added annual profit shown in the right-hand columns of Exhibit XXXIII are those for a product's first full year of operation. Exhibit XXXIV shows, for the same list of projects, the capital outlay which each project will require, showing the year(s) in which the money will be spent, the added annual marketing expense which will result from the project, and the year(s) involved. The two exhibits together require divisions to think through, in a systematic manner, the cost and revenue implications of their research and development activities.

The last segment of a division's annual profit plan is that relating to capital expenditures. It does not directly affect the profit of the budget year in the same way as do other parts of the plan, but it does directly affect the corporation's cash position and its projected balance sheet, which we have yet to consider. A summary of a division's planned capital expenditures for the next five years, showing the years in which it is expected that expenditures will actually be made, is presented by the division on Exhibit XXXV, and all major capital projects (those costing $100,000 or more) planned for the first two years are listed on Exhibit

## EXHIBIT XXXV

### CAPITAL EXPENDITURES SUMMARY

| | | Planned Period | | | Projected Period | | |
|---|---|---|---|---|---|---|---|
| | | 19— Budget | | | | | |
| | 19— Current Year | Carry-over | New Projects | 19— Yr. 2 | 19— Yr. 3 | 19— Yr. 4 | 19— Yr. 5 |
| Class I—Normal & Necessary | | | | | | | |
| (a) Cost saving | | | | | xxx | xxx | xxx |
| (b) Product improvement | | | | | xxx | xxx | xxx |
| (c) Nonproductive | | | | | xxx | xxx | xxx |
| Class II—Expansion | | | | | | | |
| (a) New products | | | | | | | |
| (b) New and exp'd facilities | | | | | | | |
| Total capital expenditure | | | | | | | |
| Property expense (related to above) | | | | | xxx | xxx | xxx |

EXHIBIT XXXVI

MAJOR CAPITAL EXPENDITURES

| | Payback Period | Planned Period | | |
|---|---|---|---|---|
| | | 19— Budget | | 19— |
| | | Carry-over | New Proj's | Yr. 2 |
| **Class I—Normal & Necessary** | | | | |
| (a) Cost saving (list) | | | | |
| (b) Product improvement (list) | | | | |
| (c) Nonproductive (list) | | | | |
| **Class II—Expansion** | | | | |
| (a) New products (list) | | | | |
| (b) New & expanded facilities (list) | | | | |

NOTE: Describe and show amount of each project with capital expenditure of $100,000 or more.

XXXVI. Each of the projects involving expenditure in the budget year will have been the subject of a capital expenditure proposal (to be discussed later), and the proposal forms will be the source of the data for the year shown on Exhibit XXXVI. The company's classification of capital projects will be looked at in more detail shortly. For the last three years of the five year period, only the totals of the "normal and necessary" projects have to be shown on the summary. For the budget year, the figures of planned expenditure are divided between the continuance of projects started in the current or an earlier year and those to be started in the budget year. These budget year expenditures have their impact, naturally, on the cash budget for the budget year and the projected balance sheet at the end thereof.

The company classifies proposed capital expenditures into two broad categories and five subcategories as follows:

Class I—Normal and necessary replacements and improvements

(a) Cost saving
This category includes normal equipment replacement, obsolescence replacements and method changes. These projects require justification in terms of their effect on profits in the period required to recover the investment.

(b) Product improvement
These expenditures are to maintain or enhance competitive position and the maintenance of profits and sales, rather than their increase, may be the only result. The expected effect on profits and cash generation for two years has to be shown on the proposal form.

(c) Nonproductive
These are the proposals required for reasons of safety, employee relations, legal requirements, etc. The expected effect on profits (usually adverse) and on cash generation for two years must be shown in the proposal.

Class II—Expansion

These projects are to be justified in terms of annual return on investment and payback period, taking into account start-up costs, possible product obsolescence, and promotion costs. Class II projects are further subdivided into two subcategories:

(a) New products

(b) New and expanded facilities
This category primarily includes expenditures designed to increase production and sales of existing products.

All Class II expansion projects are required to show at least a specified minimum before-tax rate of return on investment; and these, as well as the Class I cost-saving projects, must comply with a specified minimum period of payback while at the same time holding out promise of a service life in excess of this minimum payback period.

Exhibits XXXVII and XXXVIII are examples of capital expenditure proposals, the first being of the cost-saving type, the second being an expansion project. The same form is used for all classes of proposal, though it is not always used in precisely the same way. For example, only expansion projects have to show the expected rate of return, though other

## EXHIBIT XXXVII

### COST SAVING (OBSOLESCENCE)
### CAPITAL BUDGET PROPOSAL

YEAR 19x1

| | |
|---|---|
| Fixed capital | $40,000 |
| Property expense | — |
| TOTAL | $40,000 |

DIVISION WIDGET
UNIT/DEPT. SPRINGFIELD PLANT

DESCRIPTION: Class Ia

One King or equal 42" Boring Mill with Keller attachment

BENEFITS TO BE OBTAINED:

**This tool will replace a Betts 42" mill, No. 342—purchased in 19— and now fully depreciated**

Record of performance of obsolete machine No. 342 is as follows:

| | |
|---|---|
| (1) Scrap penalty produced—$2,400*—against average of $300—12-month penalty | $ 2,900 |
| (2) Yearly excess of repair charges over average of modern tools | 1,200 |
| (3) Penalty on production values produced per year due to down time and slow operation | 7,000 |
| (4) Estimated dollar saving in straight time operator's rate per year on a Keller controlled tool, as compared to machine No. 342 | 3,200 |
| Total yearly profit from operation of proposed tool, as compared to machine 342 | $14,300 |

* For nine months of current year.

OTHER REMARKS (or data):

Savings of production penalty calculated based on new machine operating full time thus permitting Boring Dept. to maintain a budgeted level of production with less overtime and waste motion

INVESTMENT:

| | |
|---|---|
| Land | $ |
| Buildings | |
| Machinery and equipment | 40,000 |
| Other (specify) | |
| Fixed Capital | 40,000 |
| Additional working capital | |
| Total Investment | $40,000 |

OPERATIONAL DATA:

First complete year of normal operations 19x1
Return on investment expected that year ____
Investment will be recovered in 5 yrs.
Primary service life of project 20 yrs.

Project will start (month/year) Jan. 19x1
Project will be completed (month/year) Jan. 19x1

UNIT/DEPT.: DIVISION: CORPORATION:

## EXHIBIT XXXVII (reverse)

### a) EFFECT ON PROFIT

| | 19x1 | 19x2 | 19x3 | 19x4 | 19x5 | 19— |
|---|---|---|---|---|---|---|
| 1. Net sales | $ | $ | $ | $ | $ | $ |
| 2. Costs and expense | $ | $ | $ | $ | $ | $ |
| 3. Direct labor | (3,200) | | | | | |
| 4. Direct material | | | | | | |
| 5. Indirect labor | | | | | | |
| 6. Indirect material (scrap) | (2,900) | | | | | |
| 7. Depreciation (note)* | 3,800 | 3,600 | 3,400 | 3,200 | 3,000 | |
| 8. Other mfg. expense (repairs) | (1,200) | | | | | |
| 9. Start-up | | | | | | |
| 10. Obsolescence | | | | | | |
| 11. Operating expense | | | | | | |
| 12. Production penalty—down time and slow operation | (7,000) | | | | | |
| 13. Total costs and expense | (10,500) | (10,700) | (10,900) | (11,100) | (11,300) | $ |
| 14. Net profit before tax | $10,500 | $10,700 | $10,900 | $11,100 | $11,300 | $ |

### b) RETURN ON INVESTMENT

| Investment | | | | | | |
|---|---|---|---|---|---|---|
| 15. Land | $ | $ | $ | $ | $ | $ |
| 16. Buildings | | | | | | |
| 17. Machinery & equipment | | | | | | |
| 18. Other | | | | | | |
| 19. Fixed capital | $ | $ | $ | $ | $ | $ |
| 20. Accounts receivable | | | | | | |
| Inventories | | | | | | |
| 22. Total annual investment | $ | $ | $ | $ | $ | $ |
| 23. Cumulative total investment | $ | $ | $ | $ | $ | $ |
| 24. Return on investment (Line 14 ÷ Line 23) | % | % | % | % | % | % |

### c) CASH GENERATION

| | | | | | | |
|---|---|---|---|---|---|---|
| 25. 48% of Line 14 | $ 5,040 | $ 5,140 | $ 5,230 | $ 5,340 | $ 5,420 | $ |
| 26. Add: Dep'n & obsolescence (Lines 7 and 10) | 3,800 | 3,600 | 3,400 | 3,200 | 3,000 | |
| 27. Annual cash generation | $ 8,840 | $ 8,740 | $ 8,630 | $ 8,540 | $ 8,420 | $ |
| 28. Cumulative cash generation | $ 8,840 | $17,580 | $26,210 | $34,750 | $43,170 | $ |

**CAPITAL EXPENDITURES BY QUARTERS:**

| Budget year | |
|---|---|
| 1st Quarter | $40,000 |
| 2nd Quarter | – |
| 3rd Quarter | – |
| 4th Quarter | – |
| Following year(s) | – |

*NOTE: Depreciation will be calculated based on the current book method—i.e., sum-of-the-years digits, special amortization, etc.

Basis—20-year life

**PROPERTY EXPENSE:**

| | |
|---|---|
| Demolition and site clearance | $ |
| Moving existing equipment | |
| Repair & alterations to existing equipment | |
| Other (specify) | |
| Total (include in start-up costs—Line 9) | $ None |

**PROPERTY TO BE RETIRED:**

| | | |
|---|---|---|
| Betts 42" Mill No. 342 | Book value | $18,500 |
| Purchased 1926 | Accum. dep'n | 18,500 |
| | Sound value | – |
| | Salvage | – |
| | Net (Line 10) | $ – |

## EXHIBIT XXXVIII

### NEW PRODUCT LINE
### PROPERTY BUDGET PROPOSAL

YEAR 19x1

| DIVISION | WIDGET | Fixed capital | $120,000 |
|---|---|---|---|
| UNIT/DEPT. | SPRINGFIELD PLANT | Property expense | 10,000 |
| | | TOTAL | $130,000 |

DESCRIPTION: Class IIa

Tooling, including dies, jigs, fixtures and test equipment, for a line of heat pumps 2 HP—3 HP —5 HP—7½ HP.

BENEFITS TO BE OBTAINED:

Air conditioning market will be increased by sale of heat pump adaptation of refrigeration units at present being built

Designs ready, tested and approved by Sales Dept.

OTHER REMARKS (or data):

Only intimate tooling and test equipment are needed to produce the following units: 19x1-90, 19x2-450, 19x3-720, 19x4-900. Standard machine tool capacity and existing floor space are available and adequate for project

Burden absorption due to increased production will amount to about $180,000 in 19x4

This equipment may have as short a primary service life as five years but there is a good chance that it will serve its purpose for as long as ten years. Book write-off will be over three years

NOTE: Accumulated cost of development and design—now completed—$82,000.

INVESTMENT:

| | |
|---|---|
| Land | $ – |
| Buildings | – |
| Machinery and equipment | 120,000 |
| Other (specify) | – |
| Fixed Capital | 120,000 |
| Additional working capital | 290,000 |
| Total Investment | $410,000 |

OPERATIONAL DATA:

First complete year of normal operations 19x2

Return on investment expected that year 63.9

Investment will be recovered in 4 yrs.

Primary service life of project 10 yrs.

Project will start (month/year) March 19x1

Project will be completed (month/year) Oct. 19x1

UNIT/DEPT.: DIVISION: CORPORATION:

## EXHIBIT XXXVIII (reverse)

### a) EFFECT ON PROFIT (000's Omitted)

| | 19x1 | 19x2 | 19x3 | 19x4 | 19x5 | 19— |
|---|---|---|---|---|---|---|
| 1. Net sales | $ 100 | $ 500 | $ 800 | $ 1,000 | $ 1,000 | $ |
| 2. Costs and expense | $ | $ | $ | $ | $ | $ |
| 3. Direct labor | 18 | 60 | 95 | 120 | | |
| 4. Direct material | 20 | 100 | 160 | 190 | | |
| 5. Indirect labor | 5 | 19 | 30 | 40 | | |
| 6. Indirect material | | | | | | |
| 7. Depreciation (note)* | 5 | 30 | 35 | 50 | | |
| 8. Other mfg. expense | 10 | 50 | 80 | 100 | | |
| 9. Start-up | 30 | | | | | |
| 10. Obsolescence | | | | | | |
| 11. Operating expense | | 75 | 120 | 150 | | |
| 12. | | | | | | |
| 13. Total costs and expense | $ 88 | $ 334 | $ 520 | $ 650 | $ 600 | $ |
| 14. Net profit before tax | $ 12 | $ 166 | $ 280 | $ 350 | $ 400 | $ |

### b) RETURN ON INVESTMENT (000's Omitted)

| Investment | | | | | | |
|---|---|---|---|---|---|---|
| 15. Land | $ | $ | $ | $ | $ | $ |
| 16. Buildings | | | | | | |
| 17. Machinery & equipment | 120 | | | | | |
| 18. Other | | | | | | |
| 19. Fixed capital | $ 120 | $ | $ | $ | $ | $ |
| 20. Accounts receivable | | 40 | 30 | 20 | | |
| 21. Inventories | | 100 | 65 | 35 | | |
| 22. Total annual investment | $ 120 | $ 140 | $ 95 | $ 55 | $ | $ |
| 23. Cumulative total investment | $ 120 | $ 260 | $ 355 | $ 410 | $ 410 | $ |
| 24. Return on investment (Line 14 ÷ Line 23) | 10.0% | 63.9% | 78.9% | 85.4% | 97.5% | % |

### c) CASH GENERATION (000's Omitted)

| | | | | | | |
|---|---|---|---|---|---|---|
| 25. 48% of Line 14 | $ 6 | $ 80 | $ 134 | $ 168 | $ | $ |
| 26. Add: Dep'n & obsolescence (Lines 7 and 10) | 5 | 30 | 35 | 50 | | |
| 27. Annual cash generation | $ 11 | $ 110 | $ 169 | $ 218 | $ | $ |
| 28. Cumulative cash generation | $ 11 | $ 121 | $ 290 | $ 508 | $ | $ |

**CAPITAL EXPENDITURES BY QUARTERS:** (000's Omitted)

| Budget year | |
|---|---|
| 1st Quarter | $ – |
| 2nd Quarter | 60 |
| 3rd Quarter | 60 |
| 4th Quarter | – |
| Following year(s) | – |

*NOTE: Depreciation will be calculated based on the current book method—i.e., sum-of-the-years digits, special amortization, etc.
Basis—3-year amortization
20-year life

**PROPERTY EXPENSE:** (000's Omitted)

| | |
|---|---|
| Demolition and site clearance | $ |
| Moving existing equipment | |
| Repair & alterations to existing equipment | 10 |
| Other (specify) | |
| Total (include in start-up costs—Line 9) | $ 10 |

**PROPERTY TO BE RETIRED:**

None

| | |
|---|---|
| Book value | $ |
| Accum. dep'n | |
| Sound value | |
| Salvage | |
| Net (Line 10) | $ |

projects have to show the effect on profit and cash generation. For projects under $10,000, those in each class are grouped together on one form, and the projection is made only for the next two years. This long a view is required, too, for projects over $10,000 in the product improvement and nonproductive classes, whereas those in the cost-saving and expansion classes have to be projected by years (beginning with the budget year) until the cumulative cash generation at least equals the total cumulative investment. For the most part, the proposal forms are self-explanatory. Where the benefits of a project take the form of cost savings, these are shown as negative (red) figures on lines 3 to 12 on the reverse side of the form. The 48 per cent of net profit shown on line 25 applies only to U. S. divisions.[7]

A division's final capital expenditure budget will consist of new proposals authorized for the budget year, together with unexpended balances from prior years. A proposal which has not been authorized by the budget review committee by January 1 of the budget year is deemed to have expired and must be reintroduced in the next budget, if the need for it still exists. However, proposals not planned in sufficient detail for inclusion in the budget may be presented for approval by the committee as "not on budget" projects at a later date.

Once the annual profit plan has been put into operation, it is subjected to continuous review and re-estimate throughout the year. "This review," says the company's administrative manual, "permits the assessment of the probable degree of achievement in the light of changing conditions and points out the courses of action which are necessary to reach or exceed planned objectives." To this end, a revised forecast must be submitted to the corporate head office by each division by the first working day of each month. This shows a revised forecast of the result for each of the next three months and the next three quarters. The form used also provides for the actual results for each quarter to be shown. These are filled in as the year unfolds.

With the revised forecast, the divisions submit a letter of comment which is intended to serve both as a means of self-examination and re-appraisal by the division's own management, and as a medium of communication between the division and corporate management. While divisions are not limited by instructions on reporting, a considerable list of subject matters is laid down as requiring coverage in the letter of comment. The company is, at the present time, revising the form of this letter of comment, but it may be useful to summarize the more important items on which divisions have beeen required to report hitherto:

---

[7] Readers outside the United States may need to be reminded that the U.S. rate of income tax on corporations was 52 per cent before 1964.

*Operations—forecast.* The net sales, pre-tax income and inventory, for the month just ended, the next three months and for the year ahead, are to be shown as budgeted, as forecast last month and as currently forecast. The "actual" figures for the latest month for which they have been reported are also to be shown, to indicate trends. Deviations between the budget and the latest forecasts, and plans to correct unfavorable deviations, are to be discussed.

*Operations—actual.* A statistical comparison in the following form is required:

| | *Last Month* | | | *Year to Date* | | |
|---|---|---|---|---|---|---|
| | *Actual* | *Forecast* | *Budget* | *Actual* | *Budget* | *Last Year* |
| Orders received (gross) | | | | | | |
| Backlog | | | | | | |
| Net sales | | | | | | |
| Pre-tax income | | | | | | |
| % of net sales | | | | | | |
| Gross inventory | | | | | | |

Significant deviations of last month's actual results from the forecast, and of the year-to-date's actual results from budget are to be commented on, with a discussion of plans for corrective action where necessary.

*Price changes and new or improved products.* Significant changes in list prices with effective dates, and information about expected volume and gross profit on new or improved products, are to be discussed.

*Industry comparison.* The percentage of the total industry supply, by major product lines, for the latest and the previous period and for this year and last year to date are to be reported, with comments on significant changes.

*Industry conditions.* A report is required on changes in competitive price conditions, new products, techniques and other pertinent developments within a division's industry.

*Personnel statistics.* Statistics on the size and composition of the division's labor force are to be reported in the following form:

| | *Number of Employees* | | |
|---|---|---|---|
| | *Budget* | *Last Month* | *Prior Month* |
| Hourly | | | |
| Direct | | | |
| Indirect | | | |
| Salaried | | | |
| Total | | | |

*Labor relations.* This calls for comment on labor negotiations completed or in progress, changes in wages and fringe benefits, impending and actual work stoppages, major layoffs and hirings, with an explanation of the circumstances.

*Other matters.* Suggested topics for comment under this head (though not necessarily as a matter of monthly routine) include major inventory changes and write-offs, changes in cash requirements and accounts receivable, other significant balance sheet changes, progress on capital projects, major disposals of property, pending and actual litigation, cost reduction activities, important organizational changes and developments in the fields of public relations and community relations.

On or before February 1 in each year, an annual letter of comment is submitted, discussing the accomplishments of the year as a whole compared with the goals set at the beginning of the year. This letter is primarily of a nonstatistical nature, though some of the matters discussed will have to be dealt with in quantitative terms.

Reports on the actual results of each month begin to come in very soon after the end of the month. Sales statistics are reported by wire on the fifth working day, and a statement of income (Exhibit XXXIX), with supporting schedules, is received at head office by the twelfth working day. A divisional balance sheet, with supporting detail, is also received at that time. To show the progress of each product group and product line, two reports on sales and gross profits by product line, one for the month and the other for the year to date, are submitted monthly. These show this period's figures and last period's against the budget. A breakdown of the

## EXHIBIT XXXIX

### STATEMENT OF INCOME

______________ Division

MONTH OF ________ 19___

| BUDGET | | | THIS YEAR | | LAST YEAR | |
|---|---|---|---|---|---|---|
| Amount | % | | Amount | % | Amount | % |
| | | Gross Sales<br>Returns, allow. & disc. | | | | |
| | 100.0 | NET SALES | | 100.0 | | 100.0 |
| | | Cost of goods sold | | | | |
| | | Gross Profit<br>Operating Expense | | | | |
| | | Adm. & gen. expense<br>Selling expense<br>Adv. & sales promotion<br>Research & develop.<br>Adm. service charge | | | | |
| | | Total Operating Expense | | | | |
| | | Operating Income | | | | |
| | | Other charges (net) | | | | |
| | | PRE-TAX INCOME | | | | |

YEAR TO DATE

| BUDGET | | | THIS YEAR | | LAST YEAR | |
|---|---|---|---|---|---|---|
| Amount | % | | Amount | % | Amount | % |
| | | Gross Sales<br>Returns, allow. & disc. | | | | |
| | 100.0 | NET SALES | | 100.0 | | 100.0 |
| | | Cost of goods sold | | | | |
| | | Gross Profit<br>Operating Expense | | | | |
| | | Adm. & gen. expense<br>Selling expense<br>Adv. & sales promotion<br>Research & develop.<br>Adm. service charge | | | | |
| | | Total Operating Expense | | | | |
| | | Operating Income | | | | |
| | | Other charges (net) | | | | |
| | | PRE-TAX INCOME | | | | |

## EXHIBIT XL

### DIVISION A

PRE-TAX INCOME BY PRODUCT GROUPS FOR QUARTER ENDED ______

| | Total Division | | | | Product Group 1 | | | | Product Group 2 | | | |
|---|---|---|---|---|---|---|---|---|---|---|---|---|
| | Actual | % | Budget | % | Actual | % | Budget | % | Actual | % | Budget | % |
| NET SALES | | | | | | | | | | | | |
| Mfg. Cost | | | | | | | | | | | | |
| Other Costs | | | | | | | | | | | | |
| Gross Profit | | | | | | | | | | | | |
| Operating Expense. | | | | | | | | | | | | |
| Adm. & General | | | | | | | | | | | | |
| Selling | | | | | | | | | | | | |
| Adv. & Sales Prom. | | | | | | | | | | | | |
| R&D | | | | | | | | | | | | |
| Admin. Serv. Chg. | | | | | | | | | | | | |
| Total Operating Expense | | | | | | | | | | | | |
| Operating Income | | | | | | | | | | | | |
| Other Charges Net | | | | | | | | | | | | |
| PRE-TAX INCOME | | | | | | | | | | | | |
| Investment | | | | | | | | | | | | |
| Cash | | | | | | | | | | | | |
| Acct. Rec. | | | | | | | | | | | | |
| Inventories | | | | | | | | | | | | |
| Property | | | | | | | | | | | | |
| Other | | | | | | | | | | | | |
| Total Investment | | | | | | | | | | | | |
| Turnover | | | | | | | | | | | | |
| ROI | | | | | | | | | | | | |

## EXHIBIT XLI

______________ DIVISION/COMPANY

REPORT OF PROPERTY APPROPRIATIONS

UNIT/DEPT. ______________ PERIOD ENDED ______________ 19____

| Approp. Number | Description | Capital and Expense | | Status of Project | Class | Capital Expenditures—Current Year | | | |
|---|---|---|---|---|---|---|---|---|---|
| | | | | | | Total Est. Cost to Complete | | | |
| | | Appropriation Amount | Expended To Date | | | On Budget | N.O.B. | Expended | Est. Remaining Cost to Complete |
| | | | | | | | | | |

division's pre-tax income and investment between product groups is submitted quarterly, and this form (Exhibit XL) also shows the rate of turnover of investment and the rate of return on investment by product groups.

No analysis of variances from budget are reported by divisions to the corporate management. Information on this subject is submitted each quarter to the corporate controller, however, who includes it in his reports to management. This information, broken down by product lines so far as possible, shows gross profit variances due to sales volume, net sales realization, production volume, production efficiency and expense, other cost variances and variances on operating expenses.

The last formal report we need mention is the report on property appropriations, submitted by divisions quarterly to show the progress of expenditure on capital projects. This is reproduced as Exhibit XLI. No regular form is at present in use for reporting on the operational success of new projects in their initial stages, though such a check is made when the project has been operating for 12 months.

# NONPROFIT MEASURES OF PERFORMANCE

## CHAPTER VIII

Managerial success, like success in any field, can only be assessed in terms of the progress made towards a given set of objectives. It is not always easy to say what management's objectives are. Statements of policy by companies tend to be either extremely specific, calling for stated rates of return on investment or stated profit percentages on sales, or else they are lengthy and, in attempting to say everything, end up by conveying practically nothing.

At an earlier stage of our own inquiry, we used *the excess of net earnings over the cost of capital* as a measure of short-run managerial success. The long-run counterpart of this objective is the *maximization of the discounted present value of the enterprise.* Nothing is left out of this objective because everything that happens to a business, or to any segment of it, affects its present value. The objective, therefore, is anything but narrow.

We saw, in Chapter II, that while an ideal profit figure would measure the amount which had been added to the net worth of the enterprise, and hence the progress made towards maximizing its present value, the profit figures which result from the application of "generally accepted accounting principles" are very imperfect approximations to this ideal. They therefore leave plenty of room for other measures of performance, and this is particularly true of the performance of a segment of a business such as a division. Some of these other measures are needed to support the accounting results and to throw further light on the forces helping to determine them. Others, while they have implications for profitability in the long run, are in short-range terms less directly profit-oriented.

Engineering measures of the efficiency of specific pieces of equipment have a part to play in a complete set of controls, but it is the measurement of organizational performance that we are now talking about. One such measure—the productivity index—has received more attention than most others, and it played a considerable part in European discussions of economic reconstruction after World War II. Though the productivity index has not as yet been widely put to use in the United States as a control figure, it is nevertheless worth discussing.

## Productivity Measurement

A measure of the productivity of a firm (or of one of its divisions) attempts to compare, as between the period chosen for measurement and some base period, either the output obtained per unit of input or the reciprocal of this measure, the input required per unit of output.[1] The measure may focus attention on changes in the productivity of a single kind of input (most commonly labor), the result being expressed as an index of output per man-hour. We may call this a partial productivity measure. Alternatively the measure may try to reflect changes in the productivity of all the inputs combined, giving an index of total productivity. It must be noted that, in any

---

[1] Those who wish to pursue this subject beyond the very limited discussion which is possible here will find the following references useful.

Hiram S. Davis, *Productivity Accounting,* Philadelphia: University of Pennsylvania Press, 1955.

John W. Kendrick and Daniel Creamer, *Measuring Company Productivity: Handbook With Case Studies,* Studies in Business Economics No. 74, New York: National Industrial Conference Board, 1961. This draws fairly heavily on Hiram Davis's work. It contains a case study (Case D, pp. 76-84) on "Measuring Total Productivity at the Divisional Level of an Equipment Manufacturer."

"Progress in Measuring Work," *Management Bulletin,* August 1962, Washington, D. C.: U.S. Bureau of the Budget. This provides a brief general introduction to the subject, and then provides a number of case studies of the application of productivity measurement in government agencies.

Erik Ruist, "Production Efficiency of the Industrial Firm," *Productivity Measurement Review,* Special Number, December 1961, Paris: Productivity Measurement Advisory Service of the Organization for Economic Cooperation and Development. This is a short but penetrating Swedish study which can be strongly recommended.

T. E. Easterfield, *Productivity Measurement in Great Britain—a Survey of Recent Work,* London: Department of Scientific and Industrial Research, 1959.

case, it is not an absolute yardstick of productivity which is sought; there would be no meaningful way of expressing such a thing, and it would be of very little use to anyone. It is the change in productivity between the base period and the measured period which the index expresses. If desired, it should be possible to go beyond that point and identify the causes of the change.

The nature of productivity measurement is most easily seen if we look at a simple illustration of a completely manual process (using homogeneous labor) producing a single kind of output from a single kind of material. Assume that sales always equal production. Taking 19x1 as the base year, the figures for that and the next year might be as follows:

| | 19 x 1 | 19 x 2 |
|---|---|---|
| Sales: units | 1000 | 1650 |
| value | $1250 | $2000 |
| Materials: pounds | 200 | 280 |
| cost | $ 300 | $ 450 |
| Labor: hours | 250 | 400 |
| wages | $ 625 | $1100 |

All we have to do, in a simple case such as this, is to calculate the inputs which, at 19x1 prices and at 19x1 rates of usage per unit of output, would have been required to produce the 19x2 output. Then if we compare this hypothetical total input with the actual total input for 19x2, we can easily calculate the productivity index for 19x2. How this is done can be seen in Exhibit XLII. The result is a productivity index of 107.5. We might have expressed the same information as an index of inputs per unit of output. This is, of course, the reciprocal of the productivity index multiplied by 100, 100/1.075 or 93.

Productivity measurement is not quite so simple as this in real life, because inputs and outputs are seldom, if ever, homogeneous. The basic problem, which statistical ingenuity has gone a long way towards solving, is to select characteristics of inputs and outputs which can be expressed in homogeneous units and which are, therefore, aggregable. Ideally, the characteristics sought will be physical ones, for it is physical productivity which is to be measured. However, it is usually impossible to exclude altogether the use of prices and unit costs as weights. So long as the prices and costs used ar constant, as between the base period and the measured period, thi has to be accepted.

## EXHIBIT XLII

| | Hypothetical 19x2 inputs at 19x1 prices and usage rates $ | Actual 19x inputs at 19x1 price $ |
|---|---|---|
| **Materials:** | | |
| $\$300 \times \frac{1650}{1000}$ | 495 | |
| 280 lbs. @ $1.50 | | 420 |
| **Labor:** | | |
| $\$625 \times \frac{1650}{1000}$ | 1031 | |
| 400 hrs. @ $2.50 | | 1000 |
| | 1526 | 1420 |
| **Productivity index for 19x2** | $\frac{1526}{1420} \times 100 = \underline{\underline{107.5}}$ | |

The procedure of productivity measurement may be summed up i six steps:

1. A choice must be made between measuring total productivit or partial productivity. If the latter is decided on, one type of re source has to be selected as the input whose productivity is to b measured.

2. The base period must be selected. It should be a representativ (i.e., not an abnormal) period.

3. Outputs have to be aggregated, both in the base period and th measured period. The unit used may be a physical unit (e.g., tons o steel products, yards of yarn, megawatts of electrical energy) or standard output unit (nonstandard units being suitably weighted s that they can be expressed as equivalent standard units). Output ma also be aggregated in dollars of standard cost.[2] If production statistic

[2] Constant selling prices are sometimes used. This is not satisfactory, for change in product-mix in favor of the more profitable products will raise th productivity index, when what has actually increased is not productivity but profi ability.

are not directly available, production must be ascertained by adjusting sales for inventory changes.

4. Materials, labor and capital inputs must be aggregated separately for the base year and for each measured period thereafter. Materials may be added together in "equivalent units," if such can be found (e.g., units of calorific content of different fuels), or in terms of the standard cost of material used. Labor can be aggregated in man-hours, if it does not differ too much in quality. Otherwise, the man-hours in each category must be weighted by the standard cost per hour. Capital input is hardest to measure. Various devices have been used—machine hours, base-year rate of return applied to total investment, capital equipment usage converted into man-hours (by dividing total depreciation by the weighted average standard cost per man-hour of labor employed) and several others.

5. If partial productivity measures are required in terms of one of the above inputs, divide the base-year aggregate input by the base-year output. The resultant figure of input per unit of output represents a productivity index of 100. Now multiply the base-year input per unit of output by the output of the measured period. The result is the input which would have been required to give this output if productivity had remained at 100. If it is found that actual input for the measured period is, say, only 91 per cent of this figure, then productivity for the measured period has gone up from 100 to 100/0.91 or 110.

6. To get a total productivity measure, it is usually still best to proceed as above, getting separate productivity measures for each input, and combining them by means of a weighted average. The weights to be used will usually have to be the base-year cost of each input.

There are all too many variants of this procedure, and their very multiplicity is evidence of the considerable element of arbitrariness to which productivity measurement is subject. Some of the most intractable difficulties have not even as yet been mentioned—changes in the quality of products between the base-year and the measured period, for instance, or the development of new products altogether during the interval between. Ways around these difficulties have been found; but no one pretends that the ground is yet very firm.

What can productivity measurement contribute to the control of divisional operations? A further look at the figures used in Exhibit

XLII will provide a partial answer. If the figures were those of a division, the profit in absolute terms would have increased, while the percentage of profit to sales declined, as can be seen from Exhibit XLIII.

### EXHIBIT XLIII

| | 19x1 | | 19x2 | |
|---|---|---|---|---|
| | $ | $ | $ | $ |
| Sales | | 1250 | | 2000 |
| Materials | 300 | | 450 | |
| Labor | 625 | 925 | 1100 | 1550 |
| | | 325 | | 450 |
| Per cent of sales | | 26% | | 22.5% |

Even in this simple case, it is not apparent at first glance that the change in profitability shown by the figures is the result of price effects and quantity effects which have pulled in opposite directions. In fact, the price effects have been unfavorable—selling prices have declined slightly, materials prices and wages have both risen: the quantity effects have been favorable—there has been a considerable economy in material used per unit of output and a slight saving in labor, as is apparent from Exhibit XLII. These favorable quantity effects are the factors responsible for raising the productivity index 7½ points. What the index does is to show the direction in which results would have moved if prices (all specific prices, not just the general level of prices) had remained constant, while quantities of both inputs and outputs moved in the way they did. If the adverse price movements can be shown to be outside the control of the management of the division, it is at least to be commended for improving its productivity.

What probably gives rise to scepticism on the part of business executives, when they consider the cost of productivity measurement, is the legitimate doubt whether it can contribute to management much that cannot be obtained more simply by means of standard costing. However, while productivity measurement resembles standard costing in that it separately assesses the effect of a particular factor (in this case, the factor of productive efficiency) on the fortunes of a business, productivity measurement does this by making a comparison over time. Its standard, so to speak, is the level of productive efficiency achieved in the chosen base-year.

For the comparisons to be effective, the same base must be maintained for a number of years, or at least if it is changed the appearance of a constant base must be maintained by the use of a chain index. The standards used in standard costing, on the other hand, are normally changed at least once a year. Technical improvements are therefore given expression in the changing standards. Consequently, variances from these standards cannot measure technical progress over a series of years. For the same reason, standard costing is not well adapted to provide performance comparisons between divisions, since each division has its own standards appropriate to its own products and working conditions. Divisions *can* be compared, however, by looking at the *movement* of their productivity indices over a period. They do not have to have been equally productive in the base year. It can be seen which ones are improving faster on a base-year index of 100, even though the 100 means a different level of productivity for each division. However, it does have to be remembered that it is usually easier to improve on a bad performance than on a good one, and this may be an important reservation in assessing the divisions' relative progress.

Comparisons of productivity at plant level, or a review of productivity changes for a particular process or production line, will usually be more valuable than any attempt to measure the productivity of a whole division. In any case, it is fairly easy to combine the indices for small segments of a business into an index for a larger segment, and so get the benefits of both a microcosmic and a synoptic view of productivity.

Most of the data necessary for productivity measurement is already available to those companies which have complete standard costing systems. It should not be troublesome or costly to develop a series of productivity indices for each division, virtually as a by-product of standard costing. Companies that neglect this opportunity to do so are not getting all the information they can out of their control systems.

## Marketing Effectiveness

If it were necessary to select two factors which, more than any others, are the prime ingredients of profitability, presumably high productivity would be one and marketing effectiveness would be the other. It is easier to measure the first than it is to measure the second. However, many companies expect their divisions to watch and report on their "market position" as a gauge of their success in coping with competition. Absolute sales volume, and its trend over time, reflect both competitive power and the size of the total market. Market position takes the size of the market as given, and concentrates attention on competitive power alone.

"The size of the market" is not a simple concept, for the same reason that "product" and "industry" are not simple concepts. For example, for a division which makes electric cooking ranges, does "the market" include (a) all cooking equipment or (b) all indoor ranges (gas and electric) or only (c) all electric ranges? All three are of some interest, but presumably (b) and (c) are of more interest than (a). The division's market position will be represented by the percentage of sales (or orders received, if this is a more representative figure) to total sales in the market as reported by a trade association or as otherwise ascertained by market research. Absolute precision in measurement is not important, since the trends in the figures are more informative than the percentage for any single period.

## Other Key Result Areas

The General Electric Company has given the name "key result areas" to those objectives of which it could be said that "continued failure in this area [would] prevent the attainment of management's responsibility for advancing General Electric as a leader in a strong, competitive economy, even though results in all other key result areas are good."[8] Their list includes eight areas, of which three—profitability, productivity, and market position—have already been discussed (though not necessarily with the meaning given them by GE). The remaining five are:

*Product leadership.* A divisional panel, made up of marketing, financial and engineering men, appraises each of the division's main products against those of competitors. This procedure is carried out in terms of what the customer is believed to want, and on the assump-

---

[8] Robert W. Lewis, "Measuring, Reporting and Appraising Results of Operations with Reference to Goals, Plans and Budgets," *Planning, Managing and Measuring the Business,* New York: Controllers Institute Research Foundation, 1955, p. 30. Mr. Lewis's paper reviews the key result areas. For further discussion of them, see Wm. Travers Jerome III, *Executive Control—The Catalyst,* New York: John Wiley & Sons, 1961, Chapter 14.

tion that minimum costs of production are being achieved for both the ideal and the actual products. Different grades of the same product (e.g., de luxe and economy models) must be treated as different products. The department reports the percentage of its products classified as superior, equal and inferior to those of competitors. Some products (e.g., of a military nature) and even all the products of a whole division may be unsuitable for product leadership reporting.

*Personnel development.* The information collected under this head is intended to measure the result of the personnel development process rather than the state of development at any moment of time. The figures collected by divisions (but not necessarily reported to head office) include:

(a) the number of people promoted in relation to the number promotable, and the number promotable in relation to the total number employed;
(b) the percentages of employees who are developing, who are static, and who are retrogressing;
(c) the percentages of employees who are satisfied and who are dissatisfied with their promotion prospects and other aspects of their development.

*Employee attitudes.* This area is covered by periodic questionnaires. Employees are categorized as hourly, nonexempt salaried and exempt salaried workers. The survey covers such matters as satisfaction with pay, whether the worker thinks his job worth while, his promotion prospects satisfactory, and so on. The percentages of positive and negative answers for each category of question are recorded. No report is made to top management, but average results in each category are made known to divisions so that they can assess their own results by comparison. This is, in any case, not an easy thing to do, for a high proportion of positive answers could no doubt be obtained from a workforce of satisfied morons.

For plant workers, more objective figures are also collected on absences, tardiness, grievances, participation in benefit plans, and so on. Again, averages are circulated for comparison purposes.

*Public responsibility.* This area is intended to provide information on whether the company is filling the role it has set for itself as an employer, and vis-a-vis its customers, suppliers, the Government and the community. Public responsibility is looked at from a company rather than a divisional point of view. Further work on the problem of measurement in this area remains to be done. Attitude surveys and many different kinds of measurements will no doubt have to be brought into use in the attempt to cover it. In the last analysis, it is far from sure that "public responsibility" is a sufficiently precise concept to admit of satisfactory measurement at all.

*Balance between short-run and long-range goals.* This is not a separate set of measurements but, rather, an assessment made from the measurements in the other seven areas. The relationship between long-run and short-run profits, as shown in budgets and forecasts, clearly has considerable relevance here.

General Electric's measurement project is still in process of development. Though probably few of the elements in it are unique and all of them are capable of refinement, it is unusual in offering an integrated measurement plan for a divisionalized company. As such, it serves to remind us that managerial success has many facets and accounting measurements catch only a few of them.

## Conclusion

Professor Jerome is mildly critical of GE's concept of key result areas in that "in establishing the over-all General Electric Company's objectives, . . . management has made no particular attempt to tie these broad objectives in with the eight key result areas, nor is the statement of objectives spelled out in any operational way."[4] This brings us back to the question of objectives.

Each business is entitled to go its own way in choosing its objectives. However, since only persons, not businesses, can choose goals, this statement leaves room for debate as to who, in a large company, has this right. Apart from that question, those responsible for financial control must be on the alert to see that their methods and measurements are not at variance with those chosen objectives, and do not deflect the business from its course. Motivation must come high on the list of the uses to which financial controls are put, and in divisionalized businesses nothing can be more important than the sound motivation of divisional managements. Most of the questions discussed in this book have had this thought constantly underlying them.

---

[4] *Executive Control—The Catalyst,* p. 237.

# BIBLIOGRAPHY

*(Roman numerals to left indicate chapters to which the reading is related: "G" indicates general references.)*

BOOKS


II Alexander, Sidney S., "Income Measurement in a Dynamic Economy" (revised by David Solomons) in *Studies in Accounting Theory,* Baxter & Davidson (eds.), Homewood, Ill.: Richard D. Irwin, Inc. and London: Sweet & Maxwell Ltd., 1963.

G Anderson, David and Schmidt, Leo, *Practical Controllership,* revised edition, Homewood, Ill.: Richard D. Irwin, Inc., 1961.

VII Argyris, Chris, *Impact of Budgets on People,* New York: Controllership Foundation (now Financial Executives Research Foundation), 1952.

VI Arrow, Kenneth J., "Optimization, Decentralization and Internal Pricing in Business Firms," *Contributions to Scientific Research in Management,* Berkeley, Calif.: University of California Press, 1959.

G Baxter & Davidson (eds.), *Studies in Accounting Theory,* Homewood, Ill.: Richard D. Irwin, Inc. and London: Sweet & Maxwell Ltd., 1962.

G Beyer, Robert, *Profitability Accounting for Planning and Control,* New York: Ronald Press Company, 1963.

G Bierman, Harold, Jr., *Topics in Cost Accounting and Decisions,* New York: McGraw-Hill Book Company, 1963.

VI ———, Bonini, Fouraker and Jaedicke, *Quantitative Analysis for Business Decisions,* Homewood, Ill.: Richard D. Irwin, Inc., 1965.

VII ——— and Smidt, S., *The Capital Budgeting Decision,* New York: The Macmillan Company, 1966.

G Bonini, Jaedicke and Wagner (eds.), *Management Controls: New Directions in Basic Research,* New York: McGraw-Hill Book Company, 1964.

VII Chamberlain, Neil W., *The Firm: Micro-Economic Planning and Action,* New York: McGraw-Hill Book Company, 1962.

VI Charnes, A. and Cooper, W. W., *Management Models and Industrial Applications of Linear Programming, Vols I and II,* New York: John Wiley & Sons, Inc., 1961.

III & IV Cohen, Albert H., *Apportionment and Allocation Formulae and Factors Used by States in Levying Taxes Based On or Measured by Net Income of Manufacturing, Distributive and Extractive Corporations,* New York: Controllership Foundation (now Financial Executives Research Foundation), 1954.

I Cordiner, Ralph J., *New Frontiers for Professional Managers,* New York: McGraw-Hill Book Company, 1956.

I Dale, Ernest, *The Great Organizers,* New York: McGraw-Hill Book Company, 1960.

VIII Davis, Hiram S., *Productivity Accounting,* Philadelphia: University of Pennsylvania Press, 1955.

G Dean, Joel, *Capital Budgeting,* New York: Columbia University Press, 1951.

VII Dearden, John, *Cost and Budget Analysis,* Englewood Cliffs, N. J.: Prentice-Hall, Inc., 1962.

G Dickey, Robert I. (ed.), *Accountants' Cost Handbook,* New York: Ronald Press Company, 1960.

I Drucker, Peter F., *Concept of the Corporation,* New York: The John Day Co., 1946.

VIII Easterfield, T. E., *Productivity Measurement in Great Britain—A Survey of Recent Work,* London: Department of Scientific and Industrial Research, 1959.

II Edwards, Edgar O. and Bell, Philip W., *The Theory and Measurement of Business Income,* Berkeley, Calif.: University of California Press, 1961.

G Fiske, Wyman P. and Beckett, John A. (eds.), *Industrial Accountants' Handbook,* Englewood Cliffs, N. J.: Prentice-Hall, Inc., 1954.

VI Gass, Saul, *Linear Programming: Methods and Applications,* New York, McGraw-Hill Book Company, 1958.

III & IV Goldberg, Louis, *Concepts of Depreciation,* Sydney, Australia: Law Book Co. of Australasia Pty., Ltd., 1960.

G Jerome, William Travers, III, *Executive Control—The Catalyst,* New York: John Wiley & Sons, Inc., 1961.

G Keller, I. Wayne, *Management Accounting for Profit Control,* New York: McGraw-Hill Book Company, 1957.

VIII Kendrick, John W., and Creamer, Daniel, *Measuring Company Productivity: Handbook With Case Studies,* Studies in Business Economics No. 74, New York: National Industrial Conference Board, 1961.

I Kruisinga, H. J. (ed.), *The Balance Between Centralization and Decentralization in Managerial Control,* Leiden, Netherlands: H. E. Stenfert Kroese, 1954.

G Lemke, B. C. and Edwards, James Don (eds.), *Administrative Control and Executive Action,* Columbus, Ohio: Charles E. Merrill Books, Inc., 1961.

VIII Lewis, Robert W., *Planning, Managing and Measuring the Business, A Case Study of Management Planning and Control at General Electric Company,* New York: Controllers Institute Research Foundation (now Financial Executives Research Foundation), 1955, Part V: "Measuring, Reporting, and Appraising Results of Operations With Reference to Goals, Plans, and Budgets."

G Litterer, Joseph A., *Organizations: Structure and Behavior,* New York: John Wiley & Sons, Inc., 1963.

G Mace, Myles L. and Montgomery, George G., Jr., *Management Problems of Corporate Acquisitions,* Boston: Graduate School of Business Administration, Harvard University, 1962.

VI Manne, Alan S., *Economic Analysis for Business Decisions,* New York: McGraw-Hill Book Company, 1961.

I March, J. G. and Simon, H., *Organizations,* New York: John Wiley & Sons, Inc., 1958.

III & IV Meij, J. L. (ed.), *Depreciation and Replacement Policy,* Chicago, Ill.: Quadrangle Books, 1961.

VI Naylor, Thomas H. and Byrne, Eugene T., *Linear Programming,* Belmont, Calif.: Wadsworth Publishing Company, Inc., 1963.

VI Patman, Wright, *The Robinson-Patman Act,* New York: Ronald Press Company, 1938.

II Paton, William A. and Littleton, A. C., *Introduction to Corporate Accounting Standards,* Madison, Wis.: American Accounting Association, 1940.

V Read, R. B., "Measuring Division Performance Through Return on Investment," in *Blueprinting Tomorrow's Profits,* New York: Controllers Institute of America, Inc. (now Financial Executives Institute), 1957, pp. 41-48.

VIII Rowland, Virgil K., *Managerial Performance Standards,* New York: American Management Association, 1960.

G Shillinglaw, Gordon, *Cost Accounting: Analysis and Control,* Homewood, Ill.: Richard D. Irwin, Inc., 1961.

I Shultz, G. P. and Whisler, T. L. (eds.), *Management Organization and the Computer,* Glencoe, Ill.: Free Press, 1960.

I Simon, Herbert A. *et al., Centralization versus Decentralization in Organizing the Controller's Department,* New York: Controllership Foundation (now Financial Executives Research Foundation), 1954.

G Sloan, Alfred P., Jr., *My Years With General Motors* (edited by John McDonald with Catharine Stevens), Garden City, N. Y.: Doubleday & Co., Inc., 1964.

I Smith, George Albert, Jr., *Managing Geographically Decentralized Companies,* Boston: Division of Research, Graduate School of Business Administration, Harvard University, 1958.

V Solomon, Ezra (ed.), *The Management of Corporate Capital,* Glencoe, Ill.: Free Press, 1959.

V ———, *The Theory of Financial Management,* New York: Columbia University Press, 1963.

G Solomons, David (ed.), *Studies in Cost Analysis,* London: Sweet & Maxwell, Ltd. and Homewood, Ill.: Richard D. Irwin, Inc., 1968.

VII Sord, Burnard H. and Welsch, Glenn A., *Business Budgeting, A Survey of Management Planning and Control Practices,* New York: Controllership Foundation (now Financial Executives Research Foundation), 1958.

VII Stedry, Andrew C., *Budget Control and Cost Behavior,* Englewood Cliffs, N. J.: Prentice-Hall, Inc., 1960.

VI Williams, L. S., *Controllership: Trends and Techniques,* "Pricing Products Sold Between Divisions," in New York: Controllers Institute of America (now Financial Executives Institute), 1953, pp. 110-115.

G Wixon, Rufus and Kell, Walter G. (eds.), *Accountants' Handbook,* Fourth Edition, New York: Ronald Press Company, 1956.

G Young, G. Richard *et al., Mergers and Acquisitions: Planning and Action,* New York: Financial Executives Research Foundation, 1963.

PERIODICALS

*Accounting Review* (American Accounting Association)

VI Bierman, Harold, Jr., "Pricing Intracompany Transfers," July 1959, p. 429.

III & IV Davidson, Sidney, "Accelerated Depreciation and the Allocation of Income Taxes," April 1958, pp. 173-180.

G Golembiewski, R. T., "Accountancy as a Function of Organization Theory," April 1964, pp. 333-341.

II Shillinglaw, Gordon, "Toward a Theory of Divisional Income Measurement," April 1962, pp. 208-216.

II Solomons, David, "Economic and Accounting Concepts of Income," July 1961, pp. 374-383.

VI Stone, Williard E., "Intracompany Pricing," October 1956, p. 625.

VI ———, "Legal Implications of Intracompany Pricing," January 1964, pp. 38-42.

VI ———, "Tax Considerations in Intracompany Pricing," January 1960, p. 45.

II "Accounting and Reporting Standards for Corporate Financial Statements," 1957 Revision, October 1957, p. 537.

II "Report of AAA Management Accounting Committee," July 1962, pp. 523-537.

*Advanced Management*

I Dale, Ernest, "Centralization Versus Decentralization," June 1955, pp. 11-17.

I Suojanen, Waino W., "Substantive Decentralization in the Large Corporation," September 1956, p. 16.

*Business Budgeting*

III & IV Booth, W. W., "Profit Control and Profit Measurement at Ford Motor Company," September 1956, p. 12.

VII Hartogensis, Alwyn M., "Budgeting and Controlling Indirect Labor," February 1960, p. 18.

III & IV Hindman, W. R., "Why Direct Costing?" March 1963, pp. 4-11.

V Thompson, Ira N., "A Company's Cost of Capital," January 1963, pp. 4-13.

*The Controller* (now Financial Executive)

V Allen, Richard N., "Preset Earning Standards for a Multi-division Company," June 1960, pp. 270-271.

VI Boyd, Robert, "Transfer Prices and Profitability Measurement," February 1961, pp. 88-89.

III & IV Dean, Joel, "Profit Performance Measurement of Division Managers," September 1957, p. 423.

VII Dougall, Herbert E., "Payback as an Aid in Capital Budgeting," February 1961, pp. 67-72.

VII Jones, Donald P., "Management's Use of Budgetary Controls," May 1961, pp. 2-5.

IV Kollaritsch, Felix P., "Simplification of Accounting Methods Can Lead to Distorted and Vague Facts," July 1962, pp. 323-329 ff.

IV Littlefield, W. Joseph, "Depreciation Allowances Not Fully Utilized," July 1960, pp. 324-328 ff.

V Moller, George, "Try Budgeting for Return on Capital Employed," March 1958, pp. 107-110 ff.

G Peirce, James L., "The Planning and Control Concept," September 1954, p. 403.

V Sheehan, Daniel M., "The Relation of Invested Capital to Profit," October 1956, pp. 463-465 ff.

III & IV Strong, William L., "Decentralized Operations—A Control Program," January 1958, p. 11.

I Tanner, Eugene J., "Justifying Centralized Accounting Functions," August 1964, p. 37.

V Weaver, James B., "Return on What Investment?" August 1959, pp. 366-368 ff.

III & IV Williams, T. J., "Redistribution of Selling and Administrative Expenses," January 1956, p. 23.

V Wright, John W. D., "Setting Earnings Standards for Decentralized Operations," February 1957, pp. 59-62 ff.

III & IV Wright, Wilmer L., "Why Direct Costing Provides a Better Measurement of Income," July 1962, pp. 323-329 ff.

*The Cost Accountant*

III & IV Holdsworth, A., "Some Further Considerations on the Allocation of Overheads," April 1951, p. 354.

V Stone, G. C., "Return on Investment as a Measure of Efficiency," February 1960, pp. 46-53.

*Cost and Management*

I Berghian, Peter, "Decentralizing Plant Accounting," December 1959, p. 420.

I Brayer, Herbert O., "Decentralization of Operations and Centralization of Accounting," November 1958, p. 372.

I Gookin, R. Burt, "Financial Coordination Through Top Management," July-August 1958, p. 245.

VII Gordon, W. E., "Decentralized Profit Planning and Control," March 1957, p. 106.

V Moller, George, "Measuring Management Performance," March 1958, pp. 94-99.

V Muth, F. J., "Measurement of Return on Capital Employed by Profit Centers," January 1957, pp. 7-21.

VII Sutherland, Malcolm S., "A Report on Techniques Leading to Control and Measurement of Performance," October 1956, p. 334.

*Harvard Business Review*

VII Argyris, Chris, "Human Problems With Budgets," January-February 1953, pp. 97-110.

I Burlingame, John F., "Information Technology and Decentralization," November-December 1961, pp. 121-126.

VI Cook, Paul W., Jr., "New Technique for Intracompany Pricing," July-August 1957, p. 74.

VI Dean, Joel, "Decentralization and Intracompany Pricing," July-August 1955, p. 65.

VI Dearden, John, "Case of the Disputing Divisions," May-June 1964, pp. 158-178.

VI ———, "Interdivisional Pricing," January-February 1960, p. 117.

III & IV ———, "Limits on Decentralized Profit Responsibility," July-August 1962, pp. 81-89.

G ———, "Mirage of Profit Decentralization," November-December 1962, pp. 140-154.

V ———, "Problems in Decentralized Financial Control," May-June 1961, pp. 72-80.

III & IV ———, "Problems in Decentralized Profit Responsibility," May-June 1960, pp. 79-86.

III & IV ——— and Edgerly, William S., "Bonus Formula for Division Heads," September-October 1965, pp. 83-90.

VI Henderson, A. and Schlaifer, R., "Mathematical Programming," May-June 1954, pp. 73-100.

I Kline, Bennett E. and Martin, Norman H., "Freedom, Authority, and Decentralization," May-June 1958, p. 69.

VIII Likert, Rensis, "Measuring Organizational Performance," March-April 1958, pp. 41-50.

VII MacGregor, Douglas, "An Uneasy Look at Performance Appraisal," May-June 1957, pp. 89-94.

I Murphy, Robert W., "Corporate Divisions versus Subsidiaries," November-December 1956, p. 83.

VII Peirce, James L., "The Budget Comes of Age," May-June 1954, pp. 58-66.

V Ravenscroft, Edward A., "Return on Investment: Fit the Method to Your Need," March-April 1960, pp. 97-109.

III Shillinglaw, Gordon, "Guides to Internal Profit Measurement," March-April 1957, p. 82.

I Thurston, Philip H., "Who Should Control Information Systems?" November-December 1962, pp. 135-139.

I Villers, Raymond, "Control and Freedom in a Decentralized Company," March-April 1954, p. 89.

*Journal of Accountancy*

II Arnett, Harold, "What Does 'Objectivity' Mean to Accountants?" May 1961, pp. 63-68.

G Elliott, N. J., "Management Controls and Information," January 1963, pp. 84-86.

II Grady, Paul, "The Quest for Accounting Principles," May 1962, pp. 45-50.

III & IV Jewett, Grandjean G., "The Distribution of Overhead with Electronic Calculators," June 1954, p. 698.

V Lammie, Harold R., "Return on Capital Employed," August 1958, pp. 35-41.

III & IV Miller, Robert E., "Who Should Pay the President's Salary?" March 1960, p. 61.

II Spacek, Leonard, "Are Accounting Principles Generally Accepted?" April 1961, pp. 35-46.

*Journal of Accounting Research*

II Chambers, Raymond J., "Why Bother with Postulates?" Spring 1963, pp. 3-15.

II Davidson, Sidney, "The Day of Reckoning: Accounting Theory and Management Analysis," Autumn 1963, pp. 117-126.

VI Dopuch, Nicholas and Drake, David F., "Accounting Implications of a Mathematical Programming Approach to the Transfer Price Problem," Spring 1964, pp. 10-24.

II Shillinglaw, Gordon, "The Concept of Attributable Cost," Spring 1963, pp. 73-85.

*Journal of Business*

I Caswell, W. Cameron, "Taking Stock of Divisionalization," July 1956, pp. 160-171.

VI Cook, Paul W., Jr., "Decentralization and the Transfer Price Problem," April 1955, p. 87.

VI Gould, J. R., "Internal Pricing in Firms When There Are Costs of Using an Outside Market," January 1964, pp. 61-67.

VI Hirshleifer, Jack, "Economics of the Divisionalized Firm," April 1957, pp. 96-108.

———, "On the Economics of Transfer Pricing," July 1956, p. 172.

III & IV Solomons, David, "The Determination of Asset Values," January 1962, pp. 28-47.

*Journal of Industrial Economics*

I Heflebower, R. B., "Observations on Decentralization in Large Enterprises," November 1960, pp. 7-22.

I Meij, J. L., "Some Fundamental Principles of a General Theory of Management," November 1960, pp. 16-32.

VI Menge, John A., "The Backward Art of Interdivisional Transfer Pricing," July 1961, pp. 215-232.

V Merrett, Anthony and Sykes, Allen, "Calculating the Rate of Return on Capital Projects," January 1960, pp. 98-115.

V Parker, C. L., "Capital Employed," April 1955, 134-143.

*Management Record*

III & IV "How Industry Allocates Headquarters Expenses," October 1963.

G "Managing the Decentralized Company"—five articles by Daniel L. Kurshan, E. L. Hamilton, H. J. Lang, John G. Staiger, and A. L. Fairley, Jr., January 1963, pp. 8-25.

VIII "Methods of Evaluating Decentralized Operations," Hall, W. N., January 1963, pp. 26-28.

G "Relationship Between Corporate and Divisional Staff," May 1962, pp. 23-27.

G "Staff-Staff Relationships," February 1962, pp. 2-18.

G "The Corporate Manufacturing Staff in Divisionalized Firms," March 1962, pp. 18-25.

*Management Science*

VI Baumol, William J. and Fabian, Tibor, "Decomposition, Pricing for Decentralization and External Economies," September 1964, pp. 1-32.

G Shubik, Martin, "Incentives, Decentralized Control, the Assignment of Joint Costs and Internal Pricing," April 1962, pp. 325-343.

*NA(C)A Bulletin*

III & IV Allen, Charles B., "Distribution of National and Divisional Overheads," June 1957, p. 1237.

III & IV Armstrong, George F., "Performance Information Through Responsibility Reporting," March 1960, pp. 89-93.

III & IV Ashman, Harry T., "Distribution of Overhead with Electronic Computers," February 1955, p. 798.

V Bierman, Harold, Jr., "Problems in Computation and Use of Return on Investment," December 1957, pp. 75-82.

III & IV Blegen, T. W., "Allocating Administrative Expenses to Operating Units," December 1955, p. 535.

V Bowman, Keith J., "Divisional Contribution, Product Margin and Rate-of-Return Reporting," February 1963, pp. 47-51.

III & IV Brearton, Edward T., "Contribution Margin Reporting for a Multi-unit Bakery," July 1962, pp. 77-86.

VII — Brownlee, James L., "Man-Hour Budgeting for Control of Clerical Costs," March 1955, p. 956.

VII — Clarke, Stuart A., " 'Step Reporting' for Responsibility Accounting," June 1961, p. 5.

III & IV — Crowningshield, Gerald R. and Battista, George L., "Fixing Responsibility Through Profit and Loss Analysis," December 1961, pp. 11-27.

VI — Day, C. F., " 'Shadow Prices' for Evaluating Alternative Uses of Available Capacity," May 1959, pp. 67-76.

III & IV — Dean, Joel, "An Approach to Internal Profit Measurement," March 1958, p. 5.

III & IV — DeVille, James A., "Responsibility Reporting to Management," December 1960, pp. 31-42.

VI — Drebin, Allan R., "A Proposal for Dual Pricing of Intra-company Transfers," February 1959, p. 51.

III & IV — Evans, M. K., "Accounting Problems in Measuring Performance by Organizational Units," August 1955, p. 1739.

V — Frank, George W., "Let's Develop Return-on-Investment Consciousness," October 1956, pp. 200-207.

III & IV — Franklin, W. H., "Allocation of Overhead Costs—A Shortcut," August 1951, p. 1427.

V — Gelvin, L. Millard, "Return-on-Investment Concept and Corporate Policy," July 1961, pp. 37-49.

VI — Greer, Howard C., "Divisional Profit Calculation—Notes on the Transfer Price Problem," July 1962, pp. 5-12.

I — Harris, Walter, "Centralized Data Processing for Decentralized Management," July 1956, pp. 1323-1328.

VI — Heuser, Forrest L., "Organizing for Effective Intra-company Pricing," May 1956, pp. 1100-1105.

G — Horngren, Charles, "Choosing Accounting Practices for Reporting to Management," September 1962, pp. 3-15.

I — Johnson, John E., "The Administrative Revolution," November 1962, p. 3.

V — Kamsky, Leonard, "Cost Analysis for Improved Return on Investment," July 1955, pp. 1443-1451.

V — Keller, I. Wayne, "The Return on Capital Concept," March 1958, pp. 13-21.

II — Kellogg, Martin N., "Fundamentals of Responsibility Accounting," April 1962, pp. 5-16.

III & IV — Kelsey, P. R., "Alternatives in Allocating Administrative Costs," August 1951, p. 1496.

V Knutson, P. H., "Leased Equipment and Divisional Return on Capital," November 1962, pp. 15-20.

V Kutvirt, Otakar, "Departmentalization of Return on Investment," October 1956, pp. 218-230.

VII Lagerquist, Edward A., "A Refresher on Flexible Budgeting for Departmental Cost Control," April 1956, p. 956.

III & IV Langenberg, William, "Management Accounting by Absorption Costing With Direct Costing Information," March 1963, pp. 3-13.

V Lineberger, Robert A., "A Method of Determining Return on Investment," June 1961, pp. 53-61.

V Livingston, W. G., "Clarifying Return-on-Investment Determinations," October 1956, pp. 218-230.

III & IV Longenecker, Ray E., "Converting to Direct Costing," August 1962, pp. 25-37.

III & IV Makepiece, Roger S., "Time Based Distribution of Selling and General Costs," September 1956, p. 40.

III & IV May, Paul A., "Profit Evaluation for Management, 1. The Need for Profit Evaluation for Subdivisions of a Company," September 1957, p. 27.

VI McMurray, Robert, "Where Out-of-Pocket Costs Make the Best Transfer Price," August 1961, p. 33.

V Miller, James H., "A Glimpse at Practice in Calculating and Using Return on Investment," June 1960, pp. 65-76.

V Muth, F. J., "Return on Capital Employed—A Measure of Management," February 1954, pp. 699-700.

III & IV Pearson, Gordon F., "Allocating the Costs of a Data Processing Department," May 1958, p. 61.

VII Perry, Robert C., "Control of Below-the-Line Costs," July 1955, p. 1476.

III & IV Relyea, William T., "Allocating Administrative Expense to Divisions," August 1953, p. 1626.

I Rickard, E. B., "Study in Decentralization: Controllership in a Divisional Organization," January 1950, p. 567.

III & IV Seed, A. H., "Decentralized Accounting to Divisions," August 1955, p. 1698.

V Shillinglaw, Gordon, "Divisionalization, Decentralization—and Return on Investment," December 1959, pp. 19-33.

III & IV ———, "Problems in Divisional Profit Measurement," March 1961, p. 33.

III & IV Spencer, Leland G., "Integrating Control and Allocation of Service Section Expense," January 1960, p. 63.

VII Stromberg, Bert E. and Bareuther, Ernst E., "Budgeting Policy and Practice in a Decentralized Company," October 1957, pp. 36-44.

V Vatter, William J., "Does the Rate of Return Measure Business Efficiency?" January 1959, pp. 33-48.

VIII Whalen, John M., "Adding Performance Control to Cost Control," August 1962, pp. 67-74.

VII Wickendon, W. C., "Subjecting Maintenance Costs to Budgetary Control," September 1953, p. 72.

III & IV Wright, Wilmer L., "Direct Costing—Profit Measurement," September 1959, pp. 57-68.

VI ———, "Direct Costs Are Better for Pricing," April 1960, p. 17.

OTHER PERIODICALS

VI *Accountancy*—Gould, J. R., "The Pricing of Transactions Between Members of a Group of Companies," June 1960, pp. 345-348.

VIII *Administrative Science Quarterly*—Ridgway, V. F., "Dysfunctional Consequences of Performance Measurements," September 1956, pp. 240-247.

I *American Business*—Trundle, Robert C., "Trends in Decentralization," December 1955, p. 14.

VI *American Economic Review*—Dorfman, Robert, "Mathematical or 'Linear' Programming," December 1953, pp. 797-825.

I *British Management Review*—Brech, E. F. L., "The Balance Between Centralization and Decentralization in Managerial Control," July 1954, p. 187.

I *California Management Review*—Hund, James M., "Decentralization in a Wider Context," Fall 1961, pp. 65-73.

G *Canadian Journal of Economics and Political Science*—Tannenbaum, Robert and Massarik, Fred, "Participation by Subordinates in the Managerial Decision-Making Process," August 1950, pp. 408-418.

I *Dun's Review* and *Modern Industry*—Maughan, John, "Who Makes the Profit Decisions?" September 1962, pp. 28-29 ff.

VI *Economica*—Gould, J. R., "The Firm's Demand for Intermediate Products," February 1960, pp. 32-41.

III & IV *Journal of Marketing*—Watson, R. H., "Bases for Allocating Distribution Costs," July 1951, p. 29.

III & IV *Management Review*—Axelson, H. S., "Effective Control Through Responsibility Reporting," May 1961, p. 59.

I *Michigan Business Review*—Moore, Franklin G., "Is Divisionalization on the Way Out?" May 1964, pp. 26-32.

I *Personnel Administration*—Frazer, Chalmus F., "Decentralization: An Antidote to Bigness," May-June 1960, p. 15.

VIII *Productivity Measurement Review* (special number), Productivity Measurement Advisory Service of the Organization for Economic Cooperation and Development, Paris, France—Ruist, Erik, "Production Efficiency of the Industrial Firm," December 1961.

I *The Accountant*—Hourston, J. P., "Autonomous Units," July 7, 1951, pp. 8-9.

II *The Business Quarterly*—Parker, John R. E., " 'Profits' and Accounting Principles," Fall 1962, pp. 54-59.

III & IV *The Federal Government Accountant*—Stromberg, Bert E. and Donovan, John F., "Negative Income Tax Allocations," June 1962, pp. 93-109.

V *The Ohio Certified Public Accountant*—Edson, Harvey O., "Return on Investment—Analysis by Synthesis," Spring 1959, pp. 65-77.

PAMPHLETS, MONOGRAPHS AND OTHER REFERENCES

*American Institute of Certified Public Accountants*

II *Accounting Research Bulletins Nos. 1-51,* Committee on Accounting Procedure, 1959.

II Grady, Paul, *Inventory of Generally Accepted Accounting Principles for Business Enterprises,* Accounting Research Study No. 7, 1965.

II Moonitz, Maurice, *The Basic Postulates of Accounting,* Accounting Research Study No. 1, 1961.

II Sprouse, Robert T. and Moonitz, Maurice, *A Tentative Set of Broad Accounting Principles for Business Enterprises,* Accounting Research Study No. 3, 1962.

*American Management Association*

I Cordiner, Ralph J., *Problems of Management in a Large Decentralized Organization,* General Management Series No. 159, 1952.

I Dale, Ernest, *Planning and Developing the Company Organization Structure,* Research Report No. 20, 1952.

VIII Enell, John W. and Haas, George H., *Setting Standards for Executive Performance,* Research Study No. 42, 1960.

G Gibson, Edwin T., *Policies and Principles of Decentralized Management,* General Management Series No. 144, 1949, pp. 12-20.

V *How the du Pont Organization Appraises Its Performance,* Financial Management Series No. 94, 1950.

G *Problems and Policies of Decentralized Management,* General Management Series No. 154, 1952.

V *Return on Investment—Tool of Modern Management,* Financial Management Series No. 111, 1956.

*National Association of Accountants*

VI *Accounting for Intra-company Transfers,* Research Series No. 30, June 1956.

III & IV *Assignment of Non-manufacturing Costs for Managerial Decisions,* Research Series No. 19, May 1951.

IV *Current Applications of Direct Costing,* Research Report No. 37, January 1961.

IV *Current Practice in Accounting for Depreciation,* Research Report No. 33, April 1958.

IV *Direct Costing,* Research Report No. 23, April 1953.

G Evans, Marshall K., *Accounting Problems in Measuring Performance by Organizational Units,* NAA Conference Proceedings, 1955, pp. 1739-1748.

V *Experience with Return on Capital to Appraise Management Performance,* Accounting Practice Report No. 14, February 1962.

VII *The Capital Expenditure Control Program,* March 1959.

V *Return on Capital as a Guide to Managerial Decisions,* Research Report No. 35, December 1959.

*National Industrial Conference Board*

I *Administration of Electronic Data Processing,* Studies in Business Policy No. 98, 1961.

III & IV *Allocating Corporate Expenses,* Studies in Business Economics No. 108, 1963.

I *Corporate Organization Structures,* Studies in Personal Policy No. 183, 1961.

I *Division Financial Executives,* Studies in Business Policy No. 101, 1961.

II *Inflation and Corporate Accounting,* Studies in Business Policy No. 104, 1962.

VIII Kendrick, John W. and Creamer, Daniel, *Measuring Company Productivity: Handbook with Case Studies,* Studies in Business Economics No. 74, 1961.

I *Management's Role in Electronic Data Processing,* Studies in Business Policy No. 92, 1959.

VII *Managing Capital Expenditures,* Studies in Business Policy No. 107, 1963.

I *Managing Company Cash,* Studies in Business Policy No. 99, 1961.

I *Top Management Organization in Divisionalized Companies,* Studies in Personnel Policy No. 195, 1965.

*Others*

IV *Accounting and Reporting Problems of the Accounting Profession,* Second Edition, Arthur Andersen & Co., 1962.

V *Executive Committee Control Charts,* E. I. du Pont de Nemours & Co., Inc., 1959.

G Higgins, John A., "Responsibility Accounting," *The Arthur Andersen Chronicle,* April 1952, pp. 93-113.

VIII *Progress in Measuring Work,* U.S. Bureau of the Budget, Management Bulletin, August 1962.

II *The Postulate of Accounting: What It Is, How It Is Determined, How It Should Be Used,* Arthur Andersen & Co., 1960.

VI Whinston, Andrew, *Price Coordination in Decentralized Systems,* ONR Research Memorandum No. 99, GSIA, Carnegie Institute of Technology, Pittsburgh, 1962.

# INDEX

E



F



G



I



J

## S



## T



## U